2013 STATE OF BLACK AMERICA

REDEEM *the* DREAM

JOBS REBUILD AMERICA

CONTRIBUTORS

William C. Bell, Ph.D.
Stefanie Brown James
John Hope Bryant
Esther Bush
Jonathan Capehart
Shree Chauhan
Gail Christopher, Ph.D.
Marian Wright Edelman
Michael K. Fauntroy
The Honorable Marcia L. Fudge
Darrell J. Gaskins, Ph.D.
Freeman A. Hrabowski, III
Chanelle P. Hardy, Esq.
The Honorable Dot Harris
The Honorable Eric H. Holder, Jr.
Frederick S. Humphries Jr.
Avis A. Jones-DeWeever, Ph.D.
Ambassador Ron Kirk
Thomas A. LaVeist, Ph.D.
The Honorable John Lewis
John W. Mack
Cynthia G. Marshall
Brenda W. McDuffie
David McGhee
Marc H. Morial
Janet Murguía
Laura W. Murphy
Andrew Ng
john a. powell
Patrick Richard, Ph.D.
Reverend Al Sharpton
Patricia Stokes
Vincent E. Watts
Edith G. White
Madura Wijewardena
Valerie R. Wilson, Ph.D.

A
NATIONAL URBAN LEAGUE
PUBLICATION

www.nul.org | www.iamempowered.com

ISBN-978-0-914758-15-0

2013 STATE OF BLACK AMERICA®

REDEEM *the* DREAM

JOBS REBUILD AMERICA

TABLE *of* CONTENTS

FROM THE PRESIDENT'S *desk*

MARC H. MORIAL
PRESIDENT AND CEO, NATIONAL URBAN LEAGUE

"IT IS BETTER TO BE PREPARED FOR AN OPPORTUNITY AND NOT HAVE ONE THAN TO HAVE AN OPPORTUNITY AND NOT BE PREPARED."

—WHITNEY M. YOUNG, JR.

In 1963, more than a quarter-million people came together in Washington, D.C. to march for jobs and equality. The *Great March for Jobs and Freedom* was a watershed moment in black history and—through the now-iconic speeches and multitude who gathered on that day—gave voice to the hardships facing blacks as they sought a fair shot at the American dream.

As we commemorate this event and reflect on the progress we've made toward economic equality, we are faced with the sobering truth that, while much has been achieved, so much more needs to be done. A comparison between indicators from 1963 and today reveals the tough work left to do in the pursuit of full equality and empowerment. We looked at educational achievement, income, and employment—those areas where discrimination, historically, has been most pervasive and entrenched.

Educational attainment is where we see the biggest gains over the past half-century, thanks to affirmative action and early investments in educational programs such as Head Start:

★ *The high school completion gap has closed by 57 percentage points.*

★ *There are more than triple the number of blacks enrolled in college.*

★ *For every college graduate in 1963, there are now 5.*

Coupled with educational opportunity, anti-poverty measures have been a boon to the black community and significantly raised our living standard since 1963:

★ *The percentage of blacks living in poverty has declined by 23 percentage points.*

★ *The percentage of black children living in poverty has fallen by 22 percentage points.*

★ *The percentage of blacks who own their home has grown by 14 percentage points.*

Many point to these and other apparent proofs of progress—blacks are no longer barred from living, learning and earning where they want because of their race; not to mention the election and reelection of our first black president—to conclude that we have, in fact, overcome. They use this shiny veneer of progress to justify the elimination of affirmative action in education and employment; to roll back voting rights protections and relegate this precious franchise to increasingly partisan legislatures; and to cut back on social investments that can help current and future generations survive and thrive in a fast-changing economy.

Taken alone, these achievements would be hailed as good progress in the pursuit of full equality, but against the backdrop of the larger society, the sad fact is while the African American condition has improved, these improvements have occurred largely within our own community. Economic disparities with whites persist and cast doubt on what we thought of as real and meaningful change.

★ *The income gap has only closed by 7 percentage points (now at 60%).*

★ *The unemployment rate gap has only closed by 6 percentage points (now at 52%).*

These disparities underscore the need to redouble our fight for full, meaningful and lasting economic empowerment, and for policies that drive development in those communities that have been passed over for far too long.

The National Urban League is doing its part by launching a ground-breaking endeavor, ***Jobs Rebuild America***, a series of comprehensive, public/private investments totaling more than $70 million over the next five years to put urban America back to work. This nationwide effort is targeting tens of thousands of job seekers through our affiliate network, including youth, mature workers, and entrepreneurs, to help create real and meaningful pathways to employment and upward mobility where it is so desperately needed.

The campaign includes significant investment in educational programs to prepare youth for college; guidance and support for entrepreneurs; and jobs programs aimed at those who are new to the workforce and mature workers who have been displaced by the economic downturn. ***Jobs Rebuild America*** leverages the demonstrated success of our affiliate network in creating economic opportunity and preparing people to take advantage of economic opportunities to spur upward mobility.

The ***Jobs Rebuild America*** program expansion is the latest step in the National Urban League's ongoing "War on Unemployment," launched in 2011, that included the release of our **12-Point Plan: Putting Urban America Back to Work**.

Beyond the work within our own organization, our ongoing struggle cries out for a return to the kind of coalition advocacy that drove many of the civil rights and economic victories that came in the 1960s. Last year, as the two milestone events of black history approached—the 150th anniversary of the Emancipation Proclamation and the 50th anniversary of the *Great March*—I felt the time was right to again leverage the intellectual capital and contributions of African American leaders to craft a domestic agenda that moves us closer to full equality and parity, and fulfills the promise of these events.

RATHER THAN CALLING FOR MEANINGFUL CIVIL RIGHTS LEGISLATION, WE'RE FIGHTING TO PRESERVE THOSE VERY RIGHTS OUR ANCESTORS FOUGHT AND DIED FOR.

In December 2012 and January of this year, I helped to organize a historic convening of civil rights, social justice, business and community leaders to identify and push for public policy priorities to drive economic recovery and rebirth for the African American and urban communities, and for all low-income and working-class Americans. Our policy agenda was embodied in an official Communiqúe that included specific recommendations with clearly defined objectives that we believe move us forward as a community.

When I compare the recommendations in our Communiqúe with the demands made on that August afternoon in 1963, I am struck by how little has changed.

In 1963, as today, the most pressing demands centered on economic equality; educational opportunity and parity, and civil rights—battles we're still fighting to this day. But instead of fighting against discrimination in hiring or for a $2 minimum wage, we're fighting for job training and wage equity. Instead of calling for an end to school segregation, we're demanding an end to disparities in educational investment. Rather than calling for meaningful civil rights legislation, we're fighting to preserve those very rights our ancestors fought and died for; and to retain the practical application of civil rights and equality through affirmative measures to achieve diversity in jobs and education.

Our experience as a people since the *Great March* tells us that we must be vigilant in protecting our hard-won rights. To paraphrase a famous poem, we must become the masters of our own fate to fully realize the economic prosperity we demanded in August 1963.

Just as last year's ***State of Black America: Occupy the Vote*** called on African Americans to mobilize to protect voting rights, this year's ***State of Black America, Redeem the Dream: Jobs Rebuild America*** raises an equally urgent call for an intentional focus on, and investment in, jobs for our community and our future. If we are to honor Whitney M. Young, Jr., one of the unsung visionaries of the *Great March* and the Urban League's leader from 1961–1971, we must not only be prepared to seize opportunity when it presents, we must be determined and committed to creating opportunity when it does not.

★ INTRODUCTION TO THE ★

2013 EQUALITY *index*

VALERIE RAWLSTON WILSON, PH.D.
NATIONAL URBAN LEAGUE POLICY INSTITUTE

A RETROSPECTIVE LOOK AT EQUALITY IN AMERICA

Since the National Urban League introduced the Equality Index in 2004, changes in the Equality Index from one year to the next have been barely detectable. However, it is over the longer horizon that we begin to see the results of daily battles that were hard fought and often unrecognized.

As the nation celebrates the 50th anniversary of the historic *March on Washington for Jobs and Freedom*, the National Urban League takes this opportunity to offer a 50-year retrospective look at economic and educational equality in America through the lens of the Equality Index. This special edition of the Equality Index also features perspectives from three noted champions of social and economic equality—Janet Murguía, President & CEO of the National Council of La Raza, Gail C. Christopher, Vice President for Programs at the W.K. Kellogg Foundation, and john a. powell, Executive Director of the Haas Institute for a Fair and Inclusive Society (HIFIS) and Robert D. Haas Chancellor's Chair in Equity and Inclusion at the University of California, Berkeley.

FIFTY YEARS OF ABSOLUTE PROGRESS UNMATCHED BY RELATIVE PROGRESS

Since 1963, blacks have experienced tremendous gains in school enrollment and educational attainment. Fifty years ago, only one-quarter of black adults had completed high school. Currently, only 15% of black adults are not high school completers. At the college level, there are now 3.5 times more black 18–24 year olds enrolled in college than in 1963, and 5 times as many black adults[1] hold a college degree now than in 1963. Increased access to educational and employment opportunities, brought about as a result of the Civil Rights Movement and affirmative action policies, have significantly raised the standard of living for black Americans over the last 50 years. Since 1963, the percentage of blacks living in poverty has fallen by nearly half (45%), and the percentage of black children living in poverty is down by more than one-third.

Despite notable absolute progress for Black America, there has been much less relative progress toward economic equality with whites, especially when compared to the progress made toward educational equality. In nearly 50 years, the unemployment rate gap has only closed by 6 percentage points (now at 52%), the income gap has only closed by 7 percentage points (now at 60%), and the homeownership rate gap has only closed by 6 percentage points (now at 61%). At the same time, the high school completion gap has closed by 57 percentage points (now at 112%), the college enrollment gap has closed by 30 percentage points (now at 81%) and the college graduate gap has closed by 20 percentage points (now at 62%). Put simply, African Americans have achieved much less economic parity with whites than educational parity *(Figure 1)*. And in fact, the total 2013 Equality Index of Black America stands at 71.7%, meaning that on average, African Americans enjoy less than three-fourths of the benefits and privileges offered to white Americans.

It is these persistent gaps, particularly in economic outcomes, that lead us to take a closer look at current racial gaps in unemployment and income vis-á-vis differences in education, economic status, and geographic location.

WHAT EXPLAINS THE UNEMPLOYMENT RATE GAP?

While education dramatically improves one's chances of being employed—black college graduates are 4.5 times less likely to be unemployed compared to black high school dropouts—very little of the average difference between black and white unemployment rates can be explained by differences in education. In fact, taking differences in education into account along with differences in age (or experience), occupation, industry and region of the country explains just one-fifth of the average difference between black and white unemployment rates. By contrast, differences in educational attainment explain roughly three-quarters of the average difference between Latino & white unemployment rates.

DIFFERENCES IN UNEMPLOYMENT BY EDUCATION & AGE

While it is a troubling fact that black–white unemployment rate gaps persist at all levels of education, the gaps are smallest at the top and bottom of the education ladder. On average, both blacks with a bachelor's degree or higher and blacks with less than a high school diploma have an unemployment rate that is roughly 1.7 times that of whites with similar levels of education *(Figure 2)*, but clear differences emerge when we examine these gaps separately for women and men. For example, the black–white unemployment rate gap is smallest for female college graduates (1.6 times higher for blacks) and largest for male high school graduates (more than twice as high for blacks) *(Figure 3)*. The black–white unemployment rate gap also varies by age. Older black workers, ages 55–64, experience a smaller gap (1.7 times higher for blacks) than young adults, ages 20–24 (2.2 times higher for blacks) *(Figure 4)*.

ON AVERAGE, AFRICAN AMERICANS ENJOY LESS THAN THREE-FOURTHS OF THE BENEFITS AND PRIVILEGES OFFERED TO WHITE AMERICANS.

REGIONAL DIFFERENCES IN UNEMPLOYMENT

There are also some distinctions in unemployment rate gaps based on what part of the country people live in. Average black–white unemployment rate gaps are highest in the Midwest[2] (2.6 times higher for blacks) and lowest in the Northeast[3] (2 times higher for blacks). However, these gaps also vary at different levels on the education ladder. For example, the greatest disparities in the Midwest are between blacks and whites with a high school diploma (2.6 times higher for blacks), while the greatest disparities in the Northeast are between black and white college graduates (more than twice as high for blacks). On the other hand, the smallest gap in the Midwest is between black and white college graduates (1.8 times higher for blacks) while the smallest black–white gap in the Northeast is between high school dropouts (1.6 times higher for blacks).

Black college graduates in the South[4] have unemployment rates that are closest to those of white college graduates (1.7 times higher for blacks) *(Figures 5 & 6)*.

The unemployment rate gap is lower outside metro areas (1.3 times higher for blacks) than inside metro areas (1.6 times higher for blacks). Among metros with large African American populations, the largest unemployment rate gaps are in Cleveland (3.8 times higher for blacks), San Francisco (2.8 times higher for blacks), Boston and Memphis (both 2.5 times higher for blacks). The smallest gaps are in Richmond (1.6 times higher for blacks), New Orleans (1.7 times higher for blacks) and Orlando (1.8 times higher for blacks) *(Figure 7)*. Both Cleveland and San Francisco have a relatively high black–white education gap in terms of the share of the workforce with less than a high school education—38% and 26%, respectively.

WHAT EXPLAINS THE HOUSEHOLD INCOME GAP?

Disparities in employment opportunities translate into disparities in household income. Currently, the median black household has less than two-thirds (60%) the income of the median white household. But, unlike the unemployment rate gap, the income gap changes considerably based on household or worker characteristics.

REGIONAL DIFFERENCES IN HOUSEHOLD INCOME

Place of residence, and hence access to employment opportunities, accounts for a lot of the overall disparity in income. At

FIGURE 1: *Change in Key Economic & Education Gaps Since 1963* ● 1963 ● 2013

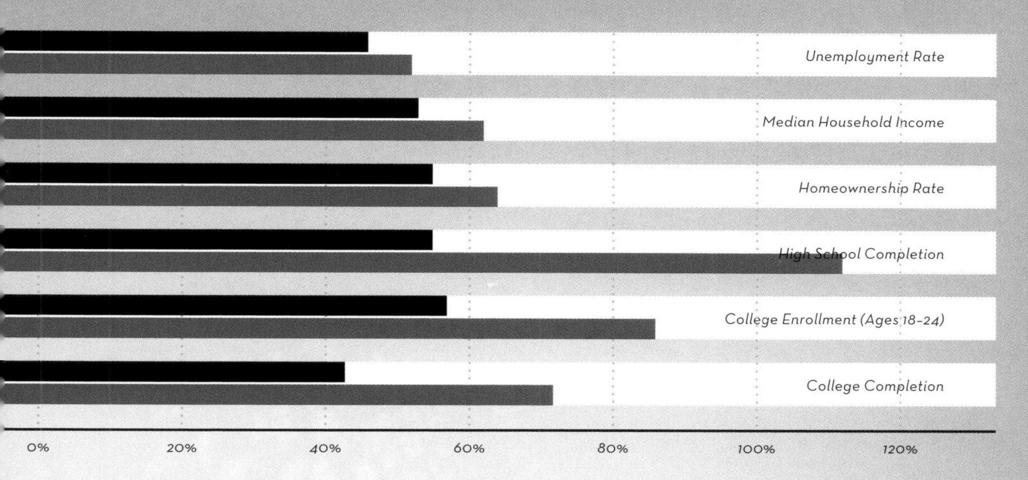

Source: 1963 to Now: Equality in Economics & Education Index

FIGURE 2: *Unemployment Rate by Race, 2012* ● White ● Black

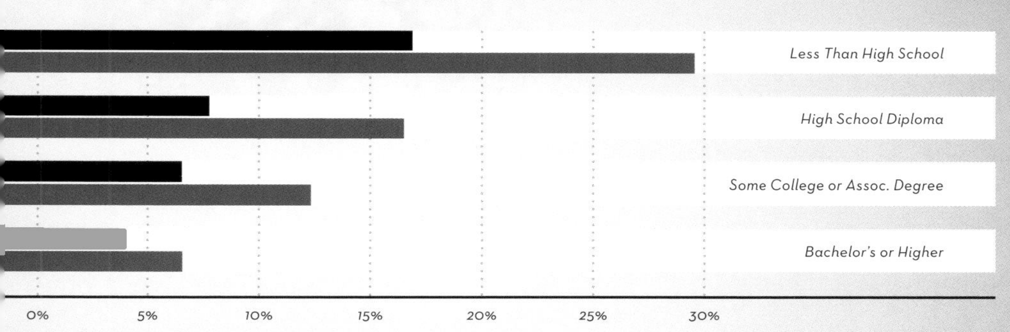

Source: Author's analysis of Current Population Survey (Jan—Dec 2012)

FIGURE 3: *Black-White Unemployment Rate Gap by Gender & Education, 2012* ● Females ● Males

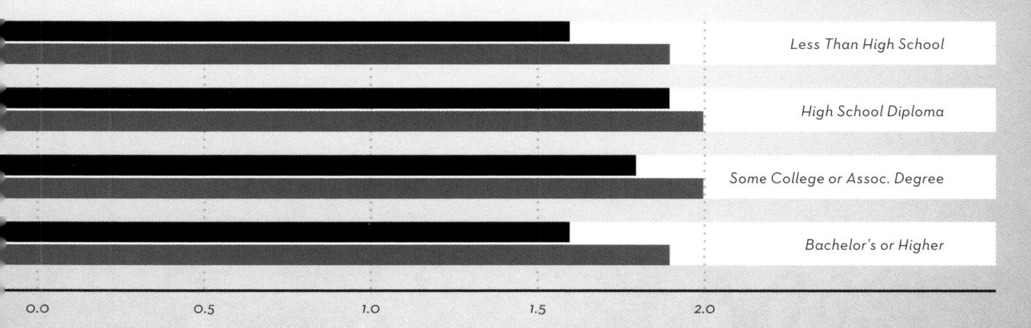

Source: Author's analysis of Current Population Survey (Jan—Dec 2012)
Numbers represent how many times higher the black unemployment rate is relative to the white unemployment rate.

the regional level, the black-white median household income gap is smallest in the South—black households have 63 cents for every dollar of white household income—and largest in the Midwest where black households have 54 cents for every dollar of white household income. At the local level, the disparity is greater in areas with a higher concentration of black population. Inside urban centers, where more than half of black households reside, the median white household income is nearly twice that of black households. However, in the suburbs, where only 38% of black households reside, median black household income is more than two-thirds that of white households.

HOUSEHOLD COMPOSITION AND SOURCES OF INCOME

The number of workers in a household also affects the income gap. In households where two or more people are working, the median income of black households is 77 cents for every dollar of white household income. But, in households where no one is working, the median black income is only 50 cents for every dollar of white household income *(Figure 8)*. More than 7 in 10 black households consist of a single worker or no workers compared to 6 in 10 white households.

When we focus on individuals' employment earnings[5]—the single largest component of household income—we find that the gap in median earnings grows with age. The black-white median earnings gap for teens is 88 cents on the dollar, compared to 73 cents on the dollar for workers age 35 to 44 *(Figure 9)*. This difference can be explained by the fact that there is little variation in educational attainment, experience or the types of jobs held by teens, so their earnings are similar. However, there is much more variation in these characteristics among adults and these differences translate into differences in earnings as illustrated by the following example.

Starting with the average weekly earnings of full-time black and white workers, we find that blacks earn 75 cents for every dollar earned by whites. If we then separate public sector from private sector workers, we find that the black-white earnings gap is smaller in the public sector than in the private sector—82 cents on the dollar compared to 73 cents on the dollar. If we further separate workers based on educational attainment, the public sector gap goes down to 89 cents on the dollar and the private sector gap goes down to 84 cents on the dollar. If we further differentiate workers based on region of the country, industry and occupation, the private sector gap goes down to 89 cents on the dollar and the public sector gap goes down to 91 cents on the dollar *(Table 1)*.

TABLE 1: *Factors Influencing the Black-White Earnings Gap, 2012*

	PUBLIC SECTOR	PRIVATE SECTOR
TOTAL BLACK-WHITE EARNINGS GAP	**$0.82**	**$0.73**
...accounting for differences in Education	$0.89	$0.84
...accounting for differences in Occupation & Industry	$0.90	$0.88
...accounting for differences by Region	$0.91	$0.89

Source: Author's analysis of Current Population Survey (Jan–Dec 2012)

FIGURE 4: *Unemployment Rate by Race & Age, 2012* ● White ● Black

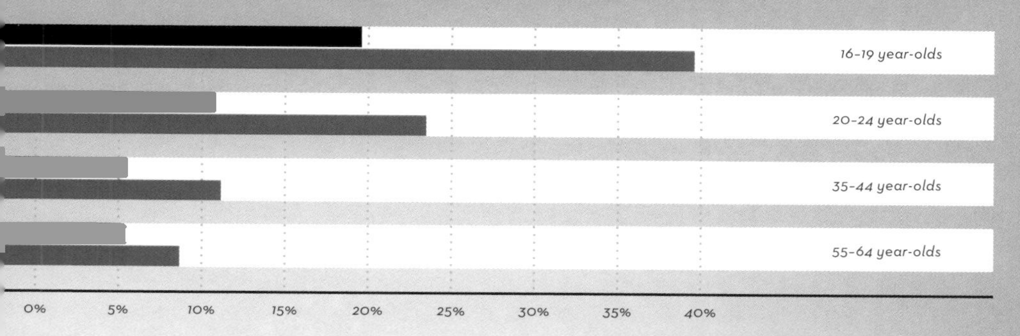

Source: Author's analysis of Current Population Survey (Jan—Dec 2012)

FIGURE 5: *Unemployment Rate by Race & Region, 2012* ● White ● Black

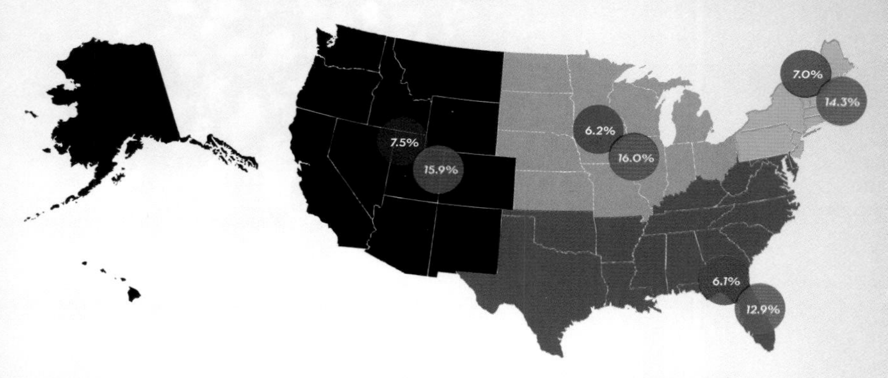

Source: Author's analysis of Current Population Survey (Jan—Dec 2012)

FIGURE 6: *Black-White Unemployment Rate Gap by Region & Education, 2012*

● West ● South ● Midwest ● South

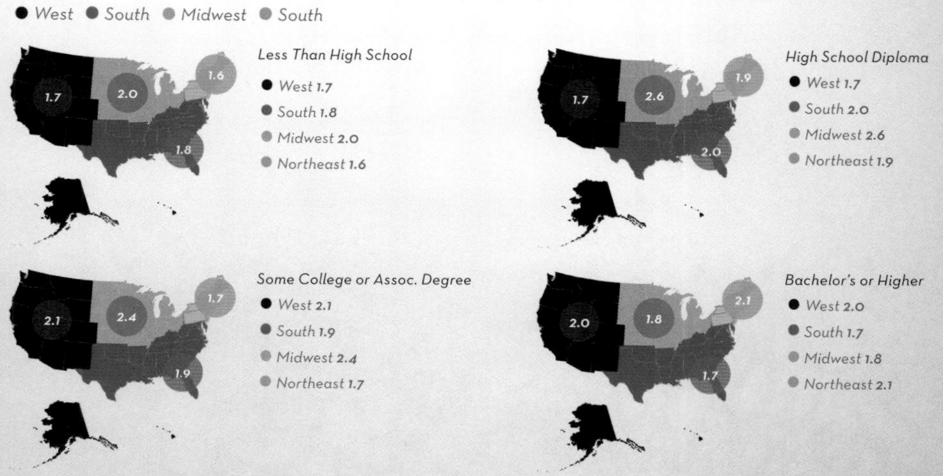

Source: Author's analysis of Current Population Survey (Jan—Dec 2012)

Numbers represent how many times higher the black unemployment rate is relative to the white unemployment rate.

THE EARNINGS GAP VARIES BY OCCUPATION

For workers with similar characteristics, the black-white earnings gap in the highest paid occupations (management and professional) is not that different from the earnings gap in the lowest paid occupations (production and transportation). However, blacks are 1.5 times less likely than whites to be employed in the highest paid occupations and 1.3 times more likely than whites to be employed in the lowest paid occupations.

For workers with similar characteristics, the smallest black-white earnings gap is in office and administrative support occupations and construction occupations. The largest earnings gap is in sales occupations and installation & maintenance occupations *(Table 2)*.

TABLE 2: *Black-White Earnings Gap by Occupation, 2012 (for workers with similar characteristics)*

	OCCUPATIONS	BLACK-WHITE GAP IN AVERAGE WEEKLY EARNINGS	SHARE OF BLACK WORKFORCE	SHARE OF WHITE WORKFORCE
HIGHEST PAID	*Management*	$0.89	11%	18%
	Professional	$0.88	18%	24%
LOWEST PAID	*Production*	$0.86	6%	5%
	Transportation	$0.86	9%	5%
SMALLEST EARNINGS GAP	*Office & Administrative*	$0.96	14%	5%
	Construction	$0.94	3%	13%
LARGEST EARNINGS GAP	*Sales*	$0.82	11%	11%
	Installation & Maintenance	$0.85	2%	4%

Source: Author's analysis of Current Population Survey (Jan–Dec 2012)

FIGURE 7: *Black-White Unemployment Rate Gap by Metro Area, 2012 (National Average is 2.1)*

Source: Author's analysis of Current Population Survey (Jan–Dec 2012)
Numbers represent how many times higher the black unemployment rate is relative to the white unemployment rate.

FIGURE 8: *Median Household Income by Race & Number of Earners, 2011* ● White ● Black

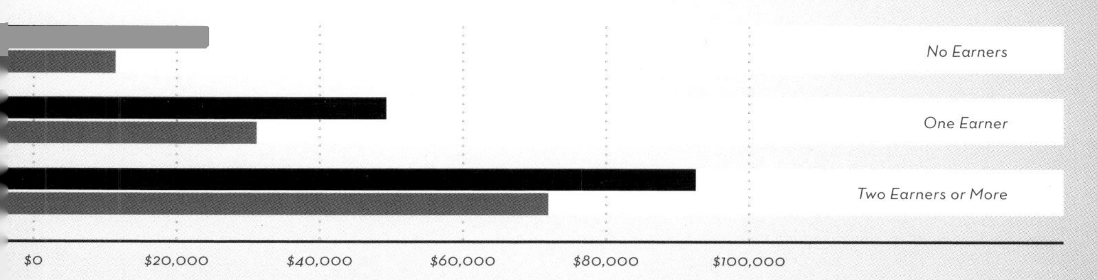

Source: Author's analysis of Current Population Survey (Jan–Dec 2012)

CONCLUSION

This analysis of the 2013 Equality Index makes a very clear and profound point. There is no doubt that African Americans have experienced tremendous gains in educational attainment since the *March on Washington for Jobs & Freedom* and these gains have increased their capacity to ascend the economic ladder. Despite these improvements however, the distance between blacks and whites on this ladder hasn't changed much over the last 50 years. In fact, employment remains the biggest barrier to economic equality in America. The roughly two-to-one unemployment rate gap between blacks and whites has persisted since the government first began reporting unemployment statistics by race, and exists at all levels of education and in all regions of the country. And in many ways, the old saying is true—the more things change, the more things stay the same. Therefore, as the nation commemorates the 150th anniversary of the Emancipation Proclamation and the 50th anniversary of the *March on Washington for Jobs & Freedom*, one question remains for the current generation. Fifty years from now, what will be said of the progress we've made toward equal access to jobs for men and women of all races & ethnicities, regardless of where or to whom they were born?

NOTES

[1] The adult population is defined as those age 25 or older.

[2] Midwestern states include IL, IN, IA, KS, MI, MN, MO, NE, ND, OH, SD, and WI.

[3] Northeastern states include CT, ME, MA, NH, NJ, NY, PA, RI, and VT.

[4] Southern states include AL, AR, DE, DC, FL, GA, KY, LA, MD, MS, NC, OK, SC, TN, TX, VA, and WV.

[5] Comparison of individual earnings is based on the weekly earnings of full-time workers in 2012.

FIGURE 9: *Median Weekly Earnings by Race & Age, 2012* ● White ● Black

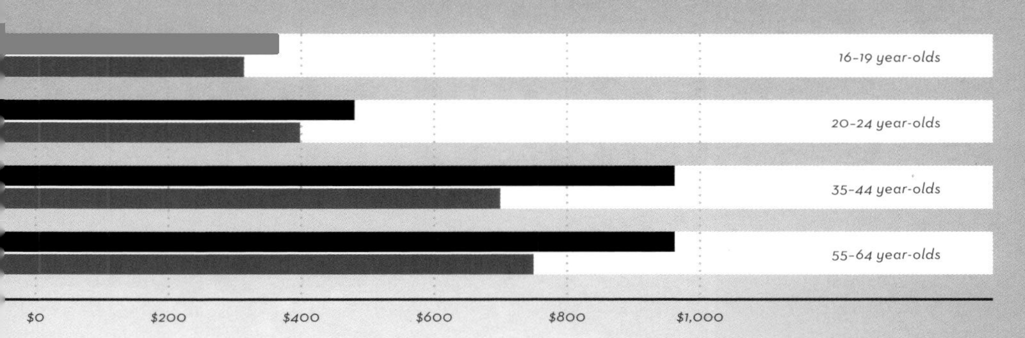

Source: Author's analysis of Current Population Survey (Jan—Dec 2012)

EDUCATION PAYS OFF MORE FOR BLACKS AT EVERY LEVEL

Blacks with a bachelor's degree or higher earn $2.40 for every dollar earned by a black high school dropout. For whites, the earnings premium for college graduates is $2.18 and for Latinos it's $2.24

FIGURE 10: *Increased Earnings at Each Level of Education by Race & Ethnicity, 2012*
(Relative to $1 In Earnings by High School Dropouts)

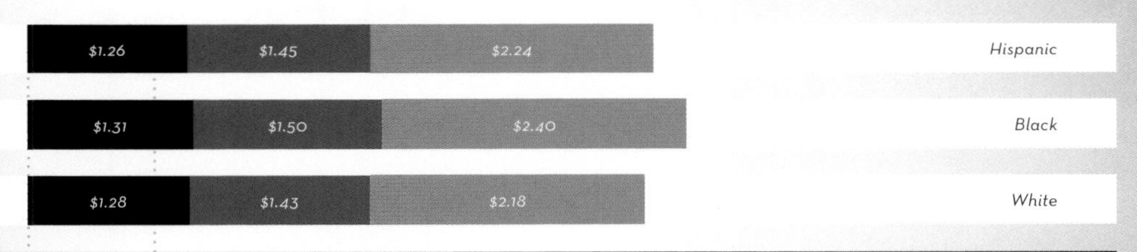

Source: Author's analysis of Current Population Survey (Jan—Dec 2012)

★ UNDERSTANDING THE ★

EQUALITY *index*

MADURA WIJEWARDENA
NATIONAL URBAN LEAGUE POLICY INSTITUTE

WHY DOES NUL PUBLISH AN EQUALITY INDEX?

Economic empowerment is the central theme of the National Urban League's mission. The Equality Index gives us a way to document progress toward this mission.

WHAT IS THE EQUALITY INDEX TRYING TO DO?

Imagine if we were to summarize how well African Americans and Hispanics are doing, compared to whites, in the areas of economics, health, education, social justice and civic engagement, and represent that by a pie.

The Equality Index measures the share of that pie which African Americans and Hispanics get.

Whites are used as the benchmark because the history of race in America has created advantages for whites that continue to persist in many of the outcomes being measured.

2013 EQUALITY INDEX OF BLACK AMERICA IS 71.7%. WHAT DOES THAT MEAN?

That means that rather than having a whole pie (100%), which would mean full equality with whites in 2013, African Americans are missing about 28% of the pie *(Figure 1)*.

FIGURE 1: *2013 Equality Index is 71.7%*

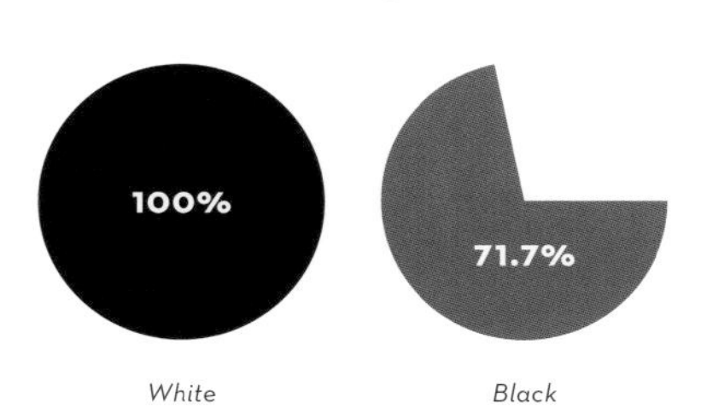

HOW IS THE EQUALITY INDEX CALCULATED?

The categories that make up the Equality Index are economics, health, education, social justice and civic engagement. In each, we calculate how well African Americans and Hispanics are doing relative to whites and add them to get the total Equality Index.

Each category is weighted, based on the importance that we give to each *(Figure 2)*.

FIGURE 2: *Different Categories That Make Up the Equality Index*

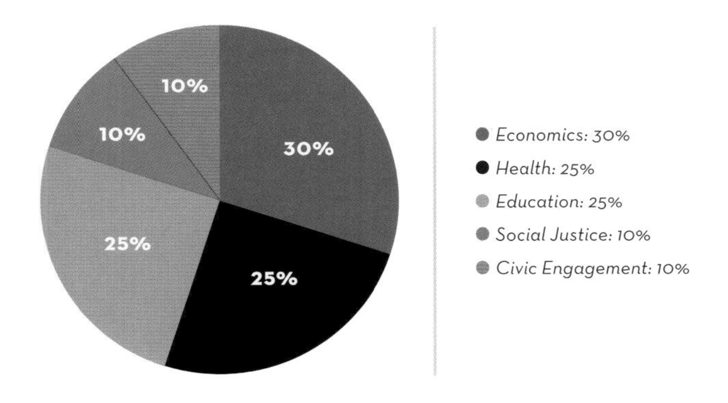

IS IT POSSIBLE TO SEE HOW WELL AFRICAN AMERICANS AND HISPANICS ARE DOING IN EACH OF THE CATEGORIES?

Yes. We show this in the tables included with the Equality Index.

Each category can be represented by a mini-pie and interpreted in the same way as the total Equality Index. So, an index of 56.3% for the economics category for African Americans in 2013 means that African Americans are missing close to half of the economics mini-pie *(Figure 3)*.

FIGURE 3: Equality Index for 2013

CATEGORY	2013
EQUALITY INDEX	**71.7%**
Economics	56.3%
Health	76.9%
Education	79.6%
Social Justice	57.1%
Civic Engagement	99.9%

IS IT POSSIBLE TO SEE HOW WELL AFRICAN AMERICANS AND HISPANICS ARE DOING OVER TIME?

Yes. The National Urban League has published the Equality Index and all the variables used to calculate it annually since 2005. We have noted the ones for 2007, 2010, and 2013 *(Figure 4)*.

FIGURE 4: Equality Index for 2007, 2010 and 2013

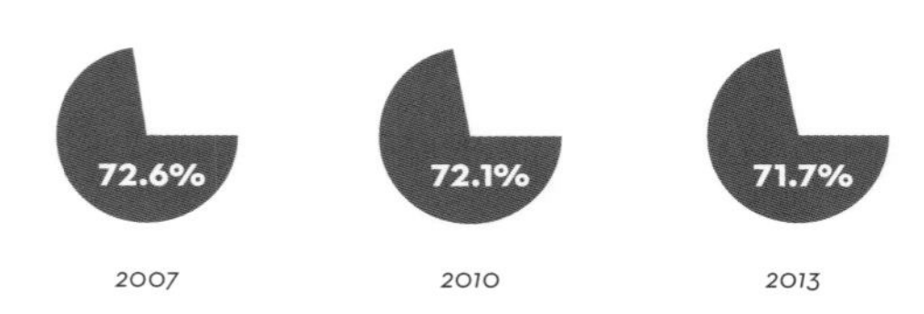

CATEGORY	2007	2010	2013
EQUALITY INDEX	**72.6%**	**72.1%**	**71.7%**
Economics	56.8%	57.9%	56.3%
Health	75.3%	76.7%	76.9%
Education	78.8%	78.3%	79.6%
Social Justice	65.4%	57.8%	57.1%
Civic Engagement	105.0%	102.2%	99.9%

IT DOESN'T LOOK LIKE THERE'S BEEN MUCH IMPROVEMENT IN THE EQUALITY INDEX—WHAT'S THE POINT?

Since the Equality Index is made up of a lot of different parts, improvements in one area are sometimes offset by losses in another area, leaving the overall index unchanged.

Change often happens slowly. The Equality Index offers solid evidence of just how slowly change happens, making it an important tool for driving policies needed in the ongoing fight against inequality.

NOT ALL AFRICAN AMERICANS ARE DOING POORLY AND NOT ALL WHITES ARE DOING WELL. WHY DOESN'T THE EQUALITY INDEX CAPTURE CLASS DIFFERENCES?

The national data used to calculate the Equality Index is reported in averages for each of the racial groups. An average includes both people who are doing well and people who are not. An average is the easiest way to summarize a large amount of information, but can mask other important differences. We provide a more detailed look at inequality in unemployment and income in this year's Equality Index chapter.

WHAT SHOULD I DO NEXT?

Support the work of the National Urban League Policy Institute as we continue to advance policies and programs to empower African American and other urban communities.

★ 1963 TO NOW ★

NATIONAL URBAN LEAGUE EQUALITY IN *ECONOMICS AND EDUCATION* index

IHS GLOBAL INSIGHT

EQUALITY IN ECONOMICS & EDUCATION, *1963 TO NOW*	1963[1]			CURRENT		
	Non-White	*White*	*Index*	*Black*	*White*	*Index*
ECONOMICS						
MEDIAN INCOME						
Median Household Income, Dollars	3,465	6,548	53%	33,223	55,305	60%
POVERTY						
Population Living Below Poverty Line, %[2]	51.0	15.3	30%	28.1	11.0	39%
Population Living Below Poverty Line (Under 18), %[2]	60.9	16.5	27%	38.8	12.5	32%
EMPLOYMENT ISSUES						
Unemployment Rate, %	10.9	5.1	46%	13.8	7.2	52%
Unemployment Rate: Male, %	10.6	4.7	44%	15.0	7.4	49%
Unemployment Rate: Female, %	11.3	5.8	51%	12.8	7.0	55%
Percent Not in Workforce: Ages 16 and Older, %	40.3	45.3	112%	38.5	36.0	94%
Labor Force Participation Rate, %	59.7	54.7	109%	61.5	64.0	96%
Employment to Pop. Ratio, %	53.2	52.0	102%	53.0	59.4	89%
HOUSING & WEALTH						
Home Ownership Rate, %[3]	31	56	55%	44.9	73.8	61%
TRANSPORTATION						
Car Ownership, %[3]	43	76	57%	68.3	87.9	78%
EDUCATION						
ENROLLMENT						
Enrollment (5–34 years old)	57.7	57.2	101%	58.6	56.5	104%
5–13	93.9	95.8	98%	96.6	97.8	99%
14–17	90.3	93.3	97%	97.1	97.3	100%
18–24	18.5	23.6	78%	46.5	50.7	92%
25–34	2.5	3.7	68%	14.9	11.6	129%
Elementary or Kindergarten	42.5	37.6	113%	30.4	28.3	107%
5–13	92.8	94.2	99%	95.8	97.3	98%
14–17	17.8	6.9	259%	10.4	7.9	133%
High School	12.7	14.4	89%	14.4	13.1	110%
5–13	1.1	1.6	67%	0.8	0.5	156%
14–17	71.9	85.0	85%	85.1	88.3	96%
18–24	7.9	2.9	271%	10.1	5.9	171%
25–34	0.5	0.2	192%	0.4	0.1	261%
College or Professional	2.5	5.3	48%	13.8	15.1	92%
14–17	0.5	1.5	37%	1.6	1.1	138%
18–24	10.4	20.6	51%	36.4	44.7	81%
25–34	2.0	3.4	57%	14.5	11.4	127%
ATTAINMENT (25 YEARS AND OLDER)						
Less Than 9th Grade	55.0	33.9	162%	3.9	2.1	182%
Some High School	20.2	17.3	117%	11.2	5.4	208%
High School Graduate	16.4	29.6	55%	34.1	30.5	112%
Some College	4.4	9.6	46%	29.6	17.1	174%
Bachelor's Degree or More	4.0	9.5	42%	21.2	34.5	62%

[1] All 1963 data (except Poverty data) from the Census' 1964 and 1965 Statistical Abstracts. The 1963 data is available only for white and non-white. The 1963 Census definition of non-white included Black, American Indian, Japanese, Chinese, Filipino, and Other; black accounted for 92% of this category.
[2] Data from Census "Poverty in the United States 1959–1968"
[3] Data for 1960–1961; Non-white refers to Black

★ COMMENTARY ON 2013 ★

BLACK–WHITE equality index

GAIL CHRISTOPHER, PH.D.
W.K. KELLOGG FOUNDATION

MOBILIZING OUR NATION TOWARD RACIAL HEALING AND EQUITY

Despite the uplifting re-election of President Obama, people of color in the U.S. continue to face conscious and unconscious bias in every aspect of society. We are discriminated against based on the color of our skin. For others, it's their ethnicity, religion or sexual preference that can adversely affect their housing, education, health, employment and environment.

For decades, the government and the courts enacted statutes and rulings ranging from *Brown v. Board of Education* to the *Civil Rights Act of 1964* to the *Fair Housing Act of 1968* that outlawed public discrimination, while purportedly providing equal opportunities. But government and courts are severely limited in their scope and reach. They enact laws, but they don't change hearts and minds.

According to the National Urban League's Equality Index, today, 38.8 percent of black children live in poverty compared to 12.5 percent of white children; black unemployment is 13.8 percent, compared to 7.2 percent for whites; and black homeownership is 44.9 percent compared to 73.8 percent for whites.

As the nation strives for a new era of racial healing and progress, a new approach is desperately needed, one making a concerted effort to change hearts and minds. Racism must be uprooted. The nation is celebrating the 150th anniversary of the Emancipation Proclamation, but unless racism is eliminated little will change over the next 150 years.

There is a prevalent belief in racial hierarchy in America, an unfair system of white privilege. Our new approach to racial healing must shatter this belief by reaching hearts and minds to create a land of equal opportunity and justice as the framers of the constitution articulated, but neither they, nor those following in their footsteps, ever established.

The American people are key to racial healing. They must embrace change. Individually and collectively, they can have an impact to shape more equitable national policies. Already, some communities fully embrace diversity by declaring that their schools, hospitals, criminal justice systems, and housing policies won't discriminate.

Oak Park, Illinois is unique, but its formula for success should be repeated. A multi-racial network of citizens, government and business leaders pronounced their community would be racially integrated and enforced laws that made it so. With a racially divided Chicago nearby, Oak Park has succeeded in achieving residential diversity.

Racial divisions often result in segregated housing patterns that spur disparities in communities of color. Residential segregation links directly to employment discrimination, segregated classrooms, and concentrated poverty, which in turn connects to violence and an unjust criminal justice system. Furthermore, environmental hazards are more prevalent in communities of color. Myriad public health and economic implications derive from persistent residential segregation.

Yet, residential segregation is not addressed in any comprehensive way because the nation usually engages superficial conversations about race. Until the racial hierarchy is dismantled, racism will continue to drive choices of where people of color live, work and are educated, diminishing our opportunities for realizing the full promise of democracy.

It's critical that a movement for racial healing mobilizes individuals and communities against racism, toward racial equity. This is our new challenge.

★ COMMENTARY ON 2013 ★

BLACK–WHITE *equality index*

JOHN A. POWELL
HAAS INSTITUTE FOR A FAIR AND INCLUSIVE SOCIETY

A THEORY OF CHANGE

The recent film, *Lincoln*, dramatized the heroic and deeply contested effort of the first post-Civil War Congress to pass the 13th Amendment, permanently abolishing racial slavery. At the center of the film is the President, a resolute, yet melancholy and tragic figure, inspiring his cabinet and his fellow Republicans, by whatever means necessary, to support the cause of ending slavery by constitutional amendment. We remember this figure as the Great Emancipator for his famous Emancipation Proclamation, issued 150 years ago, abolishing slavery by executive order.

Yet, it is worth remembering, as well, how far Lincoln traveled in just four years, and how fast the nation changed course as a result. During his failed candidacy for the U.S. Senate, Lincoln staked a very firm, but very different position against Stephen Douglas, his Democratic rival. Far from supporting abolitionism, Lincoln clearly staked his position as "non-extensionism"—opposing the further extension of slavery into the federal territories, as threatening the balance of power in the federal government between free and slave states, and further empowering the 'slave power.' Today, the not-so-subtle distinction between the two is often lost.

Also lost is the fact that for over thirty years prior, abolitionists organized and agitated public opinion in support of immediate and uncompromised abolition.

In the course of time, the Civil War was transformed from a narrow mission of preserving the union to the morally righteous cause of ending slavery. But, ending slavery alone did not ensure equality and freedom.[1] Many of the abolitionists and the Radical Republicans were not just pushing for the end of slavery but for a fully inclusive society that provided full citizenship, equality and freedom. The Radical Republicans, radical abolitionists and many blacks knew that this would require a political, social and economic strategy. Such a complete solution would not only have implications for the economy—the "promise" of forty acres and a mule—but it would change the meaning of whiteness.

During the early part of the modern Civil Rights Movement, Dr. W. E. B. Dubois would make a similar argument, rejecting the notion of civil rights separate from economic rights. And Dr. King embraced this insight as he moved to tie civil rights with the end of poverty. The failure to understand the interrelatedness of systems and structures and how they evolve and mutate, suggests that focusing on one area, be it voting or civil rights generally without tying it to other areas, is likely to produce at best, disappointing results for real equality and new forms of retrenchment.

For those of us engaged in the cause of social justice and progress, change can be frustratingly slow. The National Urban League's Equality Index illustrates both our progress and where our efforts must continue. The gains in voting and education over the last 50 years have not been matched in jobs or health. Despite the often slow pace of change, our efforts are all the more precious as they seed the ground for the political moment when the proper course becomes possible. Just as Frederick Douglass, William Lloyd Garrison, the Grimke sisters, and so many others had worked for decades in support of abolitionism until the day of Jubilee, so too must we agitate and advocate, with clear goals and a principled stance, to fight for the many causes which animate our lives. The Equality Index suggests where we might start.

NOTES

[1] For a good discussion of what ending slavery would really entail see, *The Dangerous Thirteenth Amendment.* Also for a discussion of citizenship see *Whence Comes Section One? The Abolitionist Origins of the Fourteenth Amendment.*

★ BLACK-WHITE INDEX ★

NATIONAL URBAN LEAGUE 2013 EQUALITY *index*

IHS GLOBAL INSIGHT

Updated | History Revised | Removed Weight in 2013 | No New Data

2013 EQUALITY INDEX OF BLACK AMERICA	Source	Year	Black	White	Index	Diff. ('13-'12)
Total Equality Weighted Index					71.7%	0.002
ECONOMICS (30%)						
MEDIAN INCOME (0.25)						
Median Household Income (Real), Dollars	ACS	2011	33,223	55,305	60%	(0.02)
Median Male Earnings, Dollars	ACS	2011	37,383	51,903	72%	(0.01)
Median Female Earnings, Dollars	ACS	2011	33,257	40,217	83%	0.01
POVERTY (0.15)						
Population Living Below Poverty Line, %	ACS	2011	28.1	11.0	39%	0.00
Population Living Below 50% of Poverty Line, %	ACS	2011	13.5	4.9	36%	(0.01)
Population Living Below 125% of Poverty Line, %	ACS	2011	34.8	14.7	42%	0.00
Population Living Below Poverty Line (Under 18), %	CPS ASEC	2011	38.8	12.5	32%	0.01
Population Living Below Poverty Line (18–64), %	CPS ASEC	2011	24.1	9.8	41%	(0.02)
Population Living Below Poverty Line (65 and Older), %	CPS ASEC	2011	17.3	6.7	39%	0.01
EMPLOYMENT ISSUES (0.20)						
Unemployment Rate, %	BLS	2012	13.8	7.2	52%	0.02
Unemployment Rate: Male, %	BLS	2012	15.0	7.4	49%	0.03
Unemployment Rate: Female, %	BLS	2012	12.8	7.0	55%	0.01
Unemployment Rate Persons Ages 16–19, %	BLS	2012	38.3	21.5	56%	0.04
Percent Not in Workforce: Ages 16–19, %	BLS	2012	73.1	63.1	86%	0.02
Percent Not in Workforce: Ages 16 and Older, %	BLS	2012	38.5	36.0	94%	0.02
Labor Force Participation Rate, %	BLS	2012	61.5	64.0	96%	0.01
LFPR 16–19, %	BLS	2012	26.9	36.9	73%	0.05
LFPR 20–24, %	BLS	2012	66.5	73.1	91%	0.00
LFPR Over 25: Less Than High School Grad., %	BLS	2012	36.5	47.2	77%	(0.02)
LFPR Over 25: High School Grad., No College, %	BLS	2012	61.9	58.9	105%	0.01
LFPR Over 25: Some College, No Degree, %	BLS	2012	69.4	65.3	106%	(0.01)
LFPR Over 25: Associate's Degree, %	BLS	2012	75.2	73.1	103%	0.02
LFPR Over 25: Some College or Associate Degree, %	BLS	2012	71.3	68.2	105%	(0.00)
LFPR Over 25: College Grad., %	BLS	2012	79.0	75.6	104%	0.01
Employment to Pop. Ratio, %	BLS	2012	53.0	59.4	89%	0.02
HOUSING & WEALTH (0.34)						
Home Ownership Rate, %	Census	2011	44.9	73.8	61%	(0.00)
Mortgage Application Denial Rate (Total), %	HMDA	2011	36.9	14.0	38%	(0.01)
Mortgage Application Denial Rate (Male), %	HMDA	2011	34.6	16.2	47%	(0.01)
Mortgage Application Denial Rate (Female), %	HMDA	2011	39.3	16.3	41%	(0.02)
Mortgage Application Denial Rate (Joint), %	HMDA	2011	35.2	11.5	33%	(0.01)
Home Improvement Loans Denials (Total), %	HMDA	2011	63.6	31.3	49%	(0.02)
Home Improvement Loans Denials (Male), %	HMDA	2011	63.5	37.7	59%	(0.03)
Home Improvement Loans Denials (Female), %	HMDA	2011	67.3	38.8	58%	(0.02)
Home Improvement Loans Denials (Joint), %	HMDA	2011	51.6	22.8	44%	(0.02)

Updated | History Revised | Removed Weight in 2013 | No New Data

2013 EQUALITY INDEX OF BLACK AMERICA	Source	Year	Black	White	Index	Diff. ('13-'12)
Percent of High-Priced Loans (More Than 3% Above Treasury)	HMDA	2011	7.9	3.9	49%	(0.06)
Median Home Value, 2000 Dollars	Census	2000	80,600	123,400	65%	0.00
Median Wealth, 2010 Dollars	Census SIPP	2010	4,955	110,729	4%	0.00
Equity in Home, Dollars	Census SIPP	2010	50,000	90,000	56%	(0.03)
Percent Investing in 401(K), %	EBRI	2009	27.8	36.9	75%	0.00
Percent Investing in IRA, %	EBRI	2009	10.1	25.6	39%	0.00
U.S. Firms By Race (% Compared to Employment Share)	Census	2007	7.1	86.6	8%	(0.00)
DIGITAL DIVIDE (0.05)						
Households With Computer at Home, %	Census	2010	65.1	80.0	81%	0.12
Households With the Internet, %	NTIA	2010	57.8	74.9	77%	0.00
Adult Users With Broadband Access, %	NTIA	2010	55.5	71.8	77%	0.00
TRANSPORTATION (0.01)						
Car Ownership, %	Census	2010	68.3	87.9	78%	(0.01)
Means of Transportation to Work: Drive Alone, %	ACS	2011	71.8	79.9	90%	0.00
Means of Transportation to Work: Public Transportation, %	ACS	2011	11.2	3.0	27%	0.00
Economic Weighted Index					**56.3%**	**(0.000)**

HEALTH (25%)						
DEATH RATES & LIFE EXPECTANCY (0.45)						
Life Expectancy at Birth	CDC	2010	74.7	78.8	95%	0.00
Male	CDC	2010	71.4	76.4	93%	0.01
Female	CDC	2010	77.7	81.1	96%	0.00
Life Expectancy at 65 (Additional Expected Years)	CDC	2010	17.7	19.1	93%	0.00
Male at 65	CDC	2010	15.8	17.7	89%	0.00
Female at 65	CDC	2010	19.1	20.3	94%	0.00
Age-Adjusted Death Rates (Per 100,000): All Causes	CDC	2010	920.4	755.0	82%	0.01
Age-Adjusted Death Rates (Per 100,000): Male	CDC	2010	1,131.7	892.5	79%	0.01
Age-Adjusted Death Rates (Per 100,000): Female	CDC	2010	770.8	643.3	83%	0.01
Age-Adjusted Death Rates (Per 100,000): Heart Disease	CDC	2010	229.5	179.9	78%	0.01
Ischemic Heart Disease	CDC	2010	133.4	115.0	86%	0.01
Age-Adjusted Death Rates (Per 100,000): Stroke (Cerebrovascular)	CDC	2010	54.3	37.8	70%	0.00
Age-Adjusted Death Rates (Per 100,000): Cancer	CDC	2010	208.8	176.5	85%	(0.00)
Trachea, Bronchus, and Lung	CDC	2010	52.6	50.8	97%	(0.02)
Colon, Rectum, and Anus	CDC	2010	22.4	15.5	69%	(0.01)
Prostate (Male)	CDC	2010	49.0	20.3	41%	0.00
Breast (Female)	CDC	2010	31.3	22.1	71%	(0.02)
Age-Adjusted Death Rates (Per 100,000): Chronic Lower Respiratory	CDC	2010	29.6	46.6	157%	(0.02)
Age-Adjusted Death Rates (Per 100,000): Influenza and Pneumonia	CDC	2010	17.1	14.9	87%	(0.01)
Age-Adjusted Death Rates (Per 100,000): Chronic Liver Disease and Cirrhosis	CDC	2010	6.9	9.4	136%	0.04
Age-Adjusted Death Rates (Per 100,000): Diabetes	CDC	2010	39.6	18.2	46%	(0.00)

Updated | History Revised | Removed Weight in 2013 | No New Data

2013 EQUALITY INDEX OF BLACK AMERICA	Source	Year	Black	White	Index	Diff. ('13-'12)
Age-Adjusted Death Rates (Per 100,000): HIV	CDC	2010	12.0	1.1	9%	0.01
Unintentional Injuries	CDC	2010	32.4	42.4	131%	0.04
Motor Vehicle-Related Injuries	CDC	2010	11.4	11.9	104%	0.02
Age-Adjusted Death Rates (Per 100,000): Suicide	CDC	2010	5.4	15.0	278%	0.04
Age-Adjusted Death Rates (Per 100,000): Suicide Males	CDC	2010	9.4	24.2	257%	0.06
Death Rates (Per 100,000): Suicide Males Ages 15–24	CDC	2010	11.5	20.4	177%	(0.02)
Age-Adjusted Death Rates (Per 100,000): Suicide Females	CDC	2010	1.9	6.2	326%	0.05
Death Rates (Per 100,000): Suicide Females Ages 15–24	CDC	2010	2.1	4.4	210%	0.23
Age-Adjusted Death Rates (Per 100,000): Homicide	CDC	2010	18.6	2.5	13%	(0.00)
Age-Adjusted Death Rates (Per 100,000): Homicide Male	CDC	2010	33.1	3.3	10%	(0.00)
Death Rates (Per 100,000): Homicide Males Ages 15–24	CDC	2010	74.9	4.1	5%	(0.00)
Age-Adjusted Death Rates (Per 100,000): Homicide Female	CDC	2010	5.2	1.8	35%	0.01
Death Rates (Per 100,000): Homicide Females Ages 15–24	CDC	2010	7.9	1.8	23%	0.03
Death Rates (Per 100,000) By Age Cohort: < 1 Male	CDC	2010	1,281.5	575.9	45%	0.03
Death Rates (Per 100,000) By Age Cohort: 1–4 Male	CDC	2010	45.4	27.5	61%	(0.02)
Death Rates (Per 100,000) By Age Cohort: 5–14 Male	CDC	2010	20.7	14.3	69%	0.08
Death Rates (Per 100,000) By Age Cohort: 15–24 Male	CDC	2010	150.8	93.4	62%	(0.01)
Death Rates (Per 100,000) By Age Cohort: 25–34 Male	CDC	2010	230.8	143.6	62%	0.03
Death Rates (Per 100,000) By Age Cohort: 35–44 Male	CDC	2010	321.1	219.1	68%	0.04
Death Rates (Per 100,000) By Age Cohort: 45–54 Male	CDC	2010	739.1	508.1	69%	0.03
Death Rates (Per 100,000) By Age Cohort: 55–64 Male	CDC	2010	1,705.0	1,046.2	61%	0.01
Death Rates (Per 100,000) By Age Cohort: 65–74 Male	CDC	2010	3,274.7	2,256.9	69%	0.01
Death Rates (Per 100,000) By Age Cohort: 75–84 Male	CDC	2010	6,849.1	5,770.3	84%	(0.01)
Death Rates (Per 100,000) By Age Cohort: 85+ Male	CDC	2010	14,974.2	15,816.6	106%	0.01
Death Rates (Per 100,000) By Age Cohort: <1 Female	CDC	2010	1,055.7	480.4	46%	0.02
Death Rates (Per 100,000) By Age Cohort: 1–4 Female	CDC	2010	34.8	21.8	63%	0.08
Death Rates (Per 100,000) By Age Cohort: 5–14 Female	CDC	2010	15.5	10.9	70%	0.10
Death Rates (Per 100,000) By Age Cohort: 15–24 Female	CDC	2010	45.6	38.4	84%	0.05
Death Rates (Per 100,000) By Age Cohort: 25–34 Female	CDC	2010	99.1	66.8	67%	0.02
Death Rates (Per 100,000) By Age Cohort: 35–44 Female	CDC	2010	209.1	133.1	64%	0.00
Death Rates (Per 100,000) By Age Cohort: 45–54 Female	CDC	2010	497.4	307.7	62%	0.01
Death Rates (Per 100,000) By Age Cohort: 55–64 Female	CDC	2010	996.9	631.5	63%	0.00
Death Rates (Per 100,000) By Age Cohort: 65–74 Female	CDC	2010	2,068.1	1,535.9	74%	0.00
Death Rates (Per 100,000) By Age Cohort: 75–84 Female	CDC	2010	4,675.5	4,232.6	91%	0.01
Death Rates (Per 100,000) By Age Cohort: 85+ Female	CDC	2010	12,767.7	13,543.5	106%	0.00
PHYSICAL CONDITION (0.10)						
Overweight: 18+ Years, % of Population	CDC	2011	34.8	35.7	103%	(0.04)
Overweight: Men 20 Years and Over, % of Population	CDC	2007–2010	31.2	39.5	127%	0.08
Overweight: Women 20 Years and Over, % of Population	CDC	2007–2010	26.0	27.8	107%	0.09
Obese, % of Population	CDC	2011	36.7	26.3	72%	0.08
Obese: Men 20 Years and Over, % of Population	CDC	2007–2010	37.7	33.8	90%	0.03

Updated | History Revised | Removed Weight in 2013 | No New Data

2013 EQUALITY INDEX OF BLACK AMERICA	Source	Year	Black	White	Index	Diff. ('13-'12)
Obese: Women 20 Years and Over, % of Population	CDC	2007–2010	53.7	32.7	61%	(0.05)
Diabetes: Physician Diagnosed in Ages 20+, % of Population	CDC	2007–2010	15.0	6.7	45%	(0.05)
AIDS Cases Per 100,000 Males Ages 13+	CDC	2010	75.6	9.1	12%	(0.01)
AIDS Cases Per 100,000 Females Ages 13+	CDC	2010	33.7	1.5	4%	0.00
SUBSTANCE ABUSE (0.10)						
Binge Alcohol (5 Drinks in 1 Day, 1X a Year) Ages 18+, % of Population	CDC	2011	14.1	26.2	186%	(0.06)
Use of Illicit Drugs in the Past Month Ages 12 +, % of Population	CDC	2009	9.6	8.8	92%	0.00
Tobacco: Both Cigarette & Cigar Ages 12+, % of Population	CDC	2009	26.5	29.6	112%	0.00
MENTAL HEALTH (0.02)						
Students Who Consider Suicide: Male, %	CDC	2009	7.8	10.5	135%	0.00
Students Who Carry Out Intent and Require Medical Attention: Male, %	CDC	2007	2.5	0.9	36%	0.00
Students That Act on Suicidal Feeling: Male, %	CDC	2007	5.5	3.4	62%	0.00
Students Who Consider Suicide: Female, %	CDC	2009	18.1	16.1	89%	0.00
Students Who Carry Out Intent and Require Medical Attention: Female, %	CDC	2007	2.1	2.1	100%	0.00
Students That Act on Suicidal Feeling: Female, %	CDC	2007	9.9	7.7	78%	0.00
ACCESS TO CARE (0.05)						
Private Insurance Payment for Health Care: Under 65 Years Old, % of Distribution	CPS ASEC	2011	50.5	74.5	68%	0.02
People Without Health Insurance, % of Population	CPS ASEC	2011	19.5	11.1	57%	0.01
People 18 to 64 Without a Usual Source of Health Insurance, % of Adults	CPS ASEC	2011	26.1	15.2	58%	0.01
People 18 to 64 and in Poverty Without a Usual Source of Health Insurance, % of Adults	CPS ASEC	2011	38.8	37.7	97%	(0.03)
Population Under 65 Covered By Medicaid, % of Population	CPS ASEC	2011	28.7	12.1	42%	0.02
ELDERLY HEALTH CARE (0.03)						
Population Over 65 Covered By Medicaid, % of Population	CPS ASEC	2011	18.4	6.4	35%	0.00
Medicare Expenditures Per Beneficiary, Dollars	CDC	2009	19,211	15,938	83%	(0.09)
PREGNANCY ISSUES (0.04)						
Prenatal Care Begins in 1st Trimester	CDC	2007	75.0	87.7	86%	0.00
Prenatal Care Begins in 3rd Trimester	CDC	2007	6.0	2.3	38%	0.00
Percent of Births to Mothers 18 and Under	CDC	2010	4.9	1.7	35%	0.02
Percent of Live Births to Unmarried Mothers	CDC	2010	72.5	29.0	40%	0.00
Infant Mortality Rates Among Mothers With Less Than 12 Years Education	CDC	2005	14.8	9.3	63%	0.00
Infant Mortality Rates Among Mothers With 12 Years Education	CDC	2005	14.2	7.1	50%	0.00
Infant Mortality Rates Among Mothers With 13 or More Years Education	CDC	2005	11.4	4.1	36%	0.00
Mothers Who Smoked Cigarettes During Pregnancy, %	CDC	2007	7.7	12.7	165%	0.00
Low Birth Weight, % of Live Births	CDC	2010	13.5	7.1	53%	0.00
Very Low Birth Weight, % of Live Births	CDC	2010	3.0	1.2	39%	(0.00)
REPRODUCTION ISSUES (0.01)						
Abortions, Per 1,000 Live Births	CDC	2007	447.0	159.0	36%	0.00
Women Using Contraception, % of Population	CDC	2006–2008	54.5	64.7	84%	0.00

Updated | History Revised | Removed Weight in 2013 | No New Data

2013 EQUALITY INDEX OF BLACK AMERICA	Source	Year	Black	White	Index	Diff. ('13-'12)
DELIVERY ISSUES (0.10)						
All Infant Deaths: Neonatal and Post, Per 1,000 Live Births	CDC	2008	12.7	5.5	43%	0.02
Neonatal Deaths, Per 1,000 Live Births	CDC	2008	8.3	3.5	42%	0.02
Postneonatal Deaths, Per 1,000 Live Births	CDC	2008	4.4	2.0	45%	0.02
Maternal Mortality, Per 100,000 Live Births	CDC	2007	23.8	8.1	34%	0.00
CHILDREN'S HEALTH (0.10)						
Babies Breastfed, %	CDC	2007	58.1	76.2	76%	0.00
Children Without a Health Care Visit in Past 12 Months (Up to 6 Years Old), %	CDC	2010–2011	5.9	3.5	59%	(0.05)
Vaccinations of Children Below Poverty: Combined Vacc. Series 4:3:1:3, % of Children 19–35 Months	CDC	2009	64.0	68.0	94%	0.00
Uninsured Children, %	CPS ASEC	2011	10.2	6.8	66%	0.04
Overweight Boys 6–11 Years Old, % of Population	CDC	2007–2010	23.3	18.6	80%	(0.08)
Overweight Girls 6–11 Years Old, % of Population	CDC	2007–2010	24.5	14.0	57%	(0.11)
AIDS Cases Per 100,000 All Children Under 13	CDC	2010	0.14	0.01	9%	0.06
Health Weighted Index					**76.9%**	**0.001**

EDUCATION (25%)	Source	Year	Black	White	Index	Diff. ('13-'12)
QUALITY (0.25)						
TEACHER QUALITY (0.10)						
Middle Grades: Teacher Lacking at Least a College Minor in Subject Taught (High Vs. Low Minority Schools),* %	ET	2000	49.0	40.0	85%	0.00
HS: Teacher Lacking An Undergraduate Major in Subject Taught (High Vs. Low Poverty Secondary Schools),* %	ET	2007–2008	21.9	10.9	88%	(0.03)
Per Student Funding (High [30%] Vs. Low [0%] Poverty Districts)*, Dollars	SFF	2009	10,948	10,684	102%	0.02
Teachers With <3 Years Experience (High Vs. Low Poverty Schools)*, %	NCES	2000	21.0	10.0	48%	0.00
Distribution of Underprepared Teachers (High Vs. Low Minority Schools)*, % (California Only)	SRI	2008–2009	5.0	1.0	20%	0.00
**High poverty (high minority) values are recorded in the Black column. Low poverty (low minority) values are recorded in the White column.*						
COURSE QUALITY (0.15)						
College Completion, % of All Entrants	NCES	2002	40.1	60.2	67%	(0.02)
College Completion, % of Entrants With Strong HS Curriculum (Algebra II Plus Other Courses)	ET	1999	75.0	86.0	87%	0.00
HS Students: Enrolled in Chemistry, %	NCES	2005	63.6	67.1	95%	0.00
HS Students: Enrolled in Algebra II, %	NCES	2005	69.2	71.2	97%	0.00
Students Taking: Precalculus, %	CB	2009	36.0	55.0	65%	0.00
Students Taking: Calculus, %	CB	2009	14.0	30.0	47%	0.00
Students Taking: Physics, %	CB	2009	44.0	54.0	81%	0.00
Students Taking: English Composition, %	CB	2009	31.0	43.0	72%	0.00

Updated | History Revised | Removed Weight in 2013 | No New Data

2013 EQUALITY INDEX OF BLACK AMERICA	Source	Year	Black	White	Index	Diff. ('13-'12)
ATTAINMENT (0.20)						
Graduation Rates, 2-Year Institutions Where Students Started As Full Time, First Time Students, %	NCES	2006	27.1	32.0	85%	0.00
Graduation Rates, 4-Year Institutions Where Students Started As Full Time, First Time Students, %	NCES	2003	37.7	59.3	64%	0.00
NCAA Div. I College Freshmen Graduating Within 6 Years, %	NCAA	2005	33.0	52.0	63%	(0.04)
Degrees Earned: Associate, % of Population Aged 18–24 Yrs	NCES	2010–2011	2.8	3.4	82%	0.04
Degrees Earned: Bachelor's, % of Population Aged 18–29 Yrs	NCES	2010–2011	2.4	4.0	60%	0.02
Degrees Earned: Master's, % of Population Aged 18–34 Yrs	NCES	2010–2011	0.8	1.1	72%	0.04
Educational Attainment: at Least High School (25 Yrs. and Over), % of Population	Census	2012	85.0	92.5	91%	(0.00)
Educational Attainment: at Least Bachelor's (25 Yrs. and Over), % of Population	Census	2012	21.2	34.5	58%	(0.01)
Degrees Conferred, % Distribution, By Field						
Agriculture/Forestry	NCES	2011	0.4	1.7	24%	(0.03)
Art/Architecture	NCES	2011	0.3	0.7	47%	(0.02)
Business/Management	NCES	2011	26.3	19.7	133%	(0.00)
Communications	NCES	2011	3.9	4.0	97%	0.01
Computer and Information Sciences	NCES	2011	2.4	2.0	120%	(0.01)
Education	NCES	2011	10.8	13.2	82%	(0.00)
Engineering	NCES	2011	2.4	4.8	51%	(0.02)
English/Literature	NCES	2011	1.7	2.8	61%	(0.02)
Foreign Languages	NCES	2011	0.4	1.0	39%	0.01
Health Sciences	NCES	2011	11.0	11.2	98%	(0.00)
Liberal Arts/Humanities	NCES	2011	2.7	1.9	141%	(0.01)
Mathematics/Statistics	NCES	2011	0.4	0.9	45%	(0.03)
Natural Sciences	NCES	2011	3.6	5.2	69%	(0.01)
Philosophy/Religion/Theology	NCES	2011	0.4	0.7	64%	0.04
Psychology	NCES	2011	6.1	5.0	123%	(0.01)
Social Sciences/History	NCES	2011	6.9	7.7	90%	(0.00)
Other Fields	NCES	2011	20.2	17.7	114%	0.03
SCORES (0.25)						
PRESCHOOL 10% OF TOTAL SCORES (0.015)						
Children's School Readiness Skills (Ages 3–5), % With 3 or 4 Skills* **Recognizes all letters, counts to 20 or higher, writes name, reads or pretends to read*	NCES	2005	44.1	46.8	94%	0.00
ELEMENTARY 40% OF TOTAL SCORES (0.06)						
Average Scale Score in U.S. History, 8th Graders	NCES	2010	250	274	91%	0.00
Average Scale Score in U.S. History, 4th Graders	NCES	2010	198	224	88%	0.00
Average Scale Score in Math, 8th Graders	NCES	2011	262	293	89%	0.00
Average Scale Score in Math, 4th Graders	NCES	2011	224	249	90%	0.00
Average Scale Score in Reading, 8th Graders	NCES	2011	249	274	91%	0.00
Average Scale Score in Reading, 4th Graders	NCES	2011	205	231	89%	0.00
Average Scale Score in Science, 8th Graders	NCES	2011	129	163	79%	0.01

Updated | History Revised | Removed Weight in 2013 | No New Data

2013 EQUALITY INDEX OF BLACK AMERICA	Source	Year	Black	White	Index	Diff. ('13-'12)
Average Scale Score in Science, 4th Graders	NCES	2009	127	163	78%	0.00
Writing Proficiency at or Above Basic, 8th Graders, % of Students	NCES	2011	65	92	71%	(0.17)
Writing Proficiency at or Above Basic, 4th Graders, % of Students	NCES	2002	77	90	85%	0.00
HIGH SCHOOL 50% OF TOTAL SCORES (0.075)						
Writing Proficiency at or Above Basic, 12th Graders, % of Students	NCES	2011	61	86	71%	(0.09)
Average Scale Score in Science, 12th Graders	NCES	2005	120	156	77%	0.00
Average Scale Score in U.S. History, 12th Graders	NCES	2010	268	296	91%	0.00
Average Scale Score in Reading, 12th Graders	NCES	2009	269	296	91%	0.00
High School GPAs for Those Taking the SAT	CB	2009	3.00	3.40	88%	0.00
SAT Reasoning Test: Mean Scores	CB	2012	1,273	1,578	81%	0.00
Mathematics, Joint	CB	2012	428	536	80%	0.00
Mathematics, Male	CB	2012	436	554	79%	(0.00)
Mathematics, Female	CB	2012	422	520	81%	0.00
Critical Reading, Joint	CB	2012	428	527	81%	0.00
Critical Reading, Male	CB	2012	425	530	80%	0.00
Critical Reading, Female	CB	2012	430	525	82%	0.00
Writing, Joint	CB	2012	417	515	81%	0.00
Writing, Male	CB	2012	405	506	80%	0.00
Writing, Female	CB	2012	426	522	82%	0.00
ACT: Average Composite Score	ACT	2012	17.0	22.4	76%	0.00
ENROLLMENT (0.10)						
School Enrollment: Ages 3–34, % of Population	Census	2011	58.4	56.4	103%	0.00
Preprimary School Enrollment	Census	2011	62.8	67.0	94%	(0.06)
3 and 4 Years Old	Census	2011	55.2	56.2	98%	(0.06)
5 and 6 Years Old	Census	2011	92.0	95.8	96%	(0.03)
7 to 13 Years Old	Census	2011	97.9	98.4	100%	0.00
14 and 15 Years Old	Census	2011	98.5	98.9	100%	0.00
16 and 17 Years Old	Census	2011	95.7	95.9	100%	0.01
18 and 19 Years Old	Census	2011	74.1	72.1	103%	0.13
20 and 21 Years Old	Census	2011	41.1	56.2	73%	(0.06)
22 to 24 Years Old	Census	2011	31.2	32.9	95%	(0.08)
25 to 29 Years Old	Census	2011	18.1	15.2	119%	0.15
30 to 34 Years Old	Census	2011	11.4	7.8	146%	0.10
35 and Over	Census	2011	3.8	1.7	226%	0.30
College Enrollment (Graduate or Undergraduate): Ages 14 and Over, % of Population	Census	2011	7.7	10.3	74%	(0.05)
14 to 17 Years Old	Census	2011	1.6	1.1	138%	0.25
18 to 19 Years Old	Census	2011	44.0	52.9	83%	0.09
20 to 21 Years Old	Census	2011	39.0	54.6	71%	(0.03)
22 to 24 Years Old	Census	2011	29.5	32.4	91%	(0.07)
25 to 29 Years Old	Census	2011	17.6	14.9	118%	0.14
30 to 34 Years Old	Census	2011	11.2	7.7	145%	0.20
35 Years Old and Over	Census	2011	3.7	1.7	221%	0.35

Updated | History Revised | Removed Weight in 2013 | No New Data

2013 EQUALITY INDEX OF BLACK AMERICA	Source	Year	Black	White	Index	Diff. ('13-'12)
College Enrollment Rate As a Percent of All 18- to 24-Year-Old High School Completers, %	NCES	2011	37.1	44.7	83%	(0.01)
Adult Education Participation, % of Adult Population	NCES	2004–2005	46.0	46.0	100%	0.00
STUDENT STATUS & RISK FACTORS (0.10)						
High School Dropouts: Status Dropouts, % (Not Completed HS and Not Enrolled, Regardless of When Dropped Out)	Census	2009	11.6	9.1	78%	0.00
Children in Poverty, %	Census	2011	38.8	12.5	32%	0.01
Children in All Families Below Poverty Level, %	Census	2011	38.6	11.9	31%	0.01
Children in Families Below Poverty Level (Female Householder, No Spouse Present), %	Census	2011	54.2	35.5	65%	0.00
Children With No Parent in The Labor Force, %	AECF	2011	49.0	25.0	51%	0.24
Children (Under 18) With a Disability, %	Census	2011	5.0	3.9	79%	(0.04)
Public School Students (K-12): Repeated Grade, %	NCES	2007	20.9	8.7	42%	0.00
Public School Students (K-12): Suspended, %	NCES	2003	19.6	8.8	45%	0.00
Public School Students (K-12): Expelled, %	NCES	2003	5.0	1.4	28%	0.00
Center-Based Child Care of Preschool Children, %	NCES	2005	66.5	59.1	89%	0.00
Parental Care Only of Preschool Children, %	NCES	2005	19.5	24.1	81%	0.00
Teacher Stability: Remained in Public School, High Vs. Low Minority Schools, %	NCES	2005	79.7	85.9	93%	0.00
Teacher Stability: Remained in Private School, High Vs. Low Minority Schools, %	NCES	2005	72.7	82.8	88%	0.00
Zero Days Missed in School Year, % of 10th Graders	NCES	2002	28.3	12.1	234%	0.00
3+ Days Late to School, % of 10th Graders	NCES	2002	36.4	44.4	122%	0.00
Never Cut Classes, % of 10th Graders	NCES	2002	68.9	70.3	98%	0.00
Home Literacy Activities (Age 3 to 5)						
Read to 3 or More Times a Week	NCES	2007	78.0	90.6	86%	0.00
Told a Story at Least Once a Month	NCES	2005	54.3	53.3	102%	0.00
Taught Words or Numbers Three or More Times a Week	NCES	2005	80.6	75.7	107%	0.00
Visited a Library at Least Once in Last Month	NCES	2007	24.6	40.8	60%	0.00
Education Weighted Index					**79.6%**	**(0.000)**

SOCIAL JUSTICE (10%)						
EQUALITY BEFORE THE LAW (0.70)						
Stopped While Driving, %	BJS	2008	8.8	8.4	95%	0.00
Speeding	BJS	2002	50.0	57.0	114%	0.00
Vehicle Defect	BJS	2002	10.3	8.7	84%	0.00
Roadside Check for Drinking Drivers	BJS	2002	1.1	1.3	118%	0.00
Record Check	BJS	2002	17.4	11.3	65%	0.00
Seatbelt Violation	BJS	2002	3.5	4.4	126%	0.00
Illegal Turn/Lane Change	BJS	2002	5.1	4.5	88%	0.00
Stop Sign/Light Violation	BJS	2002	5.9	6.5	110%	0.00
Other	BJS	2002	3.7	4.0	108%	0.00
Mean Incarceration Sentence (In Average Months)	BJS	2006	42	37	88%	0.00

Updated | History Revised | Removed Weight in 2013 | No New Data

2013 EQUALITY INDEX OF BLACK AMERICA	Source	Year	Black	White	Index	Diff. ('13-'12)
Average Sentence for Incarceration (All Offenses): Male, Months	BJS	2006	45	40	89%	0.00
Average Sentence for Murder: Male, Months	BJS	2006	266	265	100%	0.00
Average Sentence for Sexual Assault	BJS	2006	125	115	92%	0.00
Average Sentence for Robbery	BJS	2006	101	89	88%	0.00
Average Sentence for Aggravated Assault	BJS	2006	48	42	88%	0.00
Average Sentence for Other Violent	BJS	2006	41	43	105%	0.00
Average Sentence for Burglary	BJS	2006	50	41	82%	0.00
Average Sentence for Larceny	BJS	2006	23	24	104%	0.00
Average Sentence for Fraud	BJS	2006	27	27	100%	0.00
Average Sentence for Drug Possession	BJS	2006	25	21	84%	0.00
Average Sentence for Drug Trafficking	BJS	2006	40	39	98%	0.00
Average Sentence for Weapon Offenses	BJS	2006	34	34	100%	0.00
Average Sentence for Other Offenses	BJS	2006	25	26	104%	0.00
Average Sentence for Incarceration (All Offenses): Female,Months	BJS	2006	25	26	104%	0.00
Average Sentence for Murder	BJS	2006	175	225	129%	0.00
Average Sentence for Sexual Assault	BJS	2006	32	72	225%	0.00
Average Sentence for Robbery	BJS	2006	54	61	113%	0.00
Average Sentence for Aggravated Assault	BJS	2006	29	30	103%	0.00
Average Sentence for Other Violent	BJS	2006	17	55	324%	0.00
Average Sentence for Burglary	BJS	2006	34	29	85%	0.00
Average Sentence for Larceny	BJS	2006	19	17	89%	0.00
Average Sentence for Fraud	BJS	2006	23	22	96%	0.00
Average Sentence for Drug Possession	BJS	2006	15	17	113%	0.00
Average Sentence for Drug Trafficking	BJS	2006	27	26	96%	0.00
Average Sentence for Weapon Offenses	BJS	2006	24	24	100%	0.00
Average Sentence for Other Offenses	BJS	2006	20	22	110%	0.00
Convicted Felons Sentenced to Probation, All Offenses,%	BJS	2006	25	29	86%	0.00
Probation Sentence for Murder, %	BJS	2006	3	4	75%	0.00
Probation Sentence for Sexual Assault, %	BJS	2006	16	16	100%	0.00
Probation Sentence for Robbery, %	BJS	2006	12	15	80%	0.00
Probation Sentence for Burglary, %	BJS	2006	20	25	80%	0.00
Probation Sentence for Fraud, %	BJS	2006	35	35	100%	0.00
Probation Sentence for Drug Offenses, %	BJS	2006	25	34	74%	0.00
Probation Sentence for Weapon Offenses, %	BJS	2006	25	23	109%	0.00
Incarceration Rate: Prisoners Per 100,000	BJS	2011	1,516	261	17%	0.01
Incarceration Rate: Prisoners Per 100,000 People: Male	BJS	2011	3,023	478	16%	0.01
Incarceration Rate: Prisoners Per 100,000 People: Female	BJS	2011	129	51	40%	0.04
Prisoners as a % of Arrests	FBI, BJS	2011	21.5	7.8	36%	0.02
VICTIMIZATION & MENTAL ANGUISH (0.30)						
Homicide Rate Per 100,000	NACJD	2009	16.7	2.8	17%	0.00
Homicide Rate Per 100,000: Firearm	NACJD	2009	13.0	1.6	12%	0.00
Homicide Rate Per 100,000: Stabbings	NACJD	2009	1.5	0.5	30%	0.00

Updated | History Revised | Removed Weight in 2013 | No New Data

2013 EQUALITY INDEX OF BLACK AMERICA	Source	Year	Black	White	Index	Diff. ('13-'12)
Homicide Rate Per 100,000: Personal Weapons	NACJD	2009	0.6	0.2	38%	0.00
Homicide Rate Per 100,000: Male	CDC	2009	34.2	3.4	10%	0.01
Homicide Rate Per 100,000: Female	CDC	2009	5.4	1.8	33%	0.04
Murder Victims, Rate Per 100,000	USDJ	2011	15.5	2.4	15%	(0.03)
Hate Crimes Victims, Rate Per 100,000	USDJ	2011	6.4	0.2	4%	(0.00)
Victims of Violent Crimes, Rate Per 1,000 Persons Age 12 or Older	BJS	2011	26.4	21.5	81%	0.11
Delinquency Cases, Year of Disposition, Rate Per 100,000	NCJJ	2009	2,684.9	1,225.2	46%	(0.01)
Prisoners Under Sentence of Death, Rate Per 100,000	BJS	2009	4.6	1.1	24%	0.00
High School Students Carrying Weapons on School Property	CDC	2011	4.6	5.1	111%	0.05
High School Students Carrying Weapons Anywhere	CDC	2011	14.2	17.0	120%	(0.09)
Firearm-Related Death Rates Per 100,000: Males, All Ages	CDC	2007	40.4	16.1	40%	0.00
Ages 1–14	CDC	2007	2.4	0.7	29%	0.00
Ages 15–24	CDC	2007	91.5	13.4	15%	0.00
Ages 25–44	CDC	2007	64.8	18.3	28%	0.00
Ages 25–34	CDC	2007	88.1	18.0	20%	0.00
Ages 35–44	CDC	2007	40.7	18.7	46%	0.00
Ages 45–64	CDC	2007	20.1	19.5	97%	0.00
Age 65 and Older	CDC	2007	11.4	27.3	241%	0.00
Firearm-Related Death Rates Per 100,000: Females, All Ages	CDC	2007	4.1	2.9	70%	0.00
Ages 1–14	CDC	2007	0.9	0.3	34%	0.00
Ages 15–24	CDC	2007	7.3	2.5	34%	0.00
Ages 25–44	CDC	2007	6.7	4.1	61%	0.00
Ages 25–34	CDC	2007	7.2	3.4	47%	0.00
Ages 35–44	CDC	2007	6.2	4.6	75%	0.00
Ages 45–64	CDC	2007	2.9	3.9	136%	0.00
Age 65 and Older	CDC	2007	1.3	2.2	172%	0.00
Social Justice Weighted Index					**57.1%**	**0.006**

CIVIC ENGAGEMENT (10%)						
DEMOCRATIC PROCESS (0.4)						
Registered Voters, % of Citizen Population	Census	2010	62.8	68.2	92%	0.00
Actually Voted, % of Citizen Population	Census	2010	43.5	48.6	90%	0.00
COMMUNITY PARTICIPATION (0.3)						
Percent of Population Volunteering for Military Reserves, %	USDD	2010	0.8	1.0	80%	0.00
Volunteerism, %	BLS	2011	20.3	28.2	72%	0.02
Civic and Political	BLS	2011	3.2	5.7	56%	(0.27)
Educational or Youth Service	BLS	2011	23.9	25.7	93%	0.07
Environmental or Animal Care	BLS	2011	0.2	2.6	8%	(0.11)
Hospital or Other Health	BLS	2011	6.4	8.0	80%	0.07
Public Safety	BLS	2011	0.8	1.4	57%	0.36

Fifty years after the historic *March on Washington for Jobs & Freedom*, the 2013 Hispanic-White Equality Index is cause for both optimism and concern. It shows Latinos climbing the ladder of opportunity and in some fields, doing better than White Americans. But, the progress they are making remains unacceptably slow.

With a 2013 Hispanic-White Equality Index of 75.4%, Hispanic Americans are experiencing only three quarters of the full benefits that America has to offer.[1] In the economic and social justice fields, Latinos are even farther behind—60.8% in economics and 61.9% in social justice. The everyday reality of this was seen at the start of this year when the Hispanic unemployment rate of 9.7% was one and a half times greater than the corresponding white American unemployment rate.[2]

Despite the enormous challenges that these numbers indicate, the Hispanic-White Equality Index is not all about hardship. It also shows that Latinos are taking the opportunities presented to them to build their own American dream. For example, between 2012 and 2013, Hispanic Americans have reduced the gap in the Equality Index between them and white Americans by 0.4 percentage points. To achieve that in the middle of a lackluster recovery speaks volumes about the tenacity and enterprise of the Latino community.

And in the health field, Hispanic Americans are actually ahead of white Americans with an index of 101% in 2013. The remarkable thing about Latino achievement in health—which has always surpassed that of White Americans—is that it has been achieved while there are far more uninsured Hispanic Americans than white Americans.

We need to build on those strengths to help face our challenges and we have to do it together with our brothers and sisters in the African American community. African Americans and Latinos often live side by side in the same communities and face the same hardships. As Dr. Martin Luther King Jr. said in a telegram to Cesar Chavez, *"the plight of your people and ours is so grave that we all desperately need the inspiring example and effective leadership you have given."*[3] We are very proud that NCLR and NUL are continuing to build on this partnership forged at the height of the civil rights movement to create the opportunities and craft the future both our communities need and deserve.

NOTES

[1] An index of 100% indicates full equality with white Americans.

[2] Bureau of Labor Statistics, Employment Situation–January 2013, February 1, 2013, Washington, D.C. found at: *http://www.bls.gov/news.release/pdf/empsit.pdf.*

[3] Telegram from Dr. Martin Luther King, Jr. to Cesar Chaves dated 3.5.1968 found at: *http://www.thekingcenter.org/archive/document/telegram-mlk-cesar-chavez.*

★ HISPANIC-WHITE INDEX ★

NATIONAL URBAN LEAGUE 2013 EQUALITY *index*

IHS GLOBAL INSIGHT

Updated | History Revised | Removed Weight in 2013 | No New Data

2013 EQUALITY INDEX OF HISPANIC AMERICA	Source	Year	Hispanic	White	Index	Diff. ('13-'12)
Total Equality Weighted Index					**75.6%**	0.004
ECONOMICS (30%)						
MEDIAN INCOME (0.25)						
Median Household Income (Real), Dollars	ACS	2011	39,589	55,305	72%	(0.03)
Median Male Earnings, Dollars	ACS	2011	31,118	51,903	60%	0.00
Median Female Earnings, Dollars	ACS	2011	27,860	40,217	69%	0.01
POVERTY (0.15)						
Population Living Below Poverty Line, %	ACS	2011	25.8	11.0	43%	(0.00)
Population Living Below 50% of Poverty Line, %	ACS	2011	10.2	4.9	48%	(0.00)
Population Living Below 125% of Poverty Line, %	ACS	2011	34.0	14.7	43%	0.00
Population Living Below Poverty Line (Under 18), %	CPS ASEC	2011	34.1	12.5	37%	0.01
Population Living Below Poverty Line (18–64), %	CPS ASEC	2011	21.1	9.8	46%	0.03
Population Living Below Poverty Line (65 and Older), %	CPS ASEC	2011	18.7	6.7	36%	(0.02)
EMPLOYMENT ISSUES (0.20)						
Unemployment Rate, %	BLS	2012	10.3	7.2	70%	0.01
Unemployment Rate: Male, %	BLS	2012	9.9	7.4	75%	0.01
Unemployment Rate: Female, %	BLS	2012	10.9	7.0	64%	0.01
Unemployment Rate Persons Ages 16 to 19, %	BLS	2012	28.6	21.5	75%	0.05
Percent Not in Workforce: Ages 16 to 19, %	BLS	2012	69.0	63.1	91%	0.03
Percent Not in Workforce: Ages 16 and Older, %	BLS	2012	33.6	36.0	107%	0.01
Labor Force Participation Rate, %	BLS	2012	66.4	64.0	104%	0.01
LFPR 16 to 19, %	BLS	2012	30.9	36.9	84%	0.07
LFPR 20 to 24, %	BLS	2012	71.2	73.1	97%	(0.01)
LFPR Over 25: Less Than High School Grad, %	BLS	2012	60.5	47.2	128%	0.01
LFPR Over 25: High School Grad., No College, %	BLS	2012	71.4	58.9	121%	(0.00)
LFPR Over 25: Some College, No Degree, %	BLS	2012	75.6	65.3	116%	0.00
LFPR Over 25: Associate's Degree, %	BLS	2012	78.7	73.1	108%	0.01
LFPR Over 25: Some College or Associate Degree, %	BLS	2012	76.7	68.2	112%	0.01
LFPR Over 25: College Grad., %	BLS	2012	80.4	75.6	106%	0.01
Employment to Pop. Ratio, %	BLS	2012	59.5	59.4	100%	0.01
HOUSING & WEALTH (0.34)						
Home Ownership Rate, %	Census	2011	46.9	73.8	64%	(0.00)
Mortgage Application Denial Rate (Total), %	HMDA	2011	24.4	14.0	57%	0.01
Mortgage Application Denial Rate (Male), %	HMDA	2011	24.6	16.2	66%	0.01
Mortgage Application Denial Rate (Female), %	HMDA	2011	25.5	16.3	64%	0.02
Mortgage Application Denial Rate (Joint), %	HMDA	2011	23.0	11.5	50%	0.00
Home Improvement Loans Denials (Total), %	HMDA	2011	56.2	31.3	56%	0.02
Home Improvement Loans Denials (Male), %	HMDA	2011	58.1	37.7	65%	0.02
Home Improvement Loans Denials (Female), %	HMDA	2011	61.4	38.8	63%	0.03
Home Improvement Loans Denials (Joint), %	HMDA	2011	45.0	22.8	51%	0.00

Updated | History Revised | Removed Weight in 2013 | No New Data

2013 EQUALITY INDEX OF HISPANIC AMERICA	Source	Year	Hispanic	White	Index	Diff. ('13-'12)
Percent of High-Priced Loans (More Than 3% Above Treasury)	HMDA	2011	10.4	3.9	38%	0.01
Median Home Value, 2000 Dollars	Census	2000	105,600	123,400	86%	0.00
Median Wealth, 2010 Dollars	Census SIPP	2010	7,424	110,729	7%	0.01
Equity in Home, Dollars	Census SIPP	2010	45,000	90,000	50%	(0.01)
Percent Investing in 401(K), %	EBRI	2009	18.0	36.9	49%	(0.03)
Percent Investing in IRA, %	EBRI	2009	6.0	25.6	23%	(0.10)
DIGITAL DIVIDE (0.05)						
Households With Computer at Home, %	Census	2010	66.6	80.0	83%	0.23
Households With The Internet, %	NTIA	2010	59.1	74.9	79%	0.00
Adult Users With Broadband Access, %	NTIA	2010	56.9	71.8	79%	0.00
TRANSPORTATION (0.01)						
Car Ownership, %	Census	2010	75.8	87.9	86%	(0.01)
Means of Transportation to Work: Drive Alone, %	ACS	2011	68.2	79.9	85%	0.01
Means of Transportation to Work: Public Transportation, %	ACS	2011	8.0	3.0	37%	0.01
Economic Weighted Index					60.8%	0.006

HEALTH (25%)						
DEATH RATES & LIFE EXPECTANCY (0.45)						
Life Expectancy at Birth	CDC	2010	81.2	78.8	103%	(0.00)
Male	CDC	2010	78.5	76.4	103%	(0.00)
Female	CDC	2010	83.8	81.1	103%	0.00
Life Expectancy at 65 (Additional Expected Years)	CDC	2010	20.6	19.1	108%	(0.02)
Male at 65	CDC	2010	18.8	17.7	106%	(0.04)
Female at 65	CDC	2010	22.0	20.3	108%	0.00
Age-Adjusted Death Rates (Per 100,000): All Causes	CDC	2010	558.6	755.0	135%	0.00
Age-Adjusted Death Rates (Per 100,000): Male	CDC	2010	677.7	892.5	132%	(0.01)
Age-Adjusted Death Rates (Per 100,000): Female	CDC	2010	463.4	643.3	139%	0.01
Age-Adjusted Death Rates (Per 100,000): Heart Disease	CDC	2010	132.8	179.9	135%	0.01
Ischemic Heart Disease	CDC	2010	92.3	115.0	125%	(0.01)
Age-Adjusted Death Rates (Per 100,000): Stroke (Cerebrovascular)	CDC	2010	32.1	37.8	118%	(0.01)
Age-Adjusted Death Rates (Per 100,000): Cancer	CDC	2010	119.7	176.5	147%	(0.01)
Trachea, Bronchus, and Lung	CDC	2010	20.4	50.8	249%	(0.04)
Colon, Rectum, and Anus	CDC	2010	12.3	15.5	126%	0.02
Prostate (Male)	CDC	2010	18.4	20.3	110%	(0.04)
Breast (Female)	CDC	2010	14.4	22.1	153%	0.01
Age-Adjusted Death Rates (Per 100,000): Chronic Lower Respiratory	CDC	2010	19.6	46.6	238%	(0.00)
Age-Adjusted Death Rates (Per 100,000): Influenza and Pneumonia	CDC	2010	13.7	14.9	109%	0.05
Age-Adjusted Death Rates (Per 100,000): Chronic Liver Disease and Cirrhosis	CDC	2010	13.7	9.4	69%	0.04
Age-Adjusted Death Rates (Per 100,000): Diabetes	CDC	2010	27.1	18.2	67%	(0.01)
Age-Adjusted Death Rates (Per 100,000): HIV	CDC	2010	2.8	1.1	39%	0.02

Updated | History Revised | Removed Weight in 2013 | No New Data

2013 EQUALITY INDEX OF HISPANIC AMERICA	Source	Year	Hispanic	White	Index	Diff. ('13-'12)
Unintentional Injuries	CDC	2010	25.8	42.4	164%	0.07
Motor Vehicle-Related Injuries	CDC	2010	9.6	11.9	124%	0.03
Age-Adjusted Death Rates (Per 100,000): Suicide	CDC	2010	5.9	15.0	254%	0.04
Age-Adjusted Death Rates (Per 100,000): Suicide Males	CDC	2010	9.9	24.2	244%	0.08
Death Rates (Per 100,000): Suicide Males Ages 15–24	CDC	2010	10.7	20.4	191%	0.09
Age-Adjusted Death Rates (Per 100,000): Suicide Females	CDC	2010	2.1	6.2	295%	(0.10)
Death Rates (Per 100,000): Suicide Females Ages 15–24	CDC	2010	3.1	4.4	142%	(0.36)
Age-Adjusted Death Rates (Per 100,000): Homicide	CDC	2010	5.3	2.5	47%	0.04
Age-Adjusted Death Rates (Per 100,000): Homicide male	CDC	2010	8.7	3.3	38%	0.03
Death Rates (Per 100,000): Homicide Males Ages 15–24	CDC	2010	19.7	4.1	21%	0.03
Age-Adjusted Death Rates (Per 100,000): Homicide female	CDC	2010	1.8	1.8	100%	0.18
Death Rates (Per 100,000): Homicide Females Ages 15–24	CDC	2010	2.6	1.8	69%	0.13
Death Rates (Per 100,000) By Age Cohort: <1 Male	CDC	2010	556.8	575.9	103%	(0.03)
Death Rates (Per 100,000) By Age Cohort: 1–4 Male	CDC	2010	25.0	27.5	110%	0.01
Death Rates (Per 100,000) By Age Cohort: 5–14 Male	CDC	2010	11.4	14.3	125%	0.25
Death Rates (Per 100,000) By Age Cohort: 15–24 Male	CDC	2010	79.4	93.4	118%	0.10
Death Rates (Per 100,000) By Age Cohort: 25–34 Male	CDC	2010	100.9	143.6	142%	0.10
Death Rates (Per 100,000) By Age Cohort: 35–44 Male	CDC	2010	146.2	219.1	150%	0.06
Death Rates (Per 100,000) By Age Cohort: 45–54 Male	CDC	2010	351.9	508.1	144%	0.08
Death Rates (Per 100,000) By Age Cohort: 55–64 Male	CDC	2010	815.1	1,046.2	128%	0.01
Death Rates (Per 100,000) By Age Cohort: 65–74 Male	CDC	2010	1,775.0	2,256.9	127%	0.00
Death Rates (Per 100,000) By Age Cohort: 75–84 Male	CDC	2010	4,461.9	5,770.3	129%	(0.03)
Death Rates (Per 100,000) By Age Cohort: 85+ Male	CDC	2010	11,779.8	15,816.6	134%	(0.04)
Death Rates (Per 100,000) By Age Cohort: <1 Female	CDC	2010	462.9	480.4	104%	0.01
Death Rates (Per 100,000) By Age Cohort: 1–4 Female	CDC	2010	20.2	21.8	108%	0.16
Death Rates (Per 100,000) By Age Cohort: 5–14 Female	CDC	2010	8.9	10.9	122%	0.33
Death Rates (Per 100,000) By Age Cohort: 15–24 Female	CDC	2010	26.3	38.4	146%	0.13
Death Rates (Per 100,000) By Age Cohort: 25–34 Female	CDC	2010	38.9	66.8	172%	0.13
Death Rates (Per 100,000) By Age Cohort: 35–44 Female	CDC	2010	75.2	133.1	177%	0.07
Death Rates (Per 100,000) By Age Cohort: 45–54 Female	CDC	2010	193.9	307.7	159%	0.02
Death Rates (Per 100,000) By Age Cohort: 55–64 Female	CDC	2010	450.1	631.5	140%	0.01
Death Rates (Per 100,000) By Age Cohort: 65–74 Female	CDC	2010	1,085.5	1,535.9	141%	0.02
Death Rates (Per 100,000) By Age Cohort: 75–84 Female	CDC	2010	3,067.4	4,232.6	138%	0.03
Death Rates (Per 100,000) By Age Cohort: 85+Female	CDC	2010	10,237.3	13,543.3	132%	(0.03)
PHYSICAL CONDITION (0.10)						
Overweight: 18+ Years, % of Population	CDC	2011	38.8	35.7	92%	(0.03)
Overweight: Men 20 Years and Over, % of Population	CDC	2007–2010	44.7	39.5	88%	(0.00)
Overweight: Women 20 Years and Over, % of Population	CDC	2007–2010	33.5	27.8	83%	(0.03)
Obese, % of Population	CDC	2011	28.8	26.3	91%	0.06
Obese: Men 20 Years and Over, % of Population	CDC	2007–2010	35.3	33.8	96%	(0.08)
Obese: Women 20 Years and Over, % of Population	CDC	2007–2010	41.6	32.7	79%	0.02
Diabetes: Physician Diagnosed in Ages 20+, % of Population	CDC	2007–2010	11.1	6.7	60%	0.07

Updated | History Revised | Removed Weight in 2013 | No New Data

2013 EQUALITY INDEX OF HISPANIC AMERICA	Source	Year	Hispanic	White	Index	Diff. ('13-'12)
AIDS Cases Per 100,000 Males Ages 13+	CDC	2010	29.1	9.1	31%	(0.03)
AIDS Cases Per 100,000 Females Ages 13+	CDC	2010	7.1	1.5	21%	0.02
SUBSTANCE ABUSE (0.10)						
Binge Alcohol (5 Drinks in 1 Day, 1X a Year) Ages 18+, % of Population	CDC	2011	21.2	26.2	124%	(0.15)
Use of Illicit Drugs in the Past Month Ages 12+, % of Population	CDC	2009	7.9	8.8	111%	0.00
Tobacco: Both Cigarette & Cigar Ages 12+, % of Population	CDC	2009	23.2	29.6	128%	0.00
MENTAL HEALTH (0.02)						
Students Who Consider Suicide: Male, %	CDC	2009	10.7	10.5	98%	0.00
Students Who Carry Out Intent and Require Medical Attention: Male, %	CDC	2007	1.8	0.9	50%	0.00
Students That Act on Suicidal Feeling: Male, %	CDC	2007	6.3	3.4	54%	0.00
Students Who Consider Suicide: Female, %	CDC	2009	20.2	16.1	80%	0.00
Students Who Carry Out Intent and Require Medical Attention: Female, %	CDC	2007	3.9	2.1	54%	0.00
Students That Act on Suicidal Feeling: Female, %	CDC	2007	14.0	7.7	55%	0.00
ACCESS TO CARE (0.05)						
Private Insurance Payment for Health Care: Under 65 Years Old, % of Distribution	CPS ASEC	2011	42.2	74.5	57%	(0.01)
People Without Health Insurance, % of Population	CPS ASEC	2011	30.1	11.1	37%	(0.01)
People 18 to 64 Without a Usual Source of Health Insurance, % of Adults	CPS ASEC	2011	40.7	15.2	37%	(0.01)
People 18 to 64 and in Poverty Without a Usual Source of Health Insurance, % of Adults	CPS ASEC	2011	55.1	37.7	68%	0.02
Population Under 65 Covered By Medicaid, % of Population	CPS ASEC	2011	27.8	12.1	44%	(0.01)
ELDERLY HEALTH CARE (0.03)						
Population Over 65 Covered By Medicaid, % of Population	CPS ASEC	2011	23.3	6.4	27%	0.01
Medicare Expenditures Per Beneficiary, Dollars	CDC	2009	14,860	15,938	107%	0.16
PREGNANCY ISSUES (0.04)						
Prenatal Care Begins in 1st Trimester	CDC	2007	72.4	87.7	83%	0.00
Prenatal Care Begins in 3rd Trimester	CDC	2007	6.2	2.3	37%	0.00
Percent of Births to Mothers 18 and Under	CDC	2010	4.7	1.7	36%	0.00
Percent of Live Births to Unmarried Mothers	CDC	2010	53.4	29.0	54%	(0.00)
Infant Mortality Rates Among Mothers With Less Than 12 Years Education	CDC	2005	5.2	9.3	179%	0.00
Infant Mortality Rates Among Mothers With 12 Years Education	CDC	2005	5.4	7.1	131%	0.00
Infant Mortality Rates Among Mothers With 13 or More Years Education	CDC	2005	4.6	4.1	89%	0.00
Mothers Who Smoked Cigarettes During Pregnancy, %	CDC	2007	2.4	12.7	529%	0.00
Low Birth Weight, % of Live Births	CDC	2010	7.0	7.1	102%	(0.01)
Very Low Birth Weight, % of Live Births	CDC	2010	1.2	1.2	97%	(0.02)
REPRODUCTION ISSUES (0.01)						
Abortions, Per 1,000 Live Births	CDC	2007	193.0	159.0	82%	0.00
Women Using Contraception, % of Population (Ages 15–44)	CDC	2006–2008	58.5	64.7	90%	0.00
DELIVERY ISSUES (0.10)						
All Infant Deaths: Neonatal and Post, Per 1,000 Live Births	CDC	2008	5.6	5.5	98%	(0.05)
Neonatal Deaths, Per 1,000 Live Births	CDC	2008	3.8	3.5	92%	(0.05)
Post Neonatal Deaths, Per 1,000 Live Births	CDC	2008	1.8	2.0	111%	(0.01)

Updated | History Revised | Removed Weight in 2013 | No New Data

2013 EQUALITY INDEX OF HISPANIC AMERICA	Source	Year	Hispanic	White	Index	Diff. ('13-'12)
Maternal Mortality, Per 100,000 Live Births	CDC	2007	7.2	8.1	113%	0.00
CHILDREN'S HEALTH (0.10)						
Babies Breastfed, %	CDC	2007	80.6	76.2	106%	0.00
Children Without a Health Care Visit in Past 12 Months (Up to 6 Years Old), %	CDC	2010–2011	6.7	3.5	52%	(0.01)
Vaccinations of Children Below Poverty: Combined Vacc. Series 4: 3: 1: 3, % of Children 19–35 Months	CDC	2009	71.0	68.0	104%	0.00
Uninsured Children, %	CPS ASEC	2011	15.1	6.8	45%	0.03
Overweight Boys 6–11 Years Old, % of Population	CDC	2007–2010	24.3	18.6	77%	0.18
Overweight Girls 6–11 Years Old, % of Population	CDC	2007–2010	22.4	14.0	63%	(0.06)
AIDS Cases Per 100,000 All Children Under 13	CDC	2010	0.04	0.01	30%	0.16
Health Weighted Index					**101.2%**	**0.003**

EDUCATION (25%)

	Source	Year	Hispanic	White	Index	Diff. ('13-'12)
QUALITY (0.25)						
TEACHER QUALITY (0.10)						
Middle Grades: Teacher Lacking at Least a College Minor in Subject Taught (High Vs. Low Minority Schools)*, %	ET	2000	49.0	40.0	85%	0.00
HS: Teacher Lacking an Undergraduate Major in Subject Taught (High Vs. Low Poverty Secondary Schools)*, %	ET	2007–2008	21.9	10.9	88%	(0.03)
Per Student Funding (High [30%] Vs. Low [0%] Poverty Districts)*, Dollars	SFF	2009	10,948	10,684	102%	0.02
Teachers With < 3 Years Experience (High Vs. Low Minority Schools)*, %	NCES	2000	21.0	10.0	48%	0.00
Distribution of Underprepared Teachers (High Vs. Low Minority Schools)*, % (California Only)	SRI	2008–2009	5.0	1.0	20%	0.00
**High poverty (high minority) values are recorded in the Hispanic column. Low poverty (low minority) values are recorded in the White column.*						
COURSE QUALITY (0.15)						
College Completion, % of All Entrants	NCES	2002	48.9	60.2	81%	0.01
College Completion, % of Entrants With Strong HS Curriculum (Algebra II Plus Other Courses)	ET	1999	79.0	86.0	92%	0.00
HS Students: Enrolled in Chemistry, %	NCES	2005	59.2	67.1	88%	0.00
HS Students: Enrolled in Algebra II, %	NCES	2005	62.7	71.2	88%	0.00
Students Taking: Precalculus, %	CB	2009	45.3	55.0	82%	0.00
Students Taking: Calculus, %	CB	2009	19.3	30.0	64%	0.00
Students Taking: Physics, %	CB	2009	47.0	54.0	87%	0.00
Students Taking: English Composition, %	CB	2009	35.0	43.0	81%	0.00
ATTAINMENT (0.20)						
Graduation Rates, 2-Year Institutions Where Students Started as Full Time, First Time Students, %	NCES	2006	32.8	32.0	103%	0.00
Graduation Rates, 4-Year Institutions Where Students Started as Full Time, First Time Students, %	NCES	2003	46.2	59.3	78%	0.00
NCAA Div. I College Freshmen Graduating Within 6 Years, %	NCAA	2005	42.0	52.0	81%	(0.02)
Degrees Earned: Associate, % of Population Aged 18–24 Yrs	NCES	2010–2011	2.0	3.4	58%	0.03
Degrees Earned: Bachelor's, % of Population Aged 18–29 Yrs	NCES	2010–2011	1.4	4.0	36%	0.03

Updated | History Revised | Removed Weight in 2013 | No New Data

2013 EQUALITY INDEX OF HISPANIC AMERICA	Source	Year	Hispanic	White	Index	Diff. ('13-'12)
Degrees Earned: Master's, % of Population Aged 18–34 Yrs	NCES	2010–2011	0.3	1.1	28%	0.01
Educational Attainment: at Least High School (25 Yrs. and Over), % of Population	Census	2012	65.0	92.5	70%	0.02
Educational Attainment: at Least Bachelor's (25 Yrs. and Over), % of Population	Census	2012	14.5	34.5	42%	0.00
Degrees Conferred, % Distribution, By Field						
Agriculture/Forestry	NCES	2011	0.8	1.7	50%	0.01
Art/Architecture	NCES	2011	0.8	0.7	127%	0.05
Business/Management	NCES	2011	21.1	19.7	107%	0.00
Communications	NCES	2011	3.9	4.0	97%	0.01
Computer and Information Sciences	NCES	2011	2.0	2.0	98%	(0.00)
Education	NCES	2011	9.6	13.2	73%	(0.04)
Engineering	NCES	2011	4.2	4.8	88%	(0.00)
English/Literature	NCES	2011	2.4	2.8	88%	0.05
Foreign Languages	NCES	2011	2.1	1.0	208%	(0.03)
Health Sciences	NCES	2011	8.3	11.2	74%	(0.02)
Liberal Arts/Humanities	NCES	2011	2.4	1.9	126%	0.03
Mathematics/Statistics	NCES	2011	0.7	0.9	78%	0.03
Natural Sciences	NCES	2011	4.7	5.2	90%	0.01
Philosophy/Religion/Theology	NCES	2011	0.5	0.7	77%	(0.01)
Psychology	NCES	2011	6.8	5.0	136%	0.03
Social Sciences/History	NCES	2011	9.4	7.7	122%	0.01
Other Fields	NCES	2011	20.4	17.7	115%	0.02
SCORES (0.15)						
PRESCHOOL 10% OF TOTAL SCORES (0.015)						
Children's School Readiness Skills (Ages 3–5), % With 3 or 4 Skills* **Recognizes All Letters, Counts to 20 or Higher, Writes Name, Reads or Pretends to Read*	NCES	2005	26.0	46.8	55%	0.00
ELEMENTARY 40% OF TOTAL SCORES (0.06)						
Average Scale Score in U.S. History, 8th Graders	NCES	2010	252	274	92%	0.00
Average Scale Score in U.S. History, 4th Graders	NCES	2010	198	224	88%	0.00
Average Scale Score in Math, 8th Graders	NCES	2011	270	293	92%	0.00
Average Scale Score in Math, 4th Graders	NCES	2011	229	249	92%	0.00
Average Scale Score in Reading, 8th Graders	NCES	2011	252	274	92%	0.00
Average Scale Score in Reading, 4th Graders	NCES	2011	206	231	89%	0.00
Average Scale Score in Science, 8th Graders	NCES	2011	137	163	84%	0.03
Average Scale Score in Science, 4th Graders	NCES	2009	131	163	80%	0.00
Writing Proficiency at or Above Basic, 8th Graders, % of Students	NCES	2011	69	92	75%	(0.11)
Writing Proficiency at or Above Basic, 4th Graders, % of Students	NCES	2002	77	90	85%	0.00
HIGH SCHOOL 50% OF TOTAL SCORES (0.075)						
Writing Proficiency at or Above Basic, 12th Graders, % of Students	NCES	2011	66	86	77%	(0.06)
Average Scale Score in Science, 12th Graders	NCES	2005	128	156	82%	0.00
Average Scale Score in U.S. History, 12th Graders	NCES	2010	275	296	93%	0.00

Updated | History Revised | Removed Weight in 2013 | No New Data

2013 EQUALITY INDEX OF HISPANIC AMERICA	Source	Year	Hispanic	White	Index	Diff. ('13-'12)
Average Scale Score in Reading, 12th Graders	NCES	2009	274	296	93%	0.00
High School GPAs for Those Taking The SAT	CB	2009	3.17	3.40	93%	0.00
SAT Reasoning Test: Mean Scores	CB	2012	1,352	1,578	86%	(0.00)
Mathematics, Joint	CB	2012	462	536	86%	(0.00)
Mathematics, Male	CB	2012	481	554	87%	(0.00)
Mathematics, Female	CB	2012	446	520	86%	(0.00)
Critical Reading, Joint	CB	2012	448	527	85%	(0.00)
Critical Reading, Male	CB	2012	453	530	86%	(0.00)
Critical Reading, Female	CB	2012	444	525	85%	(0.00)
Writing, Joint	CB	2012	442	515	86%	(0.00)
Writing, Male	CB	2012	438	506	86%	(0.00)
Writing, Female	CB	2012	446	522	85%	(0.00)
ACT: Average Composite Score	ACT	2012	18.9	22.4	84%	0.01
ENROLLMENT (0.10)						
School Enrollment: ages 3–34, % of Population	Census	2011	55.6	56.4	98%	0.05
Preprimary School Enrollment	Census	2011	55.8	67.0	83%	0.02
3 and 4 Years Old	Census	2011	41.6	56.2	74%	(0.01)
5 and 6 Years Old	Census	2011	95.6	95.8	100%	0.00
7 to 13 Years Old	Census	2011	98.4	98.4	100%	0.01
14 and 15 Years Old	Census	2011	98.2	98.9	99%	(0.00)
16 and 17 Years Old	Census	2011	94.6	95.9	99%	0.01
18 and 19 Years Old	Census	2011	65.2	72.1	90%	0.12
20 and 21 Years Old	Census	2011	45.7	56.2	81%	0.15
22 to 24 Years Old	Census	2011	23.6	32.9	72%	0.06
25 to 29 Years Old	Census	2011	10.5	15.2	69%	0.01
30 to 34 Years Old	Census	2011	4.5	7.8	58%	(0.11)
35 and Over	Census	2011	1.6	1.7	93%	(0.26)
College Enrollment (Graduate or Undergraduate): Ages 14 and Over, % of Population	Census	2011	8.1	10.3	79%	0.07
14 to 17 Years Old	Census	2011	1.1	1.1	96%	(0.21)
18 to 19 Years Old	Census	2011	43.9	52.9	83%	0.25
20 to 21 Years Old	Census	2011	43.7	54.6	80%	0.18
22 to 24 Years Old	Census	2011	22.6	32.4	70%	0.07
25 to 29 Years Old	Census	2011	10.0	14.9	67%	0.00
30 to 34 Years Old	Census	2011	4.3	7.7	56%	(0.10)
35 Years Old and Over	Census	2011	1.4	1.7	82%	(0.19)
College Enrollment Rate As a Percent of All 18- to 24-Year-Old High School Completers, %	NCES	2011	34.8	44.7	78%	(0.04)
Adult Education Participation, % of Adult Population	NCES	2004–2005	38.0	46.0	83%	0.00

Updated | History Revised | Removed Weight in 2013 | No New Data

2013 EQUALITY INDEX OF HISPANIC AMERICA	Source	Year	Hispanic	White	Index	Diff. ('13-'12)
STUDENT STATUS & RISK FACTORS (0.10)						
High School Dropouts: Status Dropouts, % (Not Completed HS and Not Enrolled, Regardless of When Dropped Out)	Census	2009	20.8	9.1	44%	0.00
Children in Poverty, %	Census	2011	34.1	12.5	37%	0.01
Children in All Families Below Poverty Level, %	Census	2011	33.7	11.9	35%	0.01
Children in Families Below Poverty Level (Female Householder, No Spouse Present), %	Census	2011	56.7	35.5	63%	0.02
Children (Under 18) With a Disability, %	Census	2011	3.7	3.9	106%	(0.08)
Public School Students (K-12): Repeated Grade, %	NCES	2007	11.8	8.7	74%	0.00
Public School Students (K-12): Suspended, %	NCES	2003	10.4	8.8	85%	0.00
Public School Students (K-12): Expelled, %	NCES	2003	1.4	1.4	100%	0.00
Center-Based Child Care of Preschool Children, %	NCES	2005	43.4	59.1	136%	0.00
Parental Care Only of Preschool Children, %	NCES	2005	38.0	24.1	158%	0.00
Teacher Stability: Remained in Public School, High Vs. Low Minority Schools, %	NCES	2005	79.7	85.9	93%	0.00
Teacher Stability: Remained in Private School, High Vs. Low Minority Schools, %	NCES	2005	72.7	82.8	88%	0.00
Zero Days Missed in School Year, % of 10th Graders	NCES	2002	16.5	12.1	137%	0.00
3+ Days Late to School, % of 10th Graders	NCES	2002	46.1	44.4	96%	0.00
Never Cut Classes, % of 10th Graders	NCES	2002	64.6	70.3	92%	0.00
Home Literacy Activities (Age 3 to 5)						
Read to 3 or More Times a Week	NCES	2007	67.6	90.6	75%	0.00
Told a Story at Least Once a Month	NCES	2005	49.8	53.3	93%	0.00
Taught Words or Numbers Three or More Times a Week	NCES	2005	74.3	75.7	98%	0.00
Visited a Library at Least Once in Last Month	NCES	2007	27.0	40.8	66%	0.00
Education Weighted Index					**76.2%**	**0.003**

SOCIAL JUSTICE (10%)

EQUALITY BEFORE THE LAW (0.70)	Source	Year	Hispanic	White	Index	Diff. ('13-'12)
Stopped While Driving, %	BJS	2008	9.1	8.4	92%	0.00
Speeding	BJS	2002	44.4	57.0	128%	0.00
Vehicle Defect	BJS	2002	14.0	8.7	62%	0.00
Roadside Check for Drinking Drivers	BJS	2002	1.6	1.3	81%	0.00
Record Check	BJS	2002	7.8	11.3	145%	0.00
Seatbelt Violation	BJS	2002	5.5	4.4	80%	0.00
Illegal Turn/Lane Change	BJS	2002	5.7	4.5	79%	0.00
Stop Sign/Light Violation	BJS	2002	11.2	6.5	58%	0.00
Other	BJS	2002	6.2	4.0	65%	0.00
Incarceration Rate: Prisoners Per 100,000	BJS	2011	672	261	39%	0.02
Incarceration Rate: Prisoners Per 100,000 People: Male	BJS	2011	1,238	478	39%	0.02
Incarceration Rate: Prisoners Per 100,000 People: Female	BJS	2011	71	51	72%	0.11

Updated | History Revised | Removed Weight in 2013 | No New Data

2013 EQUALITY INDEX OF HISPANIC AMERICA	Source	Year	Hispanic	White	Index	Diff. ('13-'12)
VICTIMIZATION & MENTAL ANGUISH (0.20)						
Homicide Rate Per 100,000: Male	CDC	2009	10.5	3.4	32%	0.03
Homicide Rate Per 100,000: Female	CDC	2009	2.3	1.8	78%	0.06
Hate Crimes Victims, Rate Per 100,000	USDJ	2011	1.0	0.2	24%	0.04
Victims of Violent Crimes, Rate Per 1,000, Persons Age 12 or Older	BJS	2011	23.8	21.5	90%	(0.19)
High School Students Carrying Weapons on School Property	CDC	2011	5.8	5.1	88%	(0.09)
High School Students Carrying Weapons Anywhere	CDC	2011	16.2	17.0	105%	(0.03)
Firearm-Related Death Rates Per 100,000: Males, All Ages	CDC	2007	13.4	16.1	120%	0.00
Ages 1–14	CDC	2007	0.8	0.7	86%	0.00
Ages 15–24	CDC	2007	30.7	13.4	44%	0.00
Ages 25–44	CDC	2007	17.7	18.3	104%	0.00
Ages 25–34	CDC	2007	21.8	18.0	82%	0.00
Ages 35–44	CDC	2007	12.6	18.7	148%	0.00
Ages 45–64	CDC	2007	9.7	19.5	202%	0.00
Age 65 and Older	CDC	2007	10.8	27.3	253%	0.00
Firearm-Related Death Rates Per 100,000: Females, All Ages	CDC	2007	1.5	2.9	187%	0.00
Ages 1–14	CDC	2007	0.3	0.3	111%	0.00
Ages 15–24	CDC	2007	2.8	2.5	87%	0.00
Ages 25–44	CDC	2007	2.3	4.1	176%	0.00
Ages 25–34	CDC	2007	2.5	3.4	136%	0.00
Ages 35–44	CDC	2007	2.1	4.6	222%	0.00
Ages 45–64	CDC	2007	1.5	3.9	262%	0.00
Age 65 and Older	CDC	2007	0.6	2.2	393%	0.00
Social Justice Weighted Index					**61.9%**	**0.002**

CIVIC ENGAGEMENT (10%)	Source	Year	Hispanic	White	Index	Diff. ('13-'12)
DEMOCRATIC PROCESS (0.4)						
Registered Voters, % of Citizen Population	Census	2010	51.6	68.2	76%	0.00
Actually Voted, % of Citizen Population	Census	2010	31.2	48.6	64%	0.00
COMMUNITY PARTICIPATION (0.3)						
Percent of Population Volunteering for Military Reserves, %	USDD	2010	0.4	1.0	40%	0.00
Volunteerism, %	BLS	2011	14.9	28.2	53%	(0.00)
Civic and Political	BLS	2011	3.8	5.7	67%	0.10
Educational or Youth Service	BLS	2011	36.6	25.7	142%	0.09
Environmental or Animal Care	BLS	2011	1.2	2.6	46%	(0.06)
Hospital or Other Health	BLS	2011	6.0	8.0	75%	0.10
Public Safety	BLS	2011	0.5	1.4	36%	(0.50)
Religious	BLS	2011	32.9	31.9	103%	(0.07)
Social or Community Service	BLS	2011	10.4	14.4	72%	(0.08)
Unpaid Volunteering of Young Adults	NCES	2000	30.7	32.2	95%	0.00

Updated | History Revised | Removed Weight in 2013 | No New Data

2013 EQUALITY INDEX OF HISPANIC AMERICA	Source	Year	Hispanic	White	Index	Diff. ('13-'12)
COLLECTIVE BARGAINING (0.2)						
Members of Unions, % of Employed	BLS	2012	9.8	11.1	88%	0.03
Represented By Unions, % of Employed	BLS	2012	10.9	12.3	89%	0.03
GOVERNMENTAL EMPLOYMENT (0.1)						
Federal Executive Branch (Nonpostal) Employment, % of Adult Population	OPM	2008	0.4	0.8	52%	0.00
State and Local Government Employment, %	EEOC	2009	1.8	2.5	73%	0.00
Civic Engagement Weighted Index					**68.0%**	**0.006**

Due to data availability, the 2012 Equality Index of Hispanic America does not include all the variables that were used to calculate the 2012 Equality Index of Black America. Therefore, weights were redistributed among the available variables and a comparable Black–White index was calculated solely to provide a consistent comparison between blacks and Hispanics.

Source	Acronym
American Community Survey	ACS
American College Testing	ACT
Annie E. Casey Foundation	AECF
U.S. Bureau of Justice Statistics	BJS
U.S. Bureau of Labor Statistics	BLS
College Board	CB
Centers for Disease Control and Prevention	CDC
U.S. Census Bureau	Census
U.S. Census Bureau, Survey of Income & Program Participation	Census SIPP
Current Population Survey: Annual Social and Economic Supplement	CPS ASEC
Employee Benefit Research Institute	EBRI
U.S. Equal Employment Opportunity Commission	EEOC
The Education Trust	ET
Federal Bureau of Investigation	FBI
Home Mortgage Disclosure Act	HMDA
National Archive of Criminal Justice Data	NACJD
National Collegiate Athletic Association	NCAA
National Center for Education Statistics	NCES
National Center for Juvenile Justice	NCJJ
National Telecommunications and Information Administration	NTIA
Office of Personal Management	OPM
Education Law Center, Is School Funding Fair?	SFF
SRI International	SRI
U.S. Department of Defense	USDD
U.S. Department of Justice	USDJ

LIFT EV'RY VOICE:

A SPECIAL COLLECTION

OF ARTICLES AND OP-EDs

SLAVERY
was abolished -
YET
UNFAIR
WHY PAY RENT,
WHEN the BUILDING
NEEDS REPAIR?
ON STRIKE
WE DEMAND
RECOGNITION

INTRODUCTION TO THE SPECIAL COLLECTION

CHANELLE P. HARDY, ESQ., NATIONAL URBAN LEAGUE POLICY INSITUTE

This is the 37th edition of *The State of Black America*. Our nation's first black president has been inaugurated for his second term in office, carried there largely by the power of a historic African American vote. We also observe two pivotal events in the history of our country and our people—the 150th anniversary of the Emancipation Proclamation and the 50th anniversary of the *Great March on Washington for Jobs and Freedom*. As we reflect on the achievement embodied by these events, we must also acknowledge the work that remains to realize their full promise.

It's no secret that African Americans were hit hard by the Great Recession and have been largely left out of the fragile economic recovery. Our jobless rate hovers around 14 percent. We still earn almost 20 percent less than whites for the same work. And, as this year's special Equality Index comparing 1963 to 2013 underscores, real parity continues to elude us—even after half a century.

★ *The income gap has only closed by 7 percentage points (now at 60%).*

★ *The unemployment rate gap has only closed by 6 percentage points (now at 52%).*

Despite this sobering assessment, some have called for the elimination of the very civil rights measures—including voting rights and affirmative action—enacted to remedy past discrimination, and to offer a roadmap to equality and dignity. They cite President Obama's election and the record black turnout that helped deliver it, as well as the presence of African Americans in nearly every walk of life to conclude that black people essentially have "overcome" and, therefore, no longer need the protections guaranteed in the Constitution.

We have, indeed, made great strides over the past half-century. More blacks graduate from high school and college; many of us have a higher standard of living; and there are more pathways for upward mobility than before. But we shouldn't confuse the *ability* to achieve with the *opportunity* to achieve. Our gains are, at best, a down payment on the freedom we demanded, and we must continue to push for our full measure. The naked racism of the past may be gone, but the subtle bigotry—cloaked in specious reasoning—is just as harmful. It, too, must be met head-on with a renewed sense of purpose and resolve.

The good news is the election of 2012 demonstrated that the African American community appears ready to embrace a new spirit of activism, and to pick up where many of our civil rights icons left off to affect real change in our own destiny.

When faced with a well-orchestrated voter suppression campaign masquerading, ironically, as voter protection efforts, civil rights groups, unions, social justice organizations and others came together in solidarity to fight back against this brazen assault. The Urban League's own *Occupy the Vote* campaign enlisted hundreds of volunteers to make calls, knock on doors and use social media to encourage our people to vote.

Two Urban League Guild members in Philadelphia, 88-year-old Jacqueline Bagwell and 94-year-old Dorothy Burton, should have been secure in their right to vote—they both had been doing so for decades. But Jackie and Dorothy recognized the end game in Pennsylvania's voter ID laws, so they joined the fight to protect for future generations the rights they had long enjoyed. They spent hours in our affiliate office making calls and getting the word out to their neighbors that their votes and this election were too important to ignore. In Philadelphia, and in communities all over the country, African Americans asserted their constitutional rights at the ballot box and, in doing so, proclaimed that they would not surrender them without a fight.

THE GOOD NEWS IS THE ELECTION OF 2012 DEMONSTRATED THAT THE AFRICAN AMERICAN COMMUNITY APPEARS READY TO EMBRACE A NEW SPIRIT OF ACTIVISM, AND TO PICK UP WHERE MANY OF OUR CIVIL RIGHTS ICONS LEFT OFF TO AFFECT REAL CHANGE IN OUR OWN DESTINY.

In total, the *Occupy the Vote* campaign reached tens of thousands of individuals who, in addition to pledging to vote, enlisted as Urban League Freedom Fighters to drive civic engagement efforts at the local level. Like so many others around the country, these Freedom Fighters have committed to take up the challenge in their own communities and work to deliver the full freedom and justice to which we are entitled.

The commemorative Special Collection in this *State of Black America, Redeem the Dream: Jobs Rebuild America* pays homage to those early freedom fighters in the civil rights movement who taught us all about perseverance and sacrifice. The heroes and heroines, those who have become iconic and those who remain unsung—like Jackie and Dorothy in Philadelphia—inspire us to push on with courage and conviction for the freedom promised 150 years ago and demanded a century after.

Looking to the road ahead on our journey to full equality, I am heartened and encouraged by a new army of activists who, perhaps moved by those highlighted in this publication, will finish the work started so long ago. As you read these essays by Rep. John Lewis, Marian Wright Edelman, Stefanie Brown James or any of the other notables, I hope you, too, will be inspired to do your part to *Redeem the Dream.*

NEW TACTICS, SAME OLD TAINT

U.S. CONGRESSMAN JOHN LEWIS

On "Bloody Sunday," nearly 50 years ago, Hosea Williams and I led 600 peaceful, non-violent protestors attempting to march from Selma to Montgomery to dramatize the need for voting rights protection in Alabama. As we crossed the Edmund Pettus Bridge, we were attacked by state troopers who tear-gassed, clubbed, whipped and trampled us with horses. I was hit in the head with a nightstick and suffered a concussion. Seventeen marchers were hospitalized that day.

In response, President Lyndon B. Johnson introduced and signed the Voting Rights Act into law. We have come a great distance since then, due in large part to the Act, but efforts to undermine the voting power of minorities did not end after 1965. They persist today.

On February 27, 2013, the Supreme Court heard one of the most important cases in our generation, *Shelby County v. Holder*. At issue is Section 5 of the Act, which requires all or parts of 16 "covered" states with long histories and contemporary records of discrimination to seek approval for voting law changes from the federal government. The question for the Court is whether Section 5 remains a necessary remedy for ongoing discrimination.

In 2006, we debated this very question in Congress over a 10 month period. We held 21 hearings, heard from over 90 witnesses, and reviewed more than 15,000 pages of evidence. We analyzed voting patterns inside and outside the 16 covered jurisdictions. We considered four amendments on the floor of the House and several in the Senate Judiciary Committee.

After all of that, Congress came to a near unanimous conclusion: while some change has occurred, the places with a legacy of entrenched state-sponsored voting discrimination still have the most persistent, flagrant, contemporary records of discrimination. While the 16 jurisdictions affected by Section 5 represent only 25 percent of the nation's population, they still represent more than 80 percent of the successful lawsuits proving cases of voting discrimination.

It is ironic that the worst perpetrators are those seeking to be relieved of the responsibilities of justice. Instead of accepting the ways in which our society has changed and dealing with the implications of true democracy, they would rather free themselves of oversight and the obligations of equal justice.

The Shelby County case is a good example. In 2008 the Justice Department found the Calera city redistricting plan discriminatory. Once an all-white suburb of Birmingham, rapid new growth created one majority black district that elected the first-ever black representative to city government, Ernest Montgomery.

However, just before the next upcoming election, the legislature decided to redraw city boundaries to include three white majority districts in an effort to dilute the voting power of black citizens. The plan was blocked by the Justice Department, but Calera held the election anyway, toppling Montgomery from his seat.

In 2012, Section 5 was used to block Texas from implementing the most restrictive voter law in the country, which threatened the rights of more than 600,000 registered voters, predominantly Latinos and African Americans. Evidence in this case was so compelling that two Republican judges found the law was intentionally discriminatory.

Kilmichael, Mississippi was blocked from cancelling elections shortly after the results of the 2010 census revealed a black voting majority that for the first time could elect the candidate of their choice.

Cases like these are numerous and exemplify the unprecedented legislative record amassed in 2006. That mountain of evidence paved the way for a bi-partisan majority in a Republican-led White House and Congress to reauthorize Section 5 by a House vote of 390–33 and 98–0 in the Senate. Every president since 1965, regardless of party or politics, has reauthorized Section 5 of the Voting Rights Act.

Opponents complain of state expense, but what is the price of justice? Their only cost is the paper, postage, and manpower required to send copies of legislation to the federal government for review, hardly a punishment. But without Section 5, victims of voting discrimination, whose rights may already be flagrantly denied, would have to bear the additional cost of an expensive lawsuit to obtain relief, which could take years to resolve. Meanwhile, discrimination would run rampant in those jurisdictions.

The Act does provide a way to bail out of Justice Department scrutiny. Unfortunately for persistent offenders, they have to show a clean record to do so. Yet no area which has applied for bailout has ever been denied.

The right to vote is the most powerful non-violent tool we have in a democracy. I risked my life defending that right. Some died in the struggle. States that trample on fundamental freedoms must be held accountable. That is the purpose of the law. Oversight can be hard to bear, but if we are to ever actualize the true meaning of equality it may be a necessary requirement of democracy.

THOUGH WE HAVE ACHIEVED MUCH, THE BATTLE CONTINUES

REVEREND AL SHARPTON

One hundred and fifty years ago, God began breaking the chains and shackles of slavery. It was on January 1, 1863, that President Abraham Lincoln issued the Emancipation Proclamation. Though the nation was still reeling from war, and freedom would take some time to come to fruition, the process of ending the horrid practice of slavery had begun. And for the next 100 years, African Americans and those on the side of justice continued fighting for greater equality in all aspects of society. While progress was clearly made, it wasn't enough. Seeking greater integration, equal access to jobs, quality education, fair housing, voting rights and much more, folks from diverse backgrounds marched for 'Jobs and Freedom' in our nation's capital in 1963. Led by a coalition of groups and organizers—including the Southern Christian Leadership Conference and the great Dr. Martin Luther King Jr.—over 250,000 rallied for change. Soon after, we saw passage of the Voting Rights Act. As we reflect on these milestones in 2013, it's important to remember that though we have achieved much, the battles continue and we must be as engaged as ever so that our children may succeed further than we ever dreamed of.

Many doubted that we would see the re-election of an African American President in 2012. But while the naysayers cast doubt, and the obstructionists put roadblocks like new voter ID laws in place, the people surpassed expectations when they once again participated in the electoral process in remarkable numbers. Pushing back against voter suppression tactics, and standing in line oftentimes for hours, the voters dictated exactly what direction they wanted their country to go. We chose greater equality for all; we chose to move forward. But unfortunately, while we may have re-elected a President that fights for the middle-class/poor, establishes health care reform and pushes for many programs that directly benefit African Americans, certain Congressional and Senate leaders stand to block his every move. Though President Obama may not be dealing with something as severe as slavery, the issues of today are nonetheless important to the well-being of this nation.

When Lincoln signed the Emancipation Proclamation, many were clearly against it. But while he diligently worked to bring opposing sides together, it's important to remember that there were countless individuals on the ground that pushed him onto the right side of history. Folks like Frederick Douglass and many abolitionists (both black and white), were busy mobilizing, organizing and fighting for change. Today, as we continue to face high unemployment, excessive violence on our streets, an unbalanced educational system, threats to vital programs like social security, Medicare and Medicaid, we must remember that President Obama cannot do it alone. We must continue to be the foot soldiers championing for progress so that progress itself may be signed into law in the halls of Washington.

In 2013, as we reflect on the 150th anniversary of the Emancipation Proclamation and the 50th anniversary of the historic *March on Washington for Jobs and Freedom,* we cannot lose focus. It's absolutely remarkable that in 150 years, we went from the bondage of slavery to the highest office in the land—that achievement should never be understated or diminished. But for those of us that want to continue on the road of justice understand, we have a few more blockades to tear down. If we fight, we can win. Let's continue moving forward.

Some say change is slow to come, but I say, the harder you push, the faster it will arrive.

THE ENDURING ICON: DR. DOROTHY HEIGHT

AVIS A. JONES-DEWEEVER, PH.D.

She stood alone, among a sea of faces on that historic day some fifty years ago. As the lone woman on the dais as Dr. Martin Luther King Jr. delivered his now historic, I Have a Dream speech, that strong, yet unassuming young woman stood there, not as a symbol, not as an aide, not as someone who inexplicably made her way into a space in which she did not authentically belong, but firmly as a peer. Dr. Dorothy Height stood there as an often unacknowledged architect of strategies for justice, and a fearless advocate for what she knew was right.

In a word, Dr. Height was brilliant. She had a photographic memory that could easily relay details of discussions between her esteemed mentor, Dr. Mary McLeod Bethune and President Franklin D. Roosevelt, while then providing a nuanced perspective regarding contemporary policy challenges. Her brilliance did not only pertain to her exceedingly sharp mind and wit. Dr. Height had it all—style, charisma and character. She was that rare person who took the air out of any room she entered. She captured attention for much more than just the bountiful collection of colorful hats that proudly crowned her head. She captured your attention because of her spirit. She, quite simply, exuded love and anyone who had the joy of experiencing her presence felt it and could become stronger because of it.

I came to know and work with Dr. Height in the final years of her life—a life filled with firsts and much exceptionalism. She dedicated her life to unflinchingly fighting on behalf of race and gender equality and justice in a world that inherently respected neither. It was clear that her devotion to both the Civil Rights Movement and the Women's Rights Movement stemmed not only from an innate sense of fairness, undying tenacity, and the courage to do what others believed could not be done, but a deep love of humanity and the desire to leave the human condition in better shape than what she found.

Today as we continue to face momentous challenges across the spectrums of both race and gender, I find strength and resolve in the lessons from her life's work that "struck a mighty blow." While her life spanned nearly a century, Dr. Height still had so much more to give and I miss her. But I will, as we all should, remember the lessons she exemplified in the life she lived.

Live up to the challenge of being the voice for the voiceless. Have the courage to stand for what's right, even if at moments, you stand alone. And most importantly, quite simply, do the work. Change is not an evolution. It must be pushed. It must be prodded. It must be fought for, each and every step of the way. This is our challenge. This is the legacy Mother Dorothy left us all.

UNFINISHED BUSINESS

U.S. CONGRESSWOMAN MARCIA L. FUDGE, CHAIR, CONGRESSIONAL BLACK CAUCUS

This year, as we celebrate the 150th anniversary of the Emancipation Proclamation and the 50th Anniversary of the *March on Washington for Jobs and Freedom*, we remember the pillars of equity, justice and perseverance on which the legacy of the African American experience in this country stand.

In the face of seemingly insurmountable obstacles and in opposition to our basic civil and human rights, African Americans have labored in their communities and in Congress to move this country to a place where every individual has the opportunity to achieve their version of the American dream. Though we have lived and seen many successes, the long-standing promise of this country is in danger. We must do everything we can to restore and protect that promise.

Many African Americans, people of color and those living in rural and urban communities continue to face the challenges that those we celebrate this year dedicated their lives to overcome. The threats to voting rights, the erosion of economic opportunity and the chance every individual should have to achieve their full potential are conversations once again leading our national debates.

The fight for civil rights is still unfinished business and can look very different than it did 50 or 60 years ago. Today, Americans are not being attacked by vicious canines or thrown up against brick walls with fire hoses. Many of the injustices of today have a much more delicate face and are talked about under new, more subtle names.

One new name is "debt and deficit reduction" at the expense of seniors' health and well being, and our children's education. Another is the fight against full implementation of the Affordable Healthcare Act that guarantees access to healthcare for all Americans. Another injustice that I hope you all are paying close attention to is the Supreme Court's review of Section 5 of the Voting Rights Act.

Members of the CBC have worked to ensure that every American, no matter what they look like or where they come from, has the right to be heard in our democracy. There should be no code that determines your station in life. This is the very foundation on which our democracy was built, and almost fifty years later it is once again being challenged in the Supreme Court of these United States.

The priorities for the Congressional Black Caucus this first session of the 113th Congress include protecting the right to vote, making sure the doors to economic opportunity and mobility in this country remain open, and immigration reform and the inclusion of its impact on people within the African Diaspora.

The CBC will also continue proposing policies that address joblessness among African Americans and protect the future of all Americans without sacrificing programs on which our community traditionally rely.

But the only way we are going to be successful is if those in our communities continue to set and prioritize their local agendas, while realizing how much we rely on one another. It is the people organizing in churches, in community centers, barber and beauty shops that volunteer their time, commit their personal resources and, as we've seen, sacrifice their lives to make sure that no injustice goes unnoticed and no voice goes unheard that bring about change. Continuing to participate in our democracy is the only way we will truly honor the rich legacy of African Americans in this country and get things accomplished.

REFLECTIONS ON NATIONAL URBAN LEAGUE'S LEGACY AND SERVICE

JOHN W. MACK

The historic *March on Washington for Jobs and Freedom* pricked the conscience of our nation and ranks as one of the most important events in its history.

The March and the Bloody Sunday March across the Edmund Pettus Bridge were game changers for America. It provided the impetus for the 1965 Voting Rights Act—which became our modern day Emancipation Proclamation—Affirmative Action legislation, the Humphrey-Hawkins equal employment legislation, and other civil rights advances.

As we reflect on the achievements since the *Great March*, we must not overlook the contributions of two Urban League leaders in advancing the cause of civil rights and economic empowerment for the nation's black community and elevating the Urban League as a leading voice in the civil rights movement.

Whitney Young, our President from 1961 to 1971, is one of the unsung heroes of the *Great March*, having worked with the leaders of the AFL-CIO, the NAACP and other groups to mobilize more than 250,000 people for the historic event. Whitney was a visionary and transformed the Urban League from a passive institution primarily operating direct service programs to a strong advocate on behalf of African Americans and the poor. Under Whitney's leadership, many doors were opened in corporate America and the public sector to jobs for our constituents.

Whitney also developed a plan to directly address the problems confronting America and the poor—called a "Domestic Marshall Plan." The plan called for significant investment in urban cities and programs to help the poor and bring blacks more into the mainstream, and key elements of it were incorporated in President Lyndon Johnson's "War on Poverty."

Additionally, Whitney mobilized our affiliate network into a more cohesive and aggressive advocacy arm for the Urban League. This "New Thrust" initiative shook up our affiliates and launched a grassroots strategy to instill self-reliance and economic empowerment through expanded community-based programs focused on education, health, civic engagement and neighborhood improvement, to name a few. "New Thrust" reinforced the Urban League Movement as a leading civil rights movement coalition partner. In 1969, I was hired by Whitney and Sterling Tucker, who headed the initiative, to coordinate this effort that impacted 50 affiliates.

I was in Whitney Young's last class at Atlanta University before he departed to head the National Urban League and he was also a key advisor to our Atlanta Student Civil Rights Movement. He was the reason that I joined the Urban League Movement.

Following Whitney's tragic drowning in Lagos, Nigeria, Vernon Jordan succeeded him as the Urban League's head and served from 1971 to 1981. Jordan raised the Urban League's profile in Washington, D.C. by promoting Ron Brown from the position of General Counsel to lead our Washington operations as Executive Director. Brown became the League's voice and a chief advocate with Congress and the White House; and helped to advance our advocacy priorities.

Jordan also established the League's credibility in research through the creation of *The State of Black America*, which has become the seminal publication for the Urban League and serves as a key resource for policy-makers, colleges and universities.

The 1963 *March on Washington* inspired thousands of us to serve our people, in our communities through the Urban League and other organizations. Whitney Young's successors built upon his legacy and the League continues as a major force to continue the fight for economic equality and empowerment. Our current leader, Marc Morial has taken the Urban League to unprecedented new levels of advocacy, direct service and national impact on behalf of our constituency and continues to move our nation closer to a level playing field for every individual and advance America's unfinished domestic agenda.

BLACK CIVIC ENGAGEMENT 2.0: IN WITH THE OLD, IN WITH THE NEW

STEFANIE BROWN JAMES

For the past two cycles, African Americans turning out to the polls made the most significant difference in the outcome of the presidential election. Period.

Contrary to what is (or is not) discussed in the media, black voter turnout has not only exceeded expectations, it set the bar on how voter participation should look in our democratic society. In 2012, voter registration among black people was up dramatically from 2008 in every battleground state—especially in Colorado, Iowa, Nevada and Florida.[1]

In the states of Ohio, Michigan and Wisconsin, African American voter turnout increased from the 2008 Presidential election, in spite of the tremendous nationwide voter suppression efforts.[2] In Ohio, increased African American voter turnout helped elect an African American, Joyce Beatty, to the United States House of Representatives.

Whether we organize at our barbershops, night clubs, churches and small businesses, our challenge and mandate is to ensure that civic engagement becomes integrated into every facet of our lives. We can no longer wait for election season to register and educate voters—it must be a year-long mission. As the 2014 mid-term elections loom here are three recommendations on increasing civic engagement in our communities:

1. POWER TO THE PEOPLE

No individual leader or organization will save us or solve all of our problems. However, the collective action of people recognizing problems and working together to address those issues can be powerful. The success of the Obama campaign came from regular people in the neighborhood deciding they wanted to do something to help their community. There were no prerequisites for who could be engaged. The first step is helping people realize their power by giving them the opportunity to bring their talents to the table without fear of rejection.

2. LOOK TO THE PAST FOR CONTEXT

The victory of the civil rights movement was not that we overcame racism and oppression altogether, but that we could level the playing field by winning victories at the ballot box and in the courtrooms. Civic engagement—ie: VOTING—is the most effective and efficient strategy to improve the social ills in our community. From the school board members who decide what text books will be used in our classrooms, to juvenile court judges who oftentimes determine the fate of our children, our votes matter! If our votes did not matter, why would people spend billions of dollars to make it harder for us to cast our ballots? As people fight to take us back to pre-1965, it's up to us to protect the democracy we've won by making voting easier for all Americans.

3. WE MUST **PACE** OURSELVES

To create real, sustainable change it is imperative that we:

- ★ **POLL:** have a clear understanding of how members in our community feel about issues;
- ★ **ANALYZE:** research the polling data to help develop a plan of action;
- ★ **COALESCE:** implement our plan with others in the community;
- ★ **EVALUATE:** determine if our work actually equates to progress being made on the ground.

Oftentimes, we can't improve the work we do because we have no data available to truly assess our effectiveness and impact. By PACE-ing ourselves and utilizing common metrics across organizations, we'll be better positioned to implement effective models of engagement to achieve our goals faster and for less money.

As we enter this next phase of civic engagement let us move forward by welcoming new tools and strategies to increase our engagement.

NOTES

[1] Denise Stewart, Strong Black Voter Turnout Translates to Obama Win, Black America Web, November 8, 2012 (see at *http://blackamericaweb.com/71150/strong-black-voter-turnout-translates-to-obama-win/*) (Accessed January 2013).

[2] David Bositis Ph.D., Blacks and the 2012 Elections: A Preliminary Analysis, Joint Center for Political and Economic Studies (see at *http://www.jointcenter.org/research/blacks-and-the-2012-elections-a-preliminary-analysis*) (Accessed January 2013).

TIME TO WAKE UP AND ACT: THE STATE OF BLACK CHILDREN

MARIAN WRIGHT EDELMAN

In 1968, the day after Dr. Martin Luther King, Jr. was shot, I went into riot-torn Washington, D.C. neighborhoods and schools urging children not to loot, get arrested and ruin their futures. A young Black boy about 12 looked me squarely in the eyes and said, "Lady, what future? I ain't got no future. I ain't got nothing to lose." I've spent my life working to prove that boy's truth wrong. I had no idea it would be so hard in our economically wealthy and militarily powerful but spiritually anemic nation.

Fifty years after the *March on Washington*, how are our Black children doing? A majority of Black American children are struggling to get a foothold in America's economy and to see a future worth striving for. I believe that today Black children face one of the greatest crises since slavery and that every Black American and American needs to wake up and act.

★ *Nearly 40 percent of Black children are poor and the younger they are, the poorer they are.*[1]

★ *Seventy-two percent are born to single mothers.*[2]

★ *Every 33 seconds a Black public high school student drops out.*[3]

★ *Every four seconds a Black public school student is suspended.*[4]

★ *Over 83 percent of Black children cannot read or compute at grade level in 4th and 8th grade.*[5]

★ *A Black boy born in 2001 has a one in three chance of going to prison in his lifetime.*[6]

In 2013, huge racial disparities with often harsh zero tolerance school discipline policies and police "stop and frisk" racial profiling policies push youths, especially Black males, into the cradle to prison and school to prison pipeline—leading to the highest mass incarceration rates in the world.[7] And re-segregating and substandard schools deny millions of poor Black children the chance to compete and find jobs in our globalizing economy.

Each of these disparities requires the most urgent attention. Together they are siren alarms signaling the need for urgent and persistent action by the Obama Administration, and all Americans, especially the Black community.

During the Civil Rights Movement Black parents and leaders sacrificed and struggled to ensure their children a better life—beginning with a decent education and the repeal of Jim Crow laws. They understood that the promise of America was still not a reality for millions of poor Black children like that boy I met in 1968. Millions of poor Black children still see no future in 2013. We must change that. I've no doubt that if he were alive today, Dr. King would be calling for a campaign to end child poverty and illiteracy. He isn't. We are. Let's get on with the job of building the next movement now to ensure that all children, including little Black boys, can see a future in their lives.

NOTES

[1] U.S. Census Bureau, CPS 2012 Annual Social and Economic Supplement, Tables POV01, September 2012. (see at *http://www.census.gov/hhes/www/cpstables/032012/pov/toc.htm*).

[2] Centers for Disease Control and Prevention. "Births: Final Data for 2010," Table 14. National Vital Statistics Reports, Vol.61 No.(1), August 2012 (see at *http://www.cdc.gov/nchs/data/nvsr/nvsr61/nvsr61_01.pdf*).

[3] Stillwell, R., and Sable, J., "Public School Graduates and Dropouts from the Common Core of Data: School Year 2009–10: First Look" (Provisional Data) (NCES 2013-309). U.S. Department of Education. Washington, D.C.: National Center for Education Statistics, January 2013 (see at *http://nces.ed.gov/pubs2013/2013309.pdf*). Calculations by Children's Defense Fund based on data in Table 6 and assumption of 180 school days of 7 hours each.

[4] U.S. Department of Education, Office of Civil Rights. "2009–10 Civil Rights Data Collection (CRDC): Suppressed Reported District-Level and School-Level Data," 2012. Calculations by the Children's Defense Fund based on assumption of 180 school days of 7 hours each.

[5] U.S. Department of Education, "NAEP Data Explorer." (see at *http://nces.ed.gov/nationsreportcard/about/naeptools.asp).*

[6] U.S. Department of Justice, Bureau of Justice Statistics, "Prevalence of Imprisonment in the U.S. Population, 1974–2001," August 2003 (see at *http://bjs.ojp.usdoj.gov/content/pub/pdf/piusp01.pdf*).

[7] Losen, Daniel J. and Jonathan Gillispie. "Opportunities Suspended: The Disparate Impact of Disciplinary Exclusion from School." The Center for Civil Rights Remedies at The Civil Rights Project, August 2012, (see at *http://civilrightsproject.ucla.edu/resources/projects/center-for-civil-rights-remedies/school-to-prison-folder/federal-reports/upcoming-ccrr-research/losen-gillespie-opportunity-suspended-2012.pdf.*
Losen, D.J. "Discipline Policies, Successful Schools, and Racial Justice." Boulder, CO: National Education Policy Center, October 2011, (see at *http://nepc.colorado.edu/publication/discipline-policies*).
International Centre for Prison Studies, Entire World-Prison Population Rates Per 100,000 of the National Population (see at *http://www.prisonstudies.org/info/worldbrief/wpb_stats.php?area=all&category=wb_poprate*)(Accessed January 15, 2012).

THE EQUITY and EXCELLENCE PROJECT: COMMUNITY-DRIVEN EDUCATION REFORM

PATRICIA STOKES AND ESTHER BUSH

★ ★ ★

Education is our nation's great economic equalizer. In fact, public education is the best way to create equal opportunities for children to succeed. But today the debate about building excellent public schools and eliminating the achievement gap fails to engage our communities in a meaningful way. The average academic achievement of black or Latino students lags up to three years of learning behind their white peers.[1] This achievement gap threatens to block students of color from success in college, work and life.

Together, the Urban League affiliates in the states of Tennessee, Pennsylvania, Ohio and Florida, and in the cities of New York, Los Angeles and New Orleans are part of the Equity and Excellence Project (EEP). The EEP is a multi-state, multi-year initiative that works to create community-driven solutions which answer parent and community needs. This project takes the reins of the education reform movement and shifts the paradigm to include civil rights organizations as a true partner in reform. Instead of reforms dictated to our communities, we are building an education reform movement led by our communities.

For over 100 hundred years, the National Urban League and the Urban League movement have been making policy and programmatic progress toward our empowerment goal of "ensuring every American child is prepared for college, work, and life." Our signature education program, *Project Ready*, targets middle- and high-school aged youth, focusing on the postsecondary success of students by emphasizing effective mentoring, robust out of school and expanded learning time opportunities, science, technology, engineering and math (STEM) academic preparation, social development and college- and career-readiness.

To date, our Tennessee and Pennsylvania affiliates serve over 2500 students annually. However, our work extends beyond the programs we provide; through the EEP and as trusted anchors in our communities we are called upon to shape the policies, reforms and innovations that will help all children succeed in our respective states. We serve as school board members, members of state, district and school improvement teams and classroom educators. Recently, our colleagues in Ohio, Florida, New York City, New Orleans and Los Angeles have joined us to highlight and support equitable education reforms that open new possibilities for urban children and youth.

In Tennessee, the affiliates in Chattanooga, Knoxville, Memphis and Nashville, have come together as the Tennessee Urban

GOALS OF THE EQUITY AND EXCELLENCE PROJECT (EEP)

The goal of the Equity and Excellence Project (EEP) is to improve outcomes for underserved students in public schools by building the capacity of parents and communities to successfully and systemically advocate on behalf of children and youth in the states of Tennessee, Pennsylvania, Ohio and Florida, and in the cities of New York, Los Angeles and New Orleans.

This project is an important part of the mission of the Urban League movement and it relies on the movement's greatest asset—local Urban League affiliates.

The EEP targets five focus areas: 1) Common Core State Standards implementation; 2) equitable and improved access to high quality curricula and effective teachers; 3) comprehensive, aligned and transparent education and employment data systems; 4) equity and excellence at scale; and 5) out of school time learning.

League Affiliates (TULA). Since 2011, TULA has ramped up its advocacy at the state and local levels. In meetings with Commissioner of Education Huffman, TULA made key recommendations to improve the implementation of the state's Elementary and Secondary Education Act (ESEA) waiver and create more opportunities for local community-based organizations to not only grow their out-of-school time programs but also have meaningful, knowledgeable involvement in reform discussions. As a part of the Educator Leader Cadre for the Partnership for Assessment of Readiness for College and Careers—the consortium developing the Common Core-aligned assessment for Tennessee—the Tennessee lead affiliate has been instrumental in raising community concerns about preparation, access and equity in the development of the new assessments for the Common Core State Standards (CCSS). For 2013, TULA is in the process of creating a statewide taskforce for achievement gap closure and a legislative agenda for the 2013–14 session.

Collectively, the four Pennsylvania Urban League affiliates in Farrell, Lancaster, Philadelphia, and Pittsburgh have formed the Pennsylvania EEP (PA EEP) consortium. They lead grassroots advocacy efforts in partnership with other advocacy groups, school district superintendents, parents and community leaders. Members of the consortium serve on and convene local committees and have begun collaboration at the state level through meetings with Governor Corbett, Secretary of Education Tomalis and Secretary of Corrections Wetzel. As the state of Pennsylvania grapples with critical education reform matters such as Common Core Standards, student assessments, ESEA waivers, teacher effectiveness and budget concerns, the PA EEP continues to raise the issues of equity and excellence in education for all students, especially students of color.

THIS PROJECT TAKES THE REINS OF THE EDUCATION REFORM MOVEMENT AND SHIFTS THE PARADIGM TO INCLUDE CIVIL RIGHTS ORGANIZATIONS AS A TRUE PARTNER IN REFORM.

In addition to state advocacy, each PA EEP affiliate is engaged in local education policy; meeting regularly with district superintendents to influence how districts gather and report meaningful data and measure effective teaching. In 2013, the consortium will continue to engage the state on a multitude of education issues including the implementation of the Common Core State Standards, with a July 2013 conference of stakeholders currently being planned.

In Tennessee and in Pennsylvania, this type of engagement effort has opened new doors for civil rights organizations to deepen and broaden our influence in education policy conversations. The relationships built have resulted in policymakers reaching out to us so we can collaboratively develop solutions to improve education across our respective states and communities. Beyond simply commenting on policies after they are fully developed and implemented, Urban League affiliates serve the important roles of thought partner, technical adviser and advocate for the effective implementation of education reforms throughout the policy and program development cycle.

We believe that it is critically important for underserved communities to hold districts and states accountable for the education of their children. The National Urban League EEP initiative, through the collaboration of its affiliates, is developing accountability standards in conjunction with the communities they serve. We envision the growth of EEP to include more states in the future. Moving forward, as educational innovation and reforms such as Common Core State Standards and Elementary and Secondary Act waivers are developed and implemented in our communities, we will continue to play a role in ensuring that they do so with equity and excellence.

The Equity and Excellence Project is a partnership between the National Urban League, select Urban League affiliates, the Education Testing Service and the Campaign for High School Equity (CHSE). Since 2009, the National Urban League's Equity and Excellence Project has been generously supported by the Bill and Melinda Gates Foundation.

NOTES

[1] Source: McKinsey & Company, The Economic Impact of the Achievement Gap on America's Schools, April 2009. (see at *http://online.wsj.com/article/SB10001424052702303513404577356422025164482.html*) and George Shultz and Eric Hanushek "Education Is the Key to a Healthy Economy" *The Wall Street Journal*, April 30, 2012 (see at *http://online.wsj.com/article/SB10001424052702303513404577356422025164482.html*).

EDUCATION: THE CRITICAL LINK BETWEEN TRADE and JOBS

U.S. TRADE REPRESENTATIVE RON KIRK

As we celebrate the 50th anniversary of the iconic *March on Washington*, and the 150th anniversary of Abraham Lincoln's paradigm-shattering Emancipation Proclamation, I've used the occasion to reflect about my own experience with the Civil Rights movement. Like so many others, I was raised in the segregated South, in Austin, Texas, an otherwise progressive city that was still segregated and governed by the rules of Jim Crow like so many other southern cities at the time. My parents were unable to vote. They were confronted with literacy tests and poll taxes when they arrived at their polling place on election day. My father, an Austin postal worker, hit a glass ceiling in his workplace because of the color of his skin. Segregation was intertwined into my daily existence, and discrimination was a fact of life.

As a child, it was difficult for me to understand why African Americans didn't enjoy the automatic benefits of citizenship, as every other American did. I remember thinking that early activists for Civil Rights were fighting for things they should not have had to fight for at all. But today, we see all around us living proof of the importance of their choice to stand up, to claim rights that may have seemed obvious but that were nonetheless being denied. And I, and so many of my contemporaries (including President Obama), are the first-generation beneficiaries of their countless actions in the struggle.

As a member of President Obama's cabinet and his principal trade advisor, negotiator, and spokesperson on trade issues, I have had the opportunity to travel around the world and witness the great changes in our global economy. Ninety-five percent of the world's consumers now live outside of the United States, many in countries like India, China, and South Africa. Yet throughout this period of great change, a crucial rule of business remains: employers look to locate their companies in areas with highly educated and highly motivated populations. The recession of 2007–2009 further amplified a global trend towards fierce competition for jobs, brainpower, and investment. Whereas our parents lived and worked where they were raised, many of our children are likely to live or work overseas, and even more will work for a global company.

THE RECESSION OF 2007–2009 FURTHER AMPLIFIED A GLOBAL TREND TOWARDS FIERCE COMPETITION FOR JOBS, BRAINPOWER, AND INVESTMENT.

In my opinion, the United States is uniquely positioned to compete in this new global economy. Businesses around the world value products and services made in America, just as parents from almost every country on earth send their sons and daughters to be educated at our colleges and universities. Our diversity is one of our greatest strengths; our status as a nation of immigrants enables our workers to communicate and engage with business owners and consumers who may not speak English, and who may live in Beijing, Mexico City, or Moscow. There are great rewards a vailable for those who are enterprising, educated, and willing to work hard.

We do, however, have intractable problems that we must address before we can unlock our country's full potential, and in my mind, everything begins and ends with education. As I tell my staff, education is the critical link between trade and jobs. I have seen thousands of young people in Africa, Asia, and everywhere in-between studying hard to get ahead. In America and around the world, millions of children take their schoolwork seriously, because their parents and leaders have emphasized education as the surest path to economic stability and success. Americans must embrace the reality that our children aren't just competing against students in the next town over; they're also going to be competing against students in Shanghai and Dubai.

This international competition is particularly significant for the African American community, because in education, we are not even keeping pace with our peers in the United States. Over the next 10 years, nearly half of all new jobs will require an education that goes beyond a high-school diploma, but, according to 2010 Census data, just 19.8 percent of African American adults currently hold a college or advanced degree. This persistent "achievement gap" is manifesting itself in the unemployment numbers as well; the African American jobless rate is about twice that of whites, a disparity that has been holding steady since the 1970s. Taken overall, the statistics paint an alarming picture. Inequality and discrimination, whether in our schools or in our workplaces, remain as pernicious forces, but our community needs to do some rigorous self-examination as well.

I can't help but think that in some ways, we are missing the sense of urgency that our parents' generation embraced, whether it is with regard to civil rights or education. Of course, access to a good education is something for which no American child, for which no American parents, should have to stand up and fight. But African Americans need to choose, again, to stand up for that which belongs to our children by right. The organizers of the Civil Rights movement used organization, information, and confrontation to achieve their goals in a peaceful way, and we can use that same strategy to confront our educational challenges. Historically Black Colleges and Universities, or HBCUs, are very important to me, and seem like a good place to start our transformation. HBCUs not only provide students with high-quality undergraduate and graduate degrees, but also help connect students to networks of friends, acquaintances, and educators which are invaluable when it comes to securing a

AMERICANS MUST EMBRACE THE REALITY THAT OUR CHILDREN AREN'T JUST COMPETING AGAINST STUDENTS IN THE NEXT TOWN OVER; THEY'RE ALSO GOING TO BE COMPETING AGAINST STUDENTS IN SHANGHAI AND DUBAI.

job. We need to invest in those colleges and universities, as they produce the building blocks for our community's future.

And at the same time, in our own families we must recapture the unyielding, unwavering attitude that our parents instilled in us as children. Even as they confronted segregation, racism, and discrimination on a daily basis, their message was always "go to school, study hard, make good grades, be a good citizen, compete in the world and succeed." They were confident that education combined with hard work would lead to success, notwithstanding the great challenges they faced.

There are many ways in which we can begin to focus on the education agenda, as a community and in our own homes. But however we choose to act, we must act now. We can't afford to fall further behind our peers in the United States and abroad. Our parents and grandparents left us a legacy of civil rights, suffrage, and empowerment. My hope is that our generation will be remembered for moving the ball forward by educating and equipping our children for success in the 21st century global economy.

THE POWER *of* EDUCATION TO EMPOWER OUR CHILDREN

DR. FREEMAN A. HRABOWSKI, III

This year marks the 50th anniversary of the Children's Crusade in Birmingham, Alabama. I am reminded lately, as we reflect on this challenging and vital period in our nation's history, that two-thirds of Americans alive today had not even been born yet at the time that it took place. This makes remembering this important event a special responsibility, especially for so many of us who lived with the severe segregation and discrimination of the time, and felt their impact on our everyday lives.

When Dr. Martin Luther King Jr., and others involved in the Civil Rights movement came to Birmingham, they encountered great hardship. But they also saw the power of education and of empowering a child to have a voice. It was at this time they suggested a demonstration by children—to show the American people the extent of the injustice experienced by so many and to illustrate that even children understood the societal toll of discrimination and inequality.

Their approach resonated with many African American parents, teachers and family members who—in the face of so much prejudice and so few resources—encouraged their children to be "twice as good." Their point was to set high expectations for us, and to teach us that if you worked very hard and strove for excellence, you could take advantage of opportunities and achieve excellence.

My parents were active in the Civil Rights Movement, but reluctant to allow me (as a 12-year-old) to get involved. At first, I only was allowed to go to church to hear Dr. King and other civil rights leaders speak. Their historic words reinforced my desire to participate, and I finally got permission to join in the Children's Crusade. The resulting painful and incredible experience—including five days spent in jail—changed my life forever. I learned, as so many others did that day, that everyone—including children—can think more critically than we realize, and that they can be empowered to change the world.

Today, 50 years since the Children's Crusade in Birmingham, America has made significant progress in giving children of all races even more opportunities to succeed academically than ever before. But obstacles persist in advancing the educational attainment of African American students of all ages, and there remains significant work to be done. High school and college graduation rates are unacceptably low, especially at a time when our nation's economic competitiveness is inextricably linked to the educational attainment of all Americans.

Providing a world-class education to all Americans is a top priority for President Obama and this Administration. And in that vein, this past July President Obama issued an Executive Order establishing the White House Initiative on Educational Excellence for African Americans. I am honored and privileged to serve as Chair of the Advisory Commission for this Initiative.[1]

The Initiative's primary goal is to ensure that all African American students receive an education that prepares them for success in high school, postsecondary education, and their careers.[2] Higher levels of academic achievement of African Americans can lead to more academic and career opportunities and, ultimately, to greater economic security for our country, while building a stronger more educated workforce. The Initiative emphasizes best practices to improve academic achievement, and the development of a national network of people, organizations, and communities to implement these practices.

Our purpose and our mission are both very clear: to identify and coordinate resources to strengthen educational outcomes for African Americans of all ages. Our work is systematically focused on the roles of communities and families in promoting safe schools; the roles of school systems to ensure effective teachers, school leaders, and academic programs; and on opportunities for educational and career advancement in all sectors. We are working to develop a national network of partnerships involving individuals, organizations, communities, and Federal programs, emphasizing strengthening academic achievement of African Americans. We are also committed to engaging the philanthropic, business, non-profit, and educational communities in a national dialogue on African American student achievement, and working to establish partnerships with stakeholders from these sectors. Finally, we are working in strong collaboration with senior officials in federal agencies across the Administration to ensure the success of our initiatives.

HIGH SCHOOL AND COLLEGE GRADUATION RATES ARE UNACCEPTABLY LOW, ESPECIALLY AT A TIME WHEN OUR NATION'S ECONOMIC COMPETITIVENESS IS INEXTRICABLY LINKED TO THE EDUCATIONAL ATTAINMENT OF ALL AMERICANS.

I come into my role as Chair of this Advisory Commission with great enthusiasm, understanding that there are high expectations about what the Commission will accomplish. We will chart our objectives early in 2013, and work throughout the year to meet our goals. In partnership with a broad community of stakeholders committed to the education of America's children, through rigorous analysis, honest dialogue, high expectations, and effective educational reform, I am confident we will achieve our goals.

In 1963, as children marching along the streets of Birmingham, we showed the world that we had a voice, and a role to play in shaping our own futures and the future of our great nation. With our neighbors, teachers, and extended family as positive role models, we knew that we could help spur real and meaningful change.

Let us all remember and draw on that spirit today, recognizing that our dreams as one nation depend on our success in closing the achievement gap and educating all of our children. The very future of our nation rests on their success, and our work is critical.

NOTES

[1] The White House, Office of the Press Secretary (July 26, 2012). Executive Order—White House Initiative on Educational Excellence for African Americans [Press release]. *(see at http://www.whitehouse.gov/the-press-office/2012/07/26/executive-order-white-house-initiative-educational-excellence-african-am).*

[2] Ibid.

THE NATIONAL TALENT STRATEGY:

IDEAS TO SECURE U.S. COMPETITIVENESS and ECONOMIC GROWTH

FREDRICK S. HUMPHRIES

For the past five years, the national unemployment rate has stubbornly stayed around 8 percent—the longest such stretch in generations. The jobless rate among African Americans is double the national rate. While the economy is slowly improving, two out of every five unemployed Americans have been out of work for more than six months.[1] So why are companies having difficulty filling certain jobs in science, technology and engineering?

The problem is the persistent and growing skills gap—the shortage of individuals with the skills needed to fill the jobs the private sector is creating.[2] Across America and a range of industries, there is an urgent demand for workers trained in the Science, Technology, Engineering and Mathematics (STEM) fields, yet there are not enough people with the necessary skills to meet that demand. Simply put, too few students are achieving the levels of education required to secure jobs in innovation-based industries, especially students from historically underserved and underrepresented communities.

WE MUST DO EVERYTHING THAT WE CAN TO ADDRESS THE OPPORTUNITY DIVIDE AND ENSURE THAT ALL OF OUR CHILDREN HAVE ACCESS TO THE EDUCATION AND TRAINING NECESSARY TO SUCCEED IN THE 21ST CENTURY ECONOMY.

The current skills gap crisis reminds me of one our nation has faced before. I was fortunate to grow up in a family that was very focused on education. My father was the first African American to receive a Ph.D. in physical chemistry at the University of Pittsburgh, and he gave me a chemistry set almost every year for Christmas. But it was not just my parents who emphasized math and science. President Eisenhower did too.

This was during the height of the Cold War when the Russians demonstrated that technology and innovation would drive progress in the 20th century. President Eisenhower asked the country to rise to the challenge and compete. America met that challenge, won the Space Race and entered the greatest period of economic expansion in our history.

We are facing similar challenges today and are in need of a clear path forward. Just as America placed an emphasis on the STEM fields in the 20th century, today we need to ensure that all of our children are prepared for 21st century jobs.

According to the Bureau of Labor Statistics every year there are an estimated 122,000 jobs that require a computer science bachelor's degree.[3] These are high paying jobs that offer significant opportunities for growth. But each year, America's colleges and universities—the best in the world—only graduate some 40,000 students with bachelor's degrees in computer science.[4]

While this presents a challenge for all Americans, it is a particularly acute challenge among African Americans and other minority communities. Consider this: In the United States last year there were 1,603 new Ph.D.s in computer science—far too few. Compounding this dearth is the fact that only 349 of those degrees went to women, 47 went to African Americans and only 17 went to Hispanics. Nearly 60% of these degree holders were foreign nationals.[5]

This is a problem that impacts all Americans. Tens of thousands of unfilled high paying jobs across a wide range of industries only serves to compound our other economic problems. Every high skilled position left vacant in America also means the loss of as many as five other jobs. Students fail to achieve their full individual potential and we fail to achieve our full national economic potential as a country. Solving these challenges means opening the promise of America to more of its people—and giving our entire economy a boost.

Like companies throughout America and across industries, Microsoft is opening up new jobs in the United States faster than we can fill them. As the company that spends more on research and development than any other throughout the world, we see the problem firsthand. We currently have over 6,000 open jobs in this country, an increase of 15 percent over the past year. Nearly 3,600 of these jobs are for researchers, developers and engineers, and this total has grown by 44 percent over the past 12 months. We know we are not unique in this challenge. The U.S. government estimates that there are 3.7 million open jobs in the U.S. economy. We must do everything that we can to address the opportunity divide and ensure that all of our children have access to the education and training necessary to succeed in the 21st century economy.

At Microsoft, we have long been committed to doing all we can to bridge this opportunity divide. We've recently launched a company-wide initiative, *Microsoft YouthSpark*, through which we're investing $500 million—including the majority of our corporate philanthropy efforts—in a wide range of programs and resources designed to create opportunities for 300 million young people worldwide.

One of these programs in particular, *DigiGirlz*, has a direct positive impact on urban communities by giving young women the opportunity to learn about careers in technology, connect with Microsoft employees, and participate in hands-on computer and technology training workshops. Since its inception, *DigiGirlz* has reached 14,000 young women in cities across the country and provided them with invaluable training and experience.

But even a big company like ours can only do so much. We need American leadership, from government at every level, from the private sector, public sector, and non-profits alike, to be dedicated to closing the opportunity gap. That's why we support efforts to develop a national talent strategy to draw attention to this problem and to advocate for broader policy reforms to begin to address this challenge.

EVERY HIGH SKILLED POSITION LEFT VACANT IN AMERICA ALSO MEANS THE LOSS OF AS MANY AS FIVE OTHER JOBS.

We support a two-pronged approach that couples long-term improvements in America's STEM education with targeted, high-skilled immigration reforms. If done correctly, we believe the latter can help fund the former. Put together, this approach can help keep jobs in the U.S. by providing a supply of skilled employees who can fill these jobs in the future.

We must ensure that a national talent strategy:

- ★ *Strengthens K-12 math and science teaching and learning to better prepare students for college and possible careers in these disciplines. This means national standards for math and science and new STEM teachers across America.*
- ★ *Broadens access to computer science across our high schools. Only 2,100 of the 42,000 high schools in America are certified to teach the AP computer science course.*
- ★ *Helps more students obtain post-secondary credentials and degrees by addressing the college completion crisis.*

To ensure that our great nation retains its global competitiveness, we must close the skills gap and ensure that all Americans receive the education and skills training needed to bridge the opportunity divide.

Throughout our nation's history, the African American community has made important contributions in the areas of science and math. From George Washington Carver's critical agricultural research at the turn of the 20th century, to Dr. Charles Drew's lifesaving medical work in World War II, to Dr. Mae Jemison serving as the first African American woman to travel to space, we must ensure that our sons and daughters are prepared to help America retain its global leadership in innovation.

It must not only be a national priority, but a priority for each one of us.

NOTES

[1] U.S. Bureau of Labor Statistics, Jobs Report, January 2013 (see at *http://www.bls.gov/news.release/empsit.t02.htm*) (Accessed February 2013).

[2] Dobbs, Richard, Susan Lund, and Anu Madgavkar, "Tensions Ahead: A CEO Briefing on Imbalance in Global Labor Pool," McKinsey Global Institute, November 2012 (see at *https://www.mckinseyquarterly.com/Talent_tensions_ahead_A_CEO_briefing_3033*)(Accessed February 2013).

[3] U.S. Bureau of Labor Statistics, Employment Projections 2010-2020 (see at *http://www.bls.gov/news.release/ecopro.nr0.htm*) (Accessed February 2013).

[4] National Center for Education Statistics (NCES), Integrated Postsecondary Education Data System, U.S. Department of Education, (see at *https://webcaspar.nsf.gov*)(Accessed January 2013).

[5] Ibid.

DIVERSITY in STEM: AN ECONOMIC IMPERATIVE

THE HONORABLE DOT HARRIS

As someone who has had a diverse career grounded in engineering, science and economics, I know firsthand the unparalleled opportunities that come from a world-class education. For America to succeed in the 21st century, we must make sure that every child gets this same opportunity.

In my current role at the Energy Department, I know that fostering diversity in Science, Technology, Engineering and Mathematics (STEM) education and careers is critical to ensuring we can solve the energy challenges of tomorrow, including maintaining America's leadership in the global race for clean energy technologies.

Currently, minorities—particularly African Americans—claim a disproportionately small share of the high-tech, high-paying jobs in the industries inventing and producing the new energy technologies that will propel American innovation and provide a foundation for future prosperity. While 70 percent of our nation's college graduates are minorities or women, only 45 percent of STEM professionals fit these demographics.[1]

At the Energy Department, we know there's a critical need for more minorities to enter the energy industry. To that end, we're providing minorities with opportunities for hands-on work in STEM fields, by exposing more students to potential career paths, supporting scholarships and fellowships, and fostering mentorships with some of the world's leading scientists and engineers.

For example, we've partnered with Historically Black Colleges and Universities (HBCUs) as well as other Minority Serving Institutions to develop innovative programs that connect minority students with the Energy Department's vast network of national laboratories, field sites and plants. In October 2012, we launched the Minority Serving Institution Partnership Program which has since provided more than $4 million in research grants to over 20 HBCUs—giving these students access to the Department's cutting edge resources and technology, and ultimately increasing interest in STEM from young minority Americans across the country.

Building on this commitment to engage students in our nation's energy issues, the Energy Department's Office of Nuclear Energy has supported research equipment upgrades and scholarships for students in nuclear engineering at four Historically Black Colleges and Universities. Additionally, through partnerships with organizations such as the Thurgood Marshall College Fund and the National Action Council for Minorities in Engineering, the Energy Department supports scholarships to minorities pursuing degrees in STEM, leveraging our resources through shared commitments.

Since 1991, the Department has hosted an annual National Science Bowl, which now brings together more than 18,000 middle and high school students from across the

WE KNOW THAT INTRODUCING STUDENTS TO SCIENCE AND MATH AT AN EARLY AGE INCREASES THE LIKELIHOOD THEY WILL PURSUE A STEM CAREER PATH.

country. We know that introducing students to science and math at an early age increases the likelihood they will pursue a STEM career path.

The Energy Department also administers a number of internship programs at our National Laboratories and headquarters offices to encourage students from Minority-Serving Institutions to join the Department of Energy workforce. The Minority Educational Institution Student Partnership Program provides stipends for students to work with the Department's talented scientists and engineers—giving them hands-on experience in a wide range of areas, from renewable energy and environmental management to nuclear security and electricity delivery. As a more specialized opportunity, the Mickey Leland Energy Fellowship is a ten-week summer internship program for minority and female students who are pursuing degrees in STEM and want an opportunity to work on fossil energy challenges.

The Energy Department knows that it is mission-critical to help more minority students pursue careers tracks in the STEM fields. I am encouraged by the National Urban League's work in this important area and look forward to finding new education and career opportunities for minority students together. By strengthening these partnerships, we can make sure that no important opportunity is missed—from investing in STEM development in our communities and generating good, high-paying jobs, to stimulating America's economic growth and leading the new innovations and markets of the 21st century.

I invite you to check out additional information about the Energy Department's work with Minority Serving Institutions and minority communities at *www.energy.gov/diversity*.

NOTES

[1] See, Executive Office of the President, President's Council of Advisors on Science and Technology, Engage to Excel: Producing One Million Additional College Graduates with Degrees in Science, Technology, Engineering, and Mathematics (February 2012) (see at *http://www.whitehouse.gov/sites/default/files/microsites/ostp/fact_sheet_final.pdf*).

STOP the FAST TRACK TO PRISON

LAURA W. MURPHY

The "school-to-prison pipeline" is one of the most important civil rights issues today. The term describes various school discipline policies that push students out of the classrooms and into jail cells. When these overly punitive policies result in students being suspended, expelled or referred to law enforcement, they have enormously negative consequences for a student's long-term prospects.

Overly punitive school discipline practices like zero-tolerance policies, the physical punishment of students and removal from school for minor infractions lead directly to lower rates of graduation, poorer employment prospects and a greater chance of being swept up by the criminal justice system as an adult.[1] Having a record impacts employment, keeps many Americans from voting and participating in the political process, and carries an indelible stigma that limits societal engagement for life. These days, getting in trouble in school can ruin lives and communities.

Students of color are overrepresented at every stage of this pipeline. According to the Department of Education's most recent data, African American students are 3.5 times more likely to be suspended, and although African American students made up only 18 percent of the sample, they accounted for 39 percent of expulsions.[2] Of students arrested or referred to law enforcement nationally, 70 percent are black or Latino.[3] Crucially, there is no evidence that students of color are any more ill-behaved than white students. In fact, the data shows that black students tend to receive harsher punishment for the exact same infractions.[4] This overrepresentation plays directly into a cycle of discrimination: students of color are subject to more school discipline more often, which leads to higher rates of arrest and incarceration as adults. As a result, their young lives are permanently marred with the label of "ex-offender" with all of its associated social and economic impacts, not only on them but also on their family as well as their community.

There are several related practices that contribute to the problem. One of the most pernicious is the zero tolerance policy, which removes a teacher's discretion in punishing student misbehavior. The consequences of such policies are obvious. Kids end up getting kicked out of school for arguably minor infractions such as giving Midol to a classmate or bringing scissors in for an art project. The zero tolerance policy mandates that more and more children are disciplined in absolute terms. In the St. Louis Public School District, for instance, zero tolerance policies, in place from 2004 through 2009, increased suspensions by 600 percent.[5]

THIS OVERREPRESENTATION PLAYS DIRECTLY INTO A CYCLE OF DISCRIMINATION: STUDENTS OF COLOR ARE SUBJECT TO MORE SCHOOL DISCIPLINE MORE OFTEN, WHICH LEADS TO HIGHER RATES OF ARREST AND INCARCERATION AS ADULTS.

Another contributing factor is the use of police in schools. The New York Police Department's School Safety Division, one of the largest units in the NYPD, has 5,000 "school safety agents" and 200 uniformed officers (versus 3,000 guidance counselors and 1,500 school social workers). Last school year alone, the NYPD arrested or ticketed more than 11 students each day, and more than 95 percent of those arrests were of black or Latino students.[6] Police data suggests that relatively few of these incidents involved actual criminal behavior.[7] In addition to discriminatory enforcement, involving the police is also often coupled with zero tolerance policies, resulting in absurd situations where students as young as five are being led out of classrooms in handcuffs for throwing a temper tantrum.[8]

Numerous other policies contribute to the school-to-prison pipeline, but one that bears special mention is the continuing use of the destructive practice of corporal punishment in schools. Physically striking a student as punishment for misbehavior is still legal in 19 states, including every state in the Deep South. African American students are disproportionately the ones being hit. According to the most recent national data, African American students made up 21.7 percent of public school students in states that allow corporal punishment, but accounted for 35.6 percent of students who were struck.[9] When asked to explain why, a Mississippi teacher said that, with respect to white and lighter-skinned students, people say "this child should get less whips, it'll leave marks."[10]

PUBLIC EDUCATION IS SUPPOSED TO BE A BULWARK AGAINST DISCRIMINATION, NOT A ROOT CAUSE OF IT.

We have to dismantle the pipeline, and there are several ways to do it. The Obama Administration should begin by finalizing and issuing guidance from the Departments of Education and Justice, which are currently collaborating on the landmark Supportive School Discipline Initiative ("SSDI"). The administration formed SSDI to ensure that school discipline conforms to the nation's civil rights laws. SSDI guidance should, among other things, instruct schools to focus on the disproportionate impact of school disciplinary policies on students of color and students with disabilities, and require schools to address that discrimination through the civil rights laws. The guidance should also promote positive behavior supports as alternatives to overly punitive measures, and clarify that police should be involved in school discipline only for serious criminal matters.

Further, corporal punishment needs to end. In addition to the obvious physical pain (including the risk of serious injury), research indicates that violent discipline can increase aggression in children, as well as contribute to absenteeism, academic disengagement and ultimately dropping out. The ACLU strongly supports federal legislation prohibiting corporal punishment, which was introduced last Congress and we hope will be introduced again in 2013.

Other steps include severely limiting "seclusion and restraint" practices; reauthorizing the Juvenile Justice and Delinquency Prevention Act, which would provide much needed funding for juvenile delinquency prevention; making data collection on school discipline cover all schools on an annual basis and including the tracking of all incidents of corporal punishment; and redirecting the significant amount of resources currently being used to support the pipeline to more effective, fair and supportive policies.

It is deplorable that schools in 2013 have become fast tracks to prison, especially for students of color. Public education is supposed to be a bulwark against discrimination, not a root cause of it. Progress must be made on ending the school-to-prison pipeline, and must be made now.

NOTES

[1] *Hearing on Ending the School-to-Prison Pipeline Before the Subcomm. on the Constitution, Civil Rights & Human Rights of the S. Comm. on the Judiciary*, 112th Cong. 2-4 (2012) (statement of Laura W. Murphy, Dir., Am. Civil Liberties Union's Washington Legislative Office, and Deborah J. Vagins, Senior Legislative Counsel).

[2] Tamar Lewin, "Black Students Face More Discipline, Data Suggests," *N.Y. Times*, Mar. 6, 2012, at A11.

[3] The Transformed Civil Rights Data Collection, Dep't of Educ., *http://www2.ed.gov/about/offices/list/ocr/docs/crdc-2012-data-summary.pdf* (last visited Jan. 7, 2013).

[4] Lewin, *supra* note 2.

[5] Mo. Dep't of Elementary & Secondary Educ., Core Data (2010), *http://mcds.dese.mo.gov/quickfacts/SitePages/DistrictInfo.aspx?ID=__bk8100130013005300130013005300.*

[6] Press Release, N.Y. Civil Liberties Union, First Full Year of NYPD Data Shows Black Students Disproportionately Arrested at School (Aug. 14, 2012), *http://www.nyclu.org/news/first-full-year-of-nypd-data-shows-black-students-disproportionately-arrested-school.*

[7] Ibid.

[8] See Antoinette Campbell, "Police Handcuff 6-Year-Old Student in Georgia," *CNN.com*, Apr. 17, 2012, *http://www.cnn.com/2012/04/17/justice/georgia-student-handcuffed/index.html*; "Handcuffed 5-Year-Old Sparks Suit," *CBSNews.com*, Feb. 11, 2009, *http://www.cbsnews.com/2100-500202_162-690601.html.*

[9] *2006 National and State Estimations, Civil Rights Data Collection*, Dep't of Educ., *http://ocrdata.ed.gov/StateNationalEstimations/projections_2006* (last visited Jan. 7, 2013). Note also that students with disabilities are also disproportionately subject to corporal punishment, often for behavior related to their disability.

[10] Alice Farmer, Am. Civil Liberties Union & Human Rights Watch, *A Violent Education: Corporal Punishment of Children in U.S. Public Schools* 76 (2008), available at *http://www.aclu.org/human-rights-racial-justice/violent-education-corporal-punishment-children-us-public-schools*; see also Deborah J. Vagins, "Making School a Safe Place for All Students," *Huffington Post*, Sept. 27, 2011, *http://www.huffingtonpost.com/deborah-j-vagins/corporal-punishment-in-schools_b_983041.html.*

Bringing HIGHER EDUCATION TO THE MASSES

A CONVERSATION WITH COURSERA CO-FOUNDER ANDREW NG, BY SHREE CHAUHAN

Massive open online courses (MOOCs) burst onto the higher education landscape just over a year ago, offering courses on wide variety of topics from computer science to Greek mythology to songwriting—for free. Anyone with an Internet connection can take a university-level course taught by a professor who often is a preeminent expert in his or her field.

Organizations that offer MOOCs are already boasting millions of users. Institutions of higher education nationally and abroad, including Ivy League institutions, are investing in MOOCs.

We sat down with one of the co-founders of Coursera, an organization which offers over 200 courses, from over 33 universities. Coursera enjoys over 2 million users and *The New York Times* has gone so far as to call 2012 the "Year of the MOOC."

QUESTION #1

While MOOCs are still in their infancy, many industry experts believe they have and will continue to disrupt the educational field tremendously. **What are your thoughts on how MOOCs are changing higher education and the overall landscape of education?**

MOOCs are dramatically increasing people's ability to access a great education. When the technology exists for one professor to teach not just 50 students at a time, but 50,000, this changes the economics of higher education. I'd like to give everyone access to a great education, and let everyone learn from the best professors at the best universities—for free.

QUESTION #2

Research shows that economic stability and mobility is related to obtaining a postsecondary education.[1] Almost all high school students aspire to go to college and the number and percentage of students attending a postsecondary institution continues to rise annually in the United States. Despite these overall gains, low-income black and Hispanic students enroll in postsecondary education at a lower rate than their white high school peers.[2] In fact, students from low-income backgrounds have the lowest rates of postsecondary enrollment—and face greater barriers to access related to their academic preparation, savings for college, and lessened social and cultural capital.[3] However, enrolling in college does not guarantee a degree, of the black students attending a 4-year postsecondary institution, only 2 of 10 graduate.[4] **Given these circumstances, how do you think MOOCs fit into the conversation of educational equity? How could MOOCs increase higher education access to underserved communities?**

Education equity has long been a major problem. I'd like to live in a world where your success in life is determined only by your hard work, guts, and talent, rather than by the wealth of your parents. Education is a great equalizer, and by offering everyone access to a great education, MOOCs are democratizing education, so that we can move toward where every child—wealthy or poor—has a chance at success.

Stanford University admits about 1800 freshmen a year. What this means is that most people in this world will never have access to a Stanford class. But with MOOCs, we're changing that. If you wake up tomorrow and want to take a class from Stanford, Princeton, Caltech...you can now do so—for free!

QUESTION # 3

According to the Bureau of Labor Statistics projections, by 2020 a third of all new jobs created will be related to health care.[5] Computer and mathematical occupations are expected to grow to lesser degree by 22 percent from 2010 to 2020.[6]

A large portion of MOOC courses currently being offered focus on computer science and mathematics. How do you believe MOOCs help meet the needs of high-demand jobs for the future?

Coursera's courses are already helping students train or re-train themselves for jobs in such high-demand areas as health care and IT. In fact, many students are already putting our certificates in their resume, and successfully using them to find better jobs.

COURSERA'S COURSES ARE ALREADY HELPING STUDENTS TRAIN OR RE-TRAIN THEMSELVES FOR JOBS IN SUCH HIGH-DEMAND AREAS AS HEALTH CARE AND IT.

More broadly, I think the old model of education—where you attend college for 4 years, and "coast" for the next 40 years on your degree—just doesn't make sense anymore. In today's rapidly changing world, all of us need to get regular "booster shots" of knowledge in order to stay current. The convenience of online courses—taught by great professors—is helping many students pursue or explore new career options.

QUESTION #4

Some criticisms of MOOCs include issues about the effectiveness of peer grading and the inability of MOOCs to mirror the quality of a classroom experience. **What do you believe are some of the drawbacks to MOOCs and how do you see MOOCs managing these challenges?**

MOOCs certainly don't replicate the on-campus experience, and nor are they meant to! If a high school student is admitted to Johns Hopkins, I'd certainly recommend that they attend the university in person rather than stay home and take free online Johns Hopkins classes.

Indeed, one key part of what Coursera does is work with our partners to improve the quality of on-campus education. We do this by helping them to implement the "flipped classroom," whereby students can watch the lecture content from home; this preserves the classroom time for deeper faculty-student and student-student interactions. For students, what this means is that rather than walking into the classroom to be lectured at by the professor, the students now come to class already having watched the lecture from home, and can use the classroom time for in-depth discussions and problem solving with the instructor and with other students. This is a much more interesting experience for the student, and many studies have also shown that these more interactive modes of learning result in much better student outcomes.

So, MOOCs are not at all intended to replace the on-campus experience. Having said that, I think online learning needs to be much more social than it is currently. We're working to give students more ways to offer support to other students, as well as receive support from other students. Just as you might have made some of your best friends in school, we'd like you to make some of your future best friends among your Coursera classmates. To let this happen, we've been piloting out features such as user profiles, live video chat, and live text chat, and will be improving the social features on our site in the coming months.

I'D LIKE TO LIVE IN A WORLD WHERE STUDENTS NO LONGER HAVE TO CHOOSE BETWEEN PAYING FOR TUITION AND PAYING FOR GROCERIES.

QUESTION #5

Many in education believe MOOCs will shake up the higher education industry. For now Coursera and other MOOC organizations do not offer degrees or enjoy official accreditation like other institutions of higher education. Nonetheless, Coursera has made some progress in its ability to transfer its courses for credit. **Knowing where MOOCs are now, where do you foresee the MOOC movement in 5 years? In a decade?**

I think helping students earn degrees is important. The American Council on Education has recommended four Coursera courses for college credit. This means that students can take those courses in our MOOCs, and have them be potentially transferred into a university for academic credit. What excites me about this is the potential to help working adults re-enter the educational system. There're a lot of people today who, for whatever reason, do not yet have a college degree. I hope that the convenience of an online class—one where you can earn academic credit—will help a lot of them take the first step towards coming back to school to earn their degree.

As for where the MOOC movement will go, I'd like to live in a world where everyone has access to the best universities. I'd like to live in a world where students no longer have to choose between paying for tuition and paying for groceries. I'd like to live in a world where a poor kid born to a single mother has near the equality of opportunity as a kid born in the wealthy suburbs of D.C. I'd like to live in a world where a great education isn't reserved just for the lucky few, isn't reserved just for the privileged, but is a fundamental human right. With technology, we're working to make this world a reality.

NOTES

[1] Ron Haskins, Harry Holzer and Robert Lerman, "Promoting Economic Mobility by Increasing Access to Postsecondary Education." *Economic Mobility Project,* 2009 *The Pew Trusts.*

[2] The National Center for Education Statistics. The Condition of Education, 2012, Indicator 34. (see at *http://nces.ed.gov/programs/coe/pdf/coe_trc.pdf*).

[3] Mark Engberg and Daniel Allen, "Uncontrolled Destinies: Improving Opportunity For Low-Income Students in American higher education." *Research in Higher Education,* 2011, 52(8), 786-807.

[4] The National Center for Education Statistics. Digest of Education Statistics, Table: 345, "Graduation rates of first-time postsecondary students who started as full-time degree/certificate-seeking students , by sex race/ethnicity, time to completion, and level and control of instution where student started: Selected cohort entry years, 1996–2007." (see at *http://nces.ed.gov/programs/digest/d11/tables/dt11_345.asp*).

[5] The Bureau of Labor Statistics. Occupation Outlook Handbook: Overview of the 2010-2020 Projections, 2011. (see at *http://www.bls.gov/ooh/About/Projections-Overview.htm*)

[6] C. Brett Lockard and Michael Wolf. Employment Outlook: 2010–2020, "Occupational Employment Projections to 2020," January 2012. p. 89. (see at *http://www.bls.gov/opub/mlr/2012/01/art5full.pdf*)

SPECIAL REPORT FROM THE NATIONAL URBAN LEAGUE POLICY INSTITUTE

THE STATE of URBAN HEALTH:

ELIMINATING HEALTH DISPARITIES TO SAVE LIVES AND CUT COSTS

DARRELL J. GASKINS, PH.D., THOMAS A. LAVEIST, PH.D. AND PATRICK RICHARD, PH.D.

For over 100 years, the National Urban League has been committed to the mission of economic empowerment in underserved communities. In these communities, the link between economic empowerment and health is in many ways a double-edged sword. On one hand, poor health threatens an individual's economic well-being through higher health care expenses and lost earnings. On the other, health status is affected when economic insecurity limits access to the resources and interventions that contribute to better health.

According to the National Urban League's 2013 Equality Index, African Americans significantly lag behind their white counterparts with respect to a number of health indicators. For example, the death rates from prostate cancer and diabetes are more than twice what they are for whites and AIDS cases among African Americans age 13 and older are 8 (for males) to 23 (for females) times what they are for whites. Closing these disparities in health outcomes matters not only to the individuals who will directly benefit from a longer and better quality of life, but also to their families, their communities and ultimately the nation.

COST OF ILLNESS STUDIES HELP POLICYMAKERS MAKE JUDGMENTS ABOUT THE SIZE OF INVESTMENT SOCIETY SHOULD MAKE TO COMBAT A PARTICULAR ILLNESS OR DISEASE.

Health disparities inflict a significant level of illness, disability, and death on the nation. In addition to excess disease and death, health disparities also impose a significant economic burden on society. LaVeist and colleagues (2010) estimated that health disparities cost the U.S. economy over $1.24 trillion over the four-year period from 2003–2006. They estimated that health disparities increased health care spending by $61 billion, reduced labor market productivity by $11 billion and incurred costs due to premature death of $243.1 billion in 2006. Waidmann (2010) estimated that disparities in hypertension, diabetes, stroke, renal disease, and poor general health increased health care spending by $23.9 billion in 2009. Waidmann (2010) also predicted that by 2050, the costs of health disparities in preventable chronic diseases will increase to an annual cost of $50.1 billion if these racial/ethnic disparities in health persist. This increase in the societal burden is due to the projection that the United States will become a "majority-minority" society by 2050.

The direct medical care costs associated with health disparities alone are as high as the total economic burden of some illnesses. For instance, the direct medical care costs of racial/ethnic health disparities are similar to those of mental health disorders ($61.3 billion) and COPD, asthma, and pneumonia combined ($66.1 billion). The nation's two most expensive illnesses are heart disease ($167.4 billion) and cancer ($103.8 billion) (NHLBI 2011) and according to the National Urban League's 2013 Equality Index, African Americans are 1.3 times more likely than whites to die of heart disease and 1.2 times more likely to die from cancer.

It is important for policymakers and the public to understand the economic burden of illness and disease. Cost of illness studies help policymakers make judgments about the size of investment society should make to combat a particular illness or disease. Policymakers can use these studies to determine whether the amount of funding to support interventions to address a particular illness is commensurate with the economic burden the illness imposes on society.

These estimates also can help policymakers balance the costs that poor health imposes on society with government outlays. For instance, in 2011, the federal government incurred a significant amount of spending for health programs such as Medicare ($480 billion), Medicaid and the Children's Health Insurance Program ($283 billion), the Center for Disease Control (CDC) and Prevention ($5.7 billion), the Health Resources and Services Administration ($6.2 billion), Indian Health Services ($4.1 billion), Substance Abuse and Mental Health Services Administration ($3.4 billion) and the Center for Medicare and Medicaid Services ($3.5 billion) (OMB 2012). Yet, the annual societal costs of health disparities exceed the annual budget of all these programs with the exception of Medicare and Medicaid outlays.

The spending on programs that directly address health disparities are modest compared to the financial resources it would require to address racial/ethnic disparities in health in the U.S. For example, CDC spends about $21.9 million on its community-based effort to reduce health disparities, the Racial and Ethnic Approaches to Community Health (REACH) program. REACH empowers community-based-organizations to address six priority health problems with well-documented racial/ethnic disparities: cardiovascular disease, diabetes, breast and cervical cancer screening and prevention, asthma, immunizations, and infant mortality. Given the complexity of factors contributing to these health disparities, eliminating them will be costly. However, inaction or action that results in further cuts to important health programs that help to address these disparities will prove to be much more costly. Therefore, allocating the appropriate amount of financial resources to reduce racial/ethnic disparities in health is not only a moral imperative, but also a fiscally responsible one.

This report presents estimates of the economic burden that health disparities impose on society through health care spending and workers' lost productivity, and identifies regions of the country and stakeholders for whom the economic burden of health disparities is most felt. Specifically, we estimate the economic impact of health disparities by census region and urban and rural areas, apportioning these costs by households, public and private health plans, and industries. We also project the long-term costs of not reducing health disparities for 2020 and 2050 given the changing demographics of the nation. The report concludes with a set of policy recommendations that will help to eliminate health disparities and realize the promise of the Affordable Care Act.

THE ECONOMIC BURDEN OF HEALTH DISPARITIES

In 2009, health disparities cost the U.S. economy $82.2 billion. This includes the costs of medical care and lost productivity but it does not include the costs of premature death.[1] A detailed description of the methodology used to compute the economic burden of disparities and tables of all the estimates can be found in the attached appendix. Generally speaking, these costs were calculated based on racial/ethnic differences in age-, gender-, and region-adjusted prevalence rates for six selected health conditions: self-reported general health status, self-reported mental health status, presence of functional limitations, obesity, diabetes and hypertension *(Table 1)*. African Americans had the highest or second

TABLE 1: Age-Adjusted Prevalence of Health Status/Health Conditions by Race/Ethnicity for Adults 18 years or Older (N=24,162; 2009 MEPS)

HEALTH STATUS/HEALTH CONDITIONS	WHITE	BLACK	HISPANIC	ASIAN
FAIR/POOR HEALTH	0.12 [b]	0.17 [a,b]	0.18 [a,b]	0.08 [a]
FAIR/POOR MENTAL HEALTH	0.06	0.09 [a,b]	0.08 [a,b]	0.05
ANY FUNCTIONAL LIMITATION	0.09 [b]	0.12 [a,b]	0.08 [b]	0.03 [a]
OBESITY	0.27 [b]	0.37 [a,b]	0.30 [a,b]	0.07 [a]
DIABETES	0.04	0.07 [a,b]	0.07 [a]	0.05
HYPERTENSION	0.26 [b]	0.41 [a,b]	0.26 [b]	0.22 [a]

Source: Author's calculations based on the 2009 MEPS. Differences were tested at the 95% confidence level and 'a' denotes statistical significant difference from whites, and 'b' denotes statistical significant difference from Asians.

highest age-adjusted prevalence rates for each of the six health conditions. Hispanics' age adjusted prevalence rates were greater than the rates for Whites for three conditions and greater than those of Asians for five conditions. Asians had lower rates than Whites for four conditions.

As a result of the aforementioned disparities in health, African Americans bore the highest economic burden with $54.9 billion, followed by Hispanics with $22 billion. The census region with the highest costs was the Southern region of the country with $35 billion. The West had the next highest with $26 billion. Asians incurred relatively lower costs of $5.2 billion; however over 60% of this cost was in the Western region of the U.S. Over 90 percent of the medical care and lost productivity costs were in urban areas *(Table 2)*.

TABLE 2: Costs Attributable to Health Disparities by Race/Ethnicity, Census Region, and Urban-Rural Location, 2009

	MILLIONS OF DOLLARS			
	BLACKS	HISPANICS	ASIANS	**TOTAL**
MSA				
NORTHEAST	8,380	5,929	1,022	**15,331**
MIDWEST	11,168	486	387	**12,042**
SOUTH	23,613	4,516	562	**28,692**
WEST	5,703	9,455	3,192	**18,350**
TOTAL MSA	48,865	20,385	5,163	**74,449**
NON-MSA				
NORTHEAST	76	17	16	**109**
MIDWEST	559	66	0	**626**
SOUTH	5,360	1,089	37	**6,486**
WEST	57	475	6	**540**
TOTAL NON-MSA	6,053	1,648	60	**7,761**
TOTAL	**54,918**	**22,033**	**5,223**	**82,210**

Source: Author's calculations based on the 2009 MEPS.

HEALTH CARE SPENDING

The larger share of the costs of health disparities came from increased health care spending of $59.6 billion in 2009. African Americans accounted for much of the health care costs ($45.3 billion), with those living in urban areas in the South and Midwest bearing most of these costs. For Hispanics, the health care costs of health disparities were largest in the West ($5.3 billion) and Northeast ($4.3 billion). The health care spending due to health disparities for Asians were largest in the West ($2 billion) *(Figure 1)*.

We examined regional differences in health care spending by comparing the distribution of health care spending due to health disparities to the adult population distribution by race/ethnicity, census region, and urban-rural designation. Regional cost differences were not totally driven by where populations were concentrated. For example, Midwestern African American adults living in urban areas (i.e. in MSAs) accounted for 15.5 percent of the health care spending but represented only 6.5 percent of minority adults in 2009. African Americans in the South were 18.4 percent of minority adults but accounted for 32.4 percent of health care spending due to health disparities *(Figure 2)*. While Asians' and Hispanics' absolute share of the health disparities health care spending is less than their share of the minority population, the regional distribution of costs were heavily skewed. For example, Asians in the West represented 44.7 percent of the Asian population but accounted for 80.7 percent of their excess health care spending due to disparities in 2009 *(Figure 3)*. Similarly, for Hispanics, health spending due to disparities was concentrated in the Northeast, which had 14.1 percent of the Hispanic population but 35.5 percent of their costs in 2009 *(Figure 4)*.

Aside from the obvious influence of population distribution, the concentration of health care costs due to disparities is also likely to be related to differences in insurance coverage and regional differences in socioeconomic status within racial and ethnic groups. The influence of these factors becomes clearer as we explore the regional breakdown of costs by payer—private insurance, out-of-pocket, and Medicare and Medicaid.

Private insurance plans paid 38.4 percent of the healthcare costs of health disparities. The second highest cost burden goes to individuals and families through out-of-pocket payments of 27.7 percent—more than Medicare and Medicaid combined. These percentages did vary by region. Medicaid share was highest in the Northeast, almost 20 percent, while out-of-pocket payments were highest in the West and South, over 30 percent in each region *(Figure 5)*. This observation might reflect the relative percentages of uninsured residents and the generosity of the Medicaid programs across regions. The percentages of the under 65 population that lacked health insurance coverage were highest in the South (17.5%) and West (16.3%) compared to the Midwest (12.2%) and East (11.6%) (DeNavas-Walt et al. 2011). The South and the West are the regions of the country where the highest percentages of the African American and Hispanic populations reside, the two groups least likely to have health insurance. In 2010, 30.7 percent of Hispanics, 20.8 percent African Americans and 18.4 percent of Asians were uninsured. Also, poverty rates are higher in the South (16.9%) and West (15.3%) compared to the Midwest (13.9%) and East (12.8%) (DeNavas-Walt et al. 2011). In most states in the South and the West, Medicaid spending was below $5,000 per enrollee compared to $7,000 per enrollee for most states in the Northeast and $6,000 per enrollee for most states in the Midwest (Snyder et al. 2012). Poverty and lack of health insurance are significant not only in the way that they affect how costs are apportioned, but also inasmuch as they contribute to the existence of health disparities by limiting access to many of the resources needed to promote good health.

LOST LABOR MARKET PRODUCTIVITY

Health disparities reduced labor market productivity by $22.3 billion in 2009. Hispanics accounted for the highest costs due to lower productivity ($9.8 billion) followed by African Americans ($9.6 billion) *(Figure 6)*. The costs of lower productivity were highest in the South ($8.8 billion) and the West ($6.8 billion). Comparing the distribution of productivity loss to that of the U.S. population shows that African Americans in all regions of the country and Hispanics in the Northeast and West accounted for a disproportionate amount of the productivity loss. These findings are consistent with patterns in population distribution described in the previous section on health care costs.

An analysis of lost productivity by industry reveals that Education, Health and Social Services Industries (22.7%) followed by Leisure, Hospitality, and Other Services Industries (15.8%) had the highest shares of potential cost savings *(Figure 7)*. These industries were important in all four Census regions. Throughout the country, these industries employ a significant number of lower wage and part-time workers who might also be less likely to have employer-provided health insurance.

PROJECTED FUTURE COSTS OF HEALTH DISPARITIES

The Census Bureau projects that the United States will become a "majority-minority" nation by 2050 (U.S. Census 2012). The increase in the minority population is driven largely by the increase in the Hispanic population from the current level of 31.9 million to 89 million in 2050, a 179% increase. Figure 8 displays the estimates of the direct and indirect costs due to health disparities based on population projections. In 2020, health disparities will cost the nation $126 billion—$87.8 billion in healthcare spending and $38.2 billion in lost productivity. In 2050, health disparities costs will rise to a projected $363.1 billion. This is a 4.4 fold increase in the burden of health disparities. The burden of excess healthcare expenditures and lost productivity on Hispanics will increase by 7.1 fold; the burden on Asians will increase by 6.2 fold and for African Americans the projected burden increases by 3.2 fold. These estimates assume the 2009 rates of health insurance coverage; however, if the ACA is successful in expanding private insurance and Medicaid coverage these costs will increase if other factors influencing health disparities are not addressed.

POLICY RECOMMENDATIONS

The historic passage of the Affordable Care Act in March 2010 marked a significant step toward establishing a coordinated approach to address and eventually eliminate health disparities. In the new

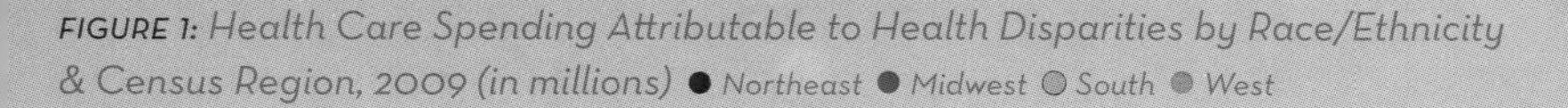

FIGURE 1: *Health Care Spending Attributable to Health Disparities by Race/Ethnicity & Census Region, 2009 (in millions)* ● Northeast ● Midwest ● South ● West

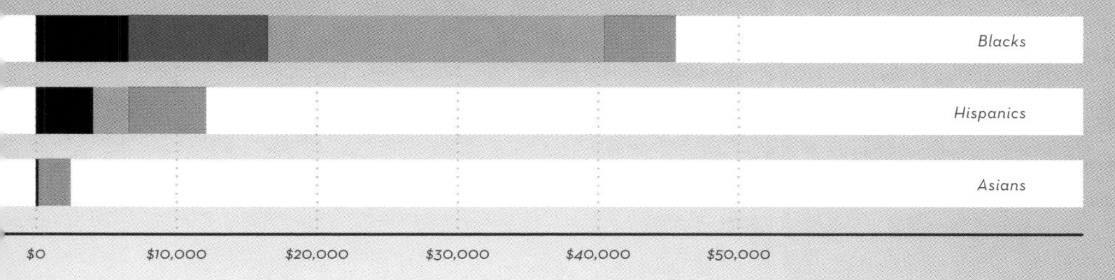

Source: Author's calculations based on the 2009 MEPS.

FIGURE 2: *African Americans as a Share of the Minority Population and Minority Health Care Spending, 2009* ● % of Minority Population ● % of Minority Health Care Spending

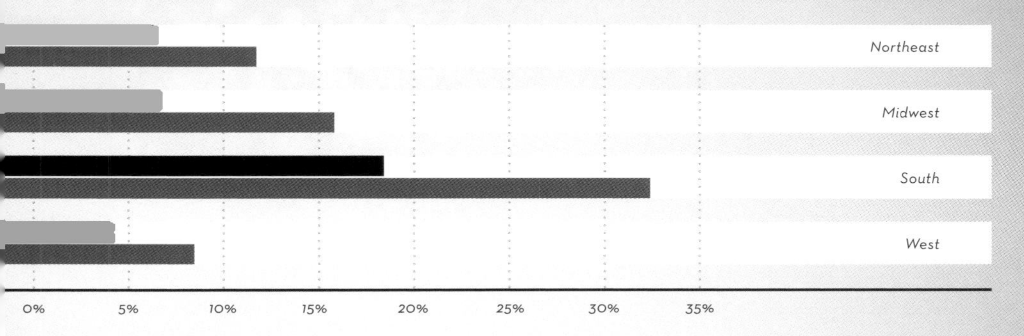

Source: Author's calculations based on the 2009 MEPS.

FIGURE 3: *Distribution of Asian Population and Health Care Spending Attributable to Health Disparities by Census Region, 2009* ● % of Asian Population ● % of Asian Health Care Spending

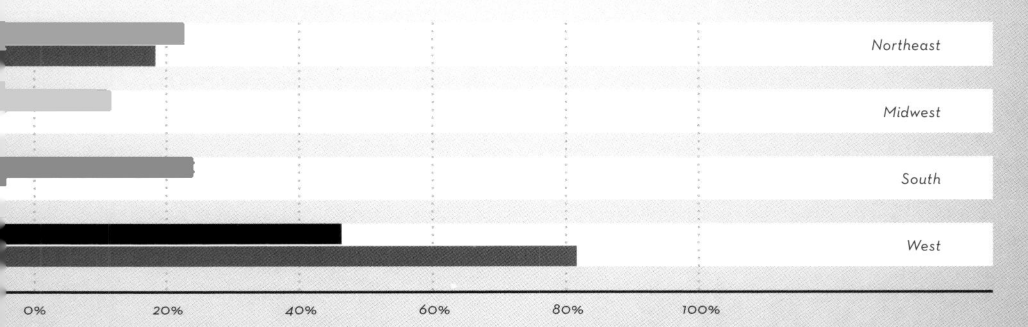

Source: Author's calculations based on the 2009 MEPS.

health care reform law there are several strong provisions, including developing research priorities, awarding community transformation grants, and evaluating and expanding effective community prevention services that will all go a long way to address health disparities, particularly in African American communities. The National Urban League believes that in addition to local and community strategies and partnerships, there are several federal policy levers that will help to eliminate disparities and help to realize the promise of the Affordable Care Act.

The following list summarizes some of those policy priorities.

MEDICARE & MEDICAID

1. Protect Medicare in the Budget
2. Cost Controls Must Protect Dual Eligible Patients
3. Incentivize Medicaid Expansion for All States

HEALTH INSURANCE EXCHANGES

4. Clear and Accessible Enrollment Process
5. Enrollment Campaigns Targeting Minorities
6. Integration and Automatic Enrollment

ENGAGING COMMUNITY-BASED ORGANIZATIONS (CBOS)

7. CBOs as Patient Navigators
8. Priority for Community Transformation Grants with Racial and Ethnic Interventions
9. Reduce Costs Through Integration of Services

HEALTHCARE WORKFORCE

10. Increase Minority Health Professionals
11. Fully Fund Community Health Worker Programs
12. Job Training Programs for Health Professions

DATA COLLECTION & REPORTING

13. Consistent Collection of Minority Health Data

But health disparities will not be eliminated through health policy alone; rather, health policy must be supported by the implementation of targeted employment, education, transportation, housing and community development policies that address the various socioeconomic contributors to health disparities, including the Urban Jobs Act, Project Ready STEM Act and others outlined in the National Urban League's *8 Point Plan to Educate, Employ and Empower and 12 Point Plan for Putting Urban America Back to Work.*

CONCLUSION

This report demonstrates that the full cost of health disparities goes well beyond the health of the individual. Closing these disparities in health outcomes matters not only to the individuals who will directly benefit from a longer and better quality of life, but also to their families, their communities and ultimately the nation. The estimated $82.2 billion that health disparities cost the U.S. economy in 2009 represents lost income for households, and money that may have otherwise been invested in education, in workforce development, in starting new businesses that create jobs or in much needed community infrastructure. Furthermore, all of these investments, when paired with the appropriate investment in preventive strategies and health programs, would go a long way in alleviating disparities in health.

FIGURE 4: *Distribution of Hispanic Population and Health Care Spending Attributable to Health Disparities by Census Region, 2009* ● *% of Hispanic Population* ● *% of Hispanic Health Care Spending*

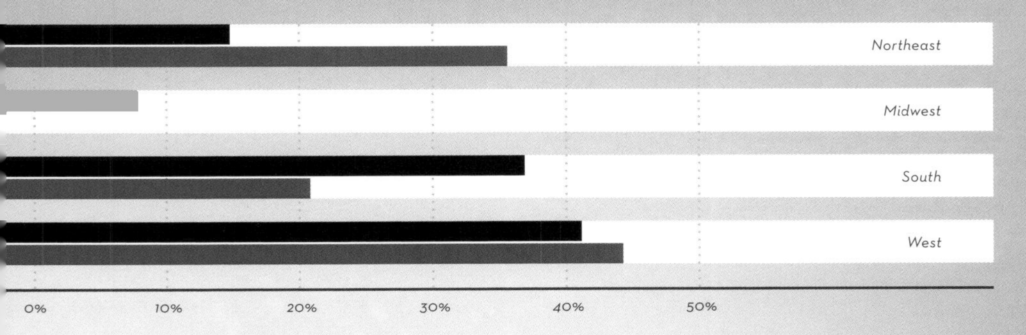

Source: Author's calculations based on the 2009 MEPS.

FIGURE 5: *Distribution of Health Care Costs Attributable to Health Disparities, by Source of Payment & Census Region (millions), 2009* ● *Out-of-Pocket* ● *Medicare* ● *Medicaid* ● *Private Insurance* ● *Other Payers*

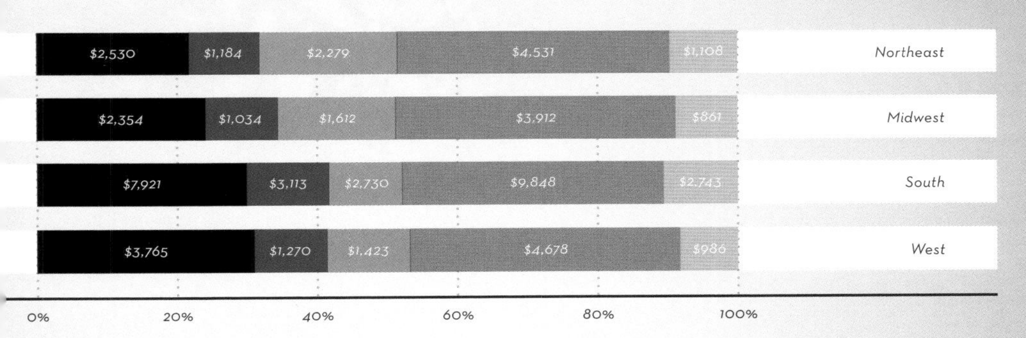

Source: Author's calculations based on the 2009 MEPS.

FIGURE 6: *Value of Lost Productivity Attributable to Health Disparities, by Race/Ethnicity & Census Region (millions), 2009* ● *Northeast* ● *Midwest* ● *South* ● *West*

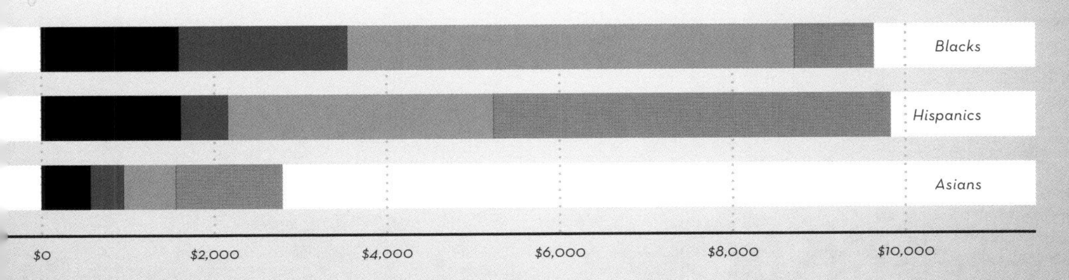

Source: Author's calculations based on the 2009 MEPS. Includes the value of lost days, hours worked, and lower wages associated with health inequity

The State of Urban Health: Eliminating Disparities to Save Lives and Cut Costs presents a sobering look at the economic impact of health inequities in America, as well as a collaborative action plan that makes the larger challenge of eliminating health disparities a more manageable and practicable goal.

Special thanks to Walgreens for their financial support and to the members of the Urban Health Advisory Panel for their guidance and feedback during the development of this report—Daniel E. Dawes, JD, Ian Duncan, FSA FIA FCIA MAAA, Jeffrey Kang, MD, MPH Allyson G. Hall, Ph.D., Daniel L. Howard, Ph.D., Camara Jones, Ph.D., Joyce Larkin, Brian D. Smedley, Ph.D., and Deborah T. Wilson.

APPENDIX

METHODS FOR ESTIMATING THE ECONOMIC BURDEN OF HEALTH DISPARITIES

The estimation of the economic impact of health disparities on society is conducted in two separate, but related economic analyses—(1) estimation of the direct medical costs, and (2) value of lost productivity associated with health disparities. We used data from the Medical Expenditure Panel Survey (MEPS) (Cohen et al. 1996/97; AHRQ 2009) for the years 2006–2009 to estimate the potential cost savings of eliminating health disparities for racial and ethnic minorities. We divided the sample into 14 cohorts based on gender and seven age groups: 18–24, 25–34, 35–44, 45–54, 55–64, 65–74, and 75 and over. Within each cohort, we computed the prevalence for several health conditions for four mutually exclusive racial/ethnic groups—African Americans, Asians, Hispanics, and whites. Hispanics are persons of Hispanic origins regardless of race. The other racial groups include only non-Hispanics. The health status and health conditions measures were:

- ★ *Self-reported general health status (ranging from excellent to poor);*
- ★ *Self-reported mental health status (ranging from excellent to poor);*
- ★ *Presence of a functional limitation;*
- ★ *Body mass index (BMI)/obesity measure;*
- ★ *Presence of chronic conditions (diabetes, asthma, asthma attack, high blood pressure, heart attack, angina, other heart disease, stroke, emphysema, joint pain, or arthritis).*

Subsequently, we determined which racial/ethnic group had the best health outcomes within each age/gender cohort for each

FIGURE 7: *Distribution of Productivity Loss Attributable to Health Disparities, by Industry, 2009*

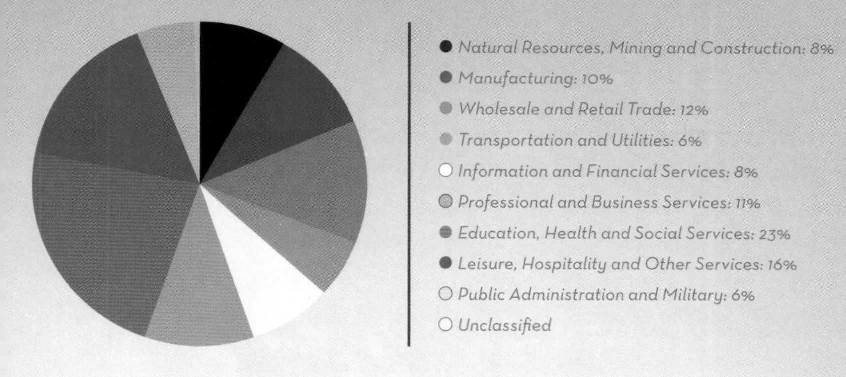

Source: Author's calculations based on the 2009 MEPS.

FIGURE 8: *Estimated Direct & Indirect Costs of Health Disparities by Race/Ethnicity (in millions),*

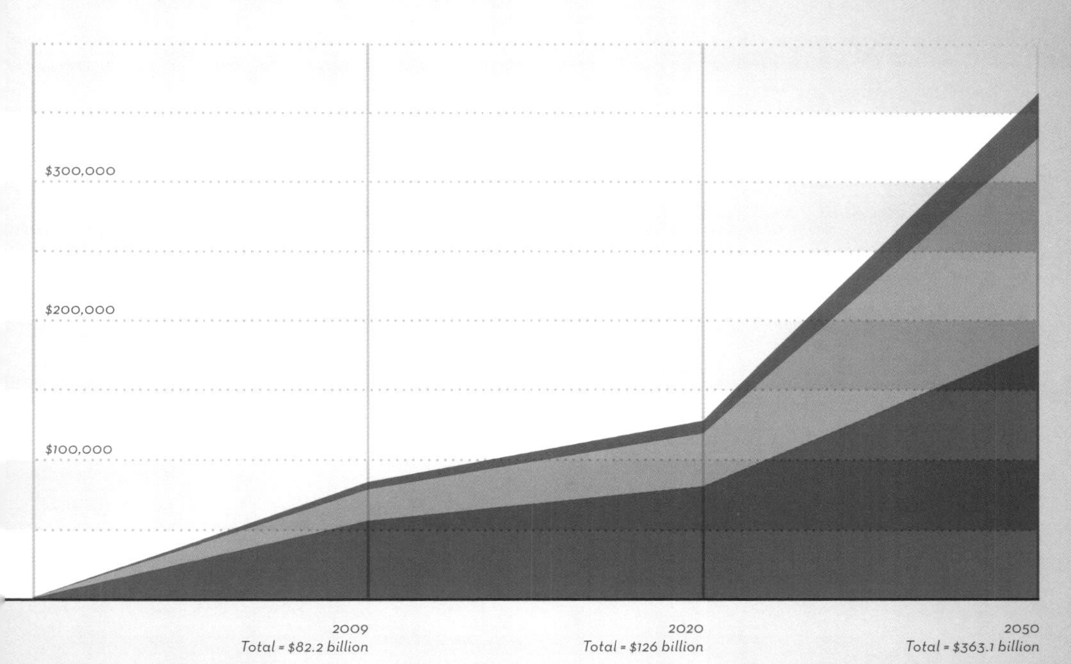

Source: Author's calculations based on the 2009 MEPS.

health status/condition. In most cases, it was whites or Asians, but in a few cases Hispanics had the best health profile within a given age/gender group. We estimated the impact of these health conditions on health care expenditures, days from work because of the health condition, annual hours off work because of the health condition, and reduced hourly wages because of the health condition. We then simulated the health care and labor market outcomes by assigning each minority group the best health profile, i.e., eliminating disparities in health in the corresponding age/gender cohort. We computed the costs of disparities as the difference between the predicted outcomes with the actual health conditions and predicted outcomes with the simulated health conditions.

DIRECT HEALTH CARE COSTS

Using 2009 data, we developed a model to estimate health care expenditures for each racial/ethnic group (African American, Asian, Hispanic, and white). Total expenditures in MEPS include both out-of-pocket and third-party payments to health care providers, but do not include health insurance premiums. Expenditures for hospital-based services include inpatient, emergency room, outpatient (hospital, clinic, and office-based visits), prescription drugs, and other services (e.g., home health services, vision care services, dental care, ambulance services, and medical equipment). Prescription drug expenditures do not include over-the-counter purchases. We estimated health care spending using demographic, socioeconomic, geographic, and health status measures. The demographic factors were age, race/ethnicity, and gender, and marital status. The socioeconomic factors were education, income, and health insurance status. The geographic factors were census region and urban-rural residence. We used geography to compute the costs of disparities by census region and urban-rural area within census region. Also, for each respondent we apportioned health care costs savings by source of payment (i.e., out-of-pocket, Medicare, Medicaid, private insurance and other third party payers).

We estimated a two-part health care expenditure model (Manning et al 2001; Buntin and Zaslavsky 2004; Manning et al , 1987;Manning, & Mullahy, 2001) to address issues of sample selection in expenditures. First, we estimated the probability of having nonzero health care expenditures during the year. The first part of the model consisted of estimating logistic regression models to estimate the probability of having any type of health care expenditures. The second part consisted of using generalized linear models to predict levels of expenditures for individuals with positive expenditures. We used a log link and gamma distribution to address the skewness in the expenditure data. We eliminated outliers, i.e., observations with expenditures greater than $100,000, less than 0.5 percent of the sample, and conducted the different diagnostic and specification tests recommended by Manning and Mullahy (1998a, 1998b, 2001). We estimated the models using the survey regression procedures in STATA 12, which appropriately incorporate the design factors and sample weights.

VALUE OF LOST PRODUCTIVITY

Similar to estimating direct medical expenditures, we used data from the 2009 MEPS to estimate two-part models of days and hours of work lost by male adults because of disability or illness. We also used a two-part model to estimate reduced wages due to a disability or illness. The functional form of the models depended upon the dependent variables. For missed days or hours of work, we estimated the impact of health on the probability of missing a workday during the year. Second, we estimated generalized linear models to predict levels of days or hours of work missed for individuals with positive days or hours of work missed. We used a log link and gamma distribution to address the skewness in the data for missed days and an inverse Gaussian distribution for hours of work. For hours worked and wages, the first equation estimated the impact of health on the probability that an adult is working. The first part of the model consisted of a probit regression. The second equation estimated the impact of health on hourly wages. Combining the results from these different parts of the models, we computed the productivity costs associated with health disparities. We used a two-step estimator for labor supply to predict lost productivity due to health disparities and adjusted the models by using an inverse mills ratio to account potential selection bias (Greene 2005, Cameron and Trivedi 2008).

We computed the estimated number of disability days and hours from work using the actual health status and health conditions from the MEPS. We subsequently computed similar predicted values to compute the potential savings assuming each racial/ethnic group had health status equal to that of the racial/ethnic group with the best health profile within each age cohort. In other words, we simulated what the labor market outcomes would be if racial/ethnic inequalities in health status and health conditions were eliminated. The productivity loss is the difference between the predicted values using actual health compared to the simulated health data. We valued disability days and hours worked at the respondents' predicted wage. We annualized the difference in wages using the respondent's predicted hours worked during the year. This analysis was restricted to working adults, ages 25–64.

PROJECTING FUTURE COSTS OF DISPARITIES

To compute savings per person for years 2020 and 2050, we used similar rates for savings per person as the Congressional Budget Office (CBO) projections of overall medical spending in the next several decades (Borger et al. 2006). Subsequently, we used Census estimates of the yearly projected population by age, sex, race and Hispanic origin. The sample was limited to those between 18 and 85 years old as the oldest person in the MEPS was 85 years old. We also limited the projected population figures for indirect savings to 65 years old. We computed both direct and indirect costs of racial/ethnic disparities in health for years 2020 and 2050 by multiplying savings per person for each racial/ethnic group and region by the number of persons in the corresponding racial/ethnic group and region of the United States. It is important to note these projections do not account for potential impact that certain provisions of the Affordable Care Act such as Medicaid expansions would have on health improvement of racial/ethnic minorities.

NOTES

[1] LaVeist and colleagues (2010) includes the costs of premature death.

TABLE A1: Distribution of Minority Population and Health Care Spending Attributable to Health Disparities by Census Region and Urban-Rural Location, 2009

ADULT POPULATION IN THOUSANDS AND PERCENT OF THE TOTAL								
	BLACKS		HISPANICS		ASIANS		TOTAL	
MSA								
NORTHEAST	4,385	6.4%	4,492	6.5%	2,290	3.3%	11,167	**16.2%**
MIDWEST	4,453	6.5%	2,106	3.1%	1,153	1.7%	7,712	**11.2%**
SOUTH	12,700	18.4%	10,700	15.5%	2,328	3.4%	25,728	**37.3%**
WEST	2,326	3.4%	12,500	18.1%	4,708	6.8%	19,534	**28.3%**
TOTAL MSA	23,864	34.6%	29,798	43.2%	10,479	15.2%	64,141	**92.9%**
NON-MSA								
NORTHEAST	27	0.0%	21	0.0%	12	0.0%	60	**0.1%**
MIDWEST	185	0.3%	358	0.5%	29	0.0%	573	**0.8%**
SOUTH	2,328	3.4%	1,075	1.6%	80	0.1%	3,483	**5.0%**
WEST	17	0.0%	694	1.0%	47	0.1%	758	**1.1%**
TOTAL NON-MSA	2,558	3.7%	2,149	3.1%	167	0.2%	4,874	**7.1%**
TOTAL	**26,422**	**38.3%**	**31,946**	**46.3%**	**10,647**	**15.4%**	**69,016**	**100%**

MILLIONS OF DOLLARS AND PERCENT OF THE TOTAL								
	BLACKS		HISPANICS		ASIANS		TOTAL	
MSA								
NORTHEAST	6,810	11.4%	4,320	7.2%	466	0.8%	11,596	**19.3%**
MIDWEST	9,280	15.5%	0	0.0%	0	0.0%	9,280	**15.5%**
SOUTH	19,400	32.4%	1,750	2.9%	0	0.0%	21,150	**35.3%**
WEST	4,810	8.0%	5,100	8.5%	1,960	3.3%	11,870	**19.8%**
TOTAL MSA	40,300	67.2%	11,170	18.6%	2,426	4.0%	59,931	**89.9%**
NON-MSA								
NORTHEAST	51	0.1%	10	0.0%	0	0.0%	61	**0.1%**
MIDWEST	495	0.8%	0	0.0%	0	0.0%	495	**0.8%**
SOUTH	4,410	7.4%	797	1.3%	4	0.0%	5,211	**8.7%**
WEST	27	0.0%	232	0.4%	0	0.0%	259	**0.4%**
TOTAL NON-MSA	4,983	8.3%	1,039	1.7%	4	0.0%	6,026	**10.1%**
TOTAL	**45,283**	**75.5%**	**12,209**	**20.4%**	**2,430**	**4.1%**	**59,957**	**100.0%**

Source: Author's calculations based on the 2009 MEPS.

TABLE A2: Distribution of Health Care Costs Due to Health Disparities, By Source of Payment and Census Region, 2009

MILLIONS OF DOLLARS					
	EAST	MIDWEST	SOUTH	WEST	**TOTAL**
TOTAL	**11,633**	**9,775**	**26,356**	**12,123**	**59,888**
OUT-OF-POCKET	2,530	2,354	7,921	3,765	**16,571**
MEDICARE	1,184	1,034	3,113	1,270	**6,602**
MEDICAID	2,279	1,612	2,730	1,423	**8,045**
PRIVATE INSURANCE	4,531	3,912	9,848	4,678	**22,971**
OTHER PAYERS	1,108	861	2,743	986	**5,699**

PERCENTAGES					
	EAST	MIDWEST	SOUTH	WEST	**TOTAL**
TOTAL	**100.0%**	**100.0%**	**100.0%**	**100.0%**	**100.0%**
OUT-OF-POCKET	21.8%	24.1%	30.1%	31.1%	**27.7%**
MEDICARE	10.2%	10.6%	11.8%	10.5%	**11.0%**
MEDICAID	19.6%	16.5%	10.4%	11.7%	**13.4%**
PRIVATE INSURANCE	38.9%	40.0%	37.4%	38.6%	**38.4%**
OTHER PAYERS	9.5%	8.8%	10.4%	8.1%	**9.5%**

Source: Author's calculations based on the 2009 MEPS.

TABLE A3: Distribution Working Age Adults Minority Population and Value of Lost Productivity Due to Health Disparities Among Working Age Adults, By Region and Urban-Rural Location, 2009

POPULATIONS IN THOUSANDS (AGES 24-65) AND PERCENT OF THE TOTAL								
	BLACKS		HISPANICS		ASIANS		TOTAL	
MSA								
NORTHEAST	3,151	6.1%	3,438	6.6%	1,797	3.5%	8,385	**16.2%**
MIDWEST	3,267	6.3%	1,652	3.2%	921	1.8%	5,840	**11.3%**
SOUTH	9,347	18.0%	8,079	15.6%	1,902	3.7%	19,329	**37.3%**
WEST	1,683	3.2%	9,730	18.8%	3,431	6.6%	14,844	**28.6%**
TOTAL MSA	17,448	33.6%	13,170	44.1%	4,620	8.9%	35,237	**93.3%**
NON-MSA								
NORTHEAST	11	0.0%	21	0.0%	12	0.0%	44	**0.1%**
MIDWEST	109	0.2%	276	0.5%	29	0.1%	413	**0.8%**
SOUTH	1,638	3.2%	753	1.5%	61	0.1%	2,452	**4.7%**
WEST	14	0.0%	523	1.0%	35	0.1%	571	**1.1%**
TOTAL NON-MSA	1,771	3.4%	1,573	3.0%	136	0.3%	3,481	**6.7%**
TOTAL	**19,219**	**37.0%**	**14,743**	**47.2%**	**4,756**	**9.2%**	**38,718**	**100%**

MILLIONS OF DOLLARS AND PERCENT OF THE TOTAL								
	BLACKS		HISPANICS		ASIANS		TOTAL	
MSA								
NORTHEAST	1,570	7.1%	1,609	7.2%	556	2.5%	3,735	**16.8%**
MIDWEST	1,888	8.5%	486	2.2%	387	1.7%	2,762	**12.4%**
SOUTH	4,213	18.9%	2,766	12.4%	562	2.5%	7,542	**33.9%**
WEST	893	4.0%	4,355	19.6%	1,232	5.5%	6,480	**29.1%**
TOTAL MSA	8,565	38.5%	9,215	41.4%	2,737	12.3%	20,518	**92.2%**
NON-MSA								
NORTHEAST	25	0.1%	7	0.0%	16	0.1%	48	**0.2%**
MIDWEST	64	0.3%	66	0.3%	0	0.0%	131	**0.6%**
SOUTH	950	4.3%	292	1.3%	33	0.1%	1,275	**5.7%**
WEST	30	0.1%	243	1.1%	6	0.0%	281	**1.3%**
TOTAL NON-MSA	1,070	4.8%	609	2.7%	56	0.3%	1,735	**7.8%**
TOTAL	**9,635**	**43.3%**	**9,824**	**44.1%**	**2,793**	**12.6%**	**22,253**	**100.0%**

Source: Author's calculations based on the 2009 MEPS. This includes the value of lost days, hours worked, and lower wages associated with health inequity.

TABLE A4: *Distribution of Productivity Loss Attributable to Health Disparities, By Industry and Census Region, 2009*

MILLIONS OF DOLLARS					
	EAST	MIDWEST	SOUTH	WEST	TOTAL
TOTAL	3,782.7	2,892.5	8,816.8	6,760.5	22,252.5
NATURAL RESOURCES, MINING AND CONSTRUCTION	176.3	113.5	799.2	770.7	1,859.7
MANUFACTURING	306.2	425.2	840.3	743.6	2,315.3
WHOLESALE AND RETAIL TRADE	447.6	282.4	1,106.8	888.1	2,724.9
TRANSPORTATION AND UTILITIES	300.6	170.4	501.2	312.2	1,284.4
INFORMATION AND FINANCIAL SERVICES	393.0	240.0	643.6	533.4	1,810.0
PROFESSIONAL AND BUSINESS SERVICES	384.3	317.1	823.3	833.6	2,358.3
EDUCATION, HEALTH AND SOCIAL SERVICES	924.4	813.5	2,072.3	1,238.8	5,049.0
LEISURE, HOSPITALITY, AND OTHER SERVICES	621.3	390.5	1,432.2	1,073.6	3,517.6
PUBLIC ADMINISTRATION AND MILITARY	199.1	124.5	567.3	350.5	1,241.4
UNCLASSIFIED	29.9	15.4	30.6	16.0	91.9

PERCENTAGES					
	EAST	MIDWEST	SOUTH	WEST	TOTAL
NATURAL RESOURCES, MINING AND CONSTRUCTION	4.7%	3.9%	9.1%	11.4%	8.4%
MANUFACTURING	8.1%	14.7%	9.5%	11.0%	10.3%
WHOLESALE AND RETAIL TRADE	11.8%	9.8%	12.6%	13.1%	12.2%
TRANSPORTATION AND UTILITIES	7.9%	5.9%	5.7%	4.6%	5.8%
INFORMATION AND FINANCIAL SERVICES	10.4%	8.3%	7.3%	7.9%	8.1%
PROFESSIONAL AND BUSINESS SERVICES	10.2%	11.0%	9.3%	12.3%	10.6%
EDUCATION, HEALTH AND SOCIAL SERVICES	24.4%	28.1%	23.5%	18.3%	22.7%
LEISURE, HOSPITALITY, AND OTHER SERVICES	16.4%	13.5%	16.2%	15.9%	15.8%
PUBLIC ADMINISTRATION AND MILITARY	5.3%	4.3%	6.4%	5.2%	5.6%
UNCLASSIFIED	0.8%	0.5%	0.3%	0.2%	0.4%

Source: Author's calculations based on the 2009 MEPS.

TABLE A5: *Projected Minority Populations, Direct and Indirect Costs of Health Disparities in 2020, by Census Region*

2020 POPULATION PROJECTIONS IN THE UNITED STATES				
	BLACKS	HISPANICS	ASIANS	TOTAL
EAST	5,066,000	5,838,000	3,014,000	**13,918,000**
MIDWEST	5,364,000	3,336,000	1,507,000	**10,207,000**
SOUTH	16,986,000	15,429,000	3,151,000	**35,566,000**
WEST	2,682,000	17,097,000	6,165,000	**25,944,000**
TOTAL	**$30,098,000**	**$41,700,000**	**$13,837,000**	**$85,635,000**

PROJECTION OF HEALTHCARE COSTS IN MILLIONS OF DOLLARS				
	BLACKS	HISPANICS	ASIANS	TOTAL
EAST	9,794	6,965	719	**17,478**
MIDWEST	14,056	0	0	**14,056**
SOUTH	33,461	4,150	0	**37,611**
WEST	6,884	8,591	3,150	**18,625**
TOTAL	**$64,194**	**$19,705**	**$3,869**	**$87,768**

PROJECTION POPULATION FOR 2020 (AGES 18–65)				
	BLACKS	HISPANICS	ASIANS	TOTAL
EAST	4,286,055	5,452,100	2,585,537	**12,323,692**
MIDWEST	4,576,819	3,050,277	1,456,425	**9,083,521**
SOUTH	14,856,852	14,057,651	2,829,608	**31,744,111**
WEST	2,280,274	16,239,972	5,128,429	**23,648,675**
TOTAL	**$26,000,000**	**$38,800,000**	**$12,000,000**	**$76,800,000**

PROJECTED INDIRECT COSTS DUE TO LOST PRODUCTIVITY IN MILLIONS OF DOLLARS				
	BLACKS	HISPANICS	ASIANS	TOTAL
EAST	2,493	2,987	1,026	**6,506**
MIDWEST	3,051	1,021	696	**4,768**
SOUTH	8,069	5,653	1,069	**14,791**
WEST	1,444	8,500	2,224	**12,168**
TOTAL	**$15,057**	**$18,161**	**$5,015**	**$38,233**
GRAND TOTAL	$79,251	$37,866	$8,884	$126,001

Source: Author's calculations based on the 2009 MEPS.

TABLE A6: Projected Minority Populations, Direct and Indirect Costs of Health Disparities in 2050, by Census Region

2050 POPULATION PROJECTIONS IN THE UNITED STATES				
	BLACKS	HISPANICS	ASIANS	TOTAL
EAST	6,379,625	12,572,756	5,621,682	24,574,063
MIDWEST	6,705,624	6,865,724	2,885,099	16,456,447
SOUTH	21,727,169	32,803,534	5,880,854	60,411,557
WEST	3,387,582	36,757,986	11,612,365	51,757,933
TOTAL	$38,200,000	$89,000,000	$26,000,000	$153,200,000

PROJECTION OF HEALTHCARE COSTS IN MILLIONS OF DOLLARS				
	BLACKS	HISPANICS	ASIANS	TOTAL
EAST	19,837	24,126	2,158	46,121
MIDWEST	28,263	0	0	28,263
SOUTH	68,842	14,191	0	83,033
WEST	13,985	29,707	9,543	53,235
TOTAL	$130,927	$68,024	$11,701	$210,652

PROJECTED POPULATIONS FOR 2050 (AGES 18-65)				
	BLACKS	HISPANICS	ASIANS	TOTAL
EAST	5,027,872	10,510,749	4,287,682	19,826,303
MIDWEST	5,368,961,	5,880,431	2,415,238	13,664,630
SOUTH	17,428,230	27,100,832	4,692,433	49,221,495
WEST	2,674,937	31,307,987	8,504,645	42,487,569
TOTAL	$30,500,000	$74,800,000	$19,899,998	$125,199,998

PROJECTED INDIRECT COSTS DUE TO LOST PRODUCTIVITY IN MILLIONS OF DOLLARS				
	BLACKS	HISPANICS	ASIANS	TOTAL
EAST	7,312	14,395	4,252	25,959
MIDWEST	8,948	4,923	2,884	16,755
SOUTH	23,664	27,246	4,434	55,344
WEST	4,236	40,970	9,220	54,426
TOTAL	$44,160	$87,534	$20,790	$152,484
GRAND TOTAL	$175,087	$155,558	$32,491	$363,136

Source: Author's calculations based on the 2009 MEPS.

REFERENCES

Agency for Healthcare Research and Quality. 2006. *National Healthcare Disparities Report.* Rockville, MD: U.S. Department of Health and Human Services, Agency for Healthcare Research and Quality. AHRQ Pub. No. 07–0012.

Agency for Healthcare Research and Quality Center for Financing, Access, and Cost Trends: Medical Expenditure Panel Survey Household Component, 2010. Table 4.a Total population and uninsured persons under age 65: Percent by selected population characteristics, United States, 2010. *http://meps.ahrq.gov/mepsweb/data_stats/summ_tables/hc/hlth_insr/2010/t4a_d10.htm accessed November 2012.*

Borger C, Smith S, Truffer C, Keehan S, Sisko A, Poisal J, Clemens MK. 2006. "Health Spending Projections Through 2015: Changes on the Horizon." *Health Affairs* 25: w61–w73.

Buettgens, M., Garrett, B., & Holahan, J. (2010). *America under the Affordable Care Act.* Urban Institute and Robert Wood Johnson Foundation Washington, D.C. accessed at *http://www.urban.org/url.cfm?ID=412267 accessed November 2012.*

Buntin MB, Zaslavsky AM. 2004. "Too Much Ado About Two-Part Models and Transformation? Comparing Methods of Modeling Medicare Expenditures." *Journal of Health Economics* 23: 525–542.

Cameron AC, Trivedi PK. 2008. *Microeconometrics Methods and Applications.* New York, NY: Cambridge University Press.

Cohen JW, Monheit AC, Beauregard KM, et al. 1996/1997. "The Medical Expenditure Panel Survey: A National Health Information Resource." *Inquiry* 33: 373–389.

Congress of the United States, Congressional Budget Office. Updated long-term projections for social security. Washington, D.C.: Congress of the United States, Congressional Budget Office; 2008. *http://www.cbo.gov/ftpdocs/96xx/doc9649/08-20-SocialSecurityUpdate.pdf.* Accessed November 2012.

CPI Detailed Report Data for September 2012—Table 25C. Historical Chained Consumer Price Index for All Urban Consumers (C-CPI-U): U.S. city average, by commodity and service group and detailed expenditure categories. *http://www.bls.gov/cpi/cpid1209.pdf.* Accessed October 2012.

DeNavas-Walt, Carmen, Bernadette D. Proctor, and Jessica C. Smith, U.S. Census Bureau, Current Population Reports, P60–239, *Income, Poverty, and Health Insurance Coverage in the United States: 2010,* U.S. Government Printing Office, Washington, D.C., 2011.

Duan N. 1983. "Smearing estimate: a nonparametric retransformation method," *Journal of American Statistical Association* 78:605–610.

Duan N, Manning WG, Morris N, Newhouse JP. 1983. "A Comparison of Alternative Models for Demand for Medical Care." *Journal of Business and Economic Statistics* 1: 115–126.

Office of Budget and Management, Executive Office of the President of the United States, Fiscal Year 2013 Budget of the U.S. Government. U.S. Government Printing Office, Washington 2010 *http://www.whitehouse.gov/sites/default/files/omb/budget/fy2013/assets/budget.pdf* accessed November 2012.

Fortune. 2009. "Global 200: Our Annual Ranking of the World's Largest Corporations." *http://money.cnn.com/magazines/fortune/global500/2008/index.html* (retrieved 2 September 2009).

Greene WH. 2005. *Econometric Analysis.* Upper Saddle River: NJ: Prentice Hall.

Humphreys JM. 2008. "The Multicultural Economy: 2008." Selig Center for Economic Growth, Terry College of Business, University of Georgia.

Killingsworth MR: *Labor supply.* New York: Cambridge University Press, 1983.

LaVeist T, Gaskin D, Richard P. (2011). Estimating the economic burden of racial health disparities in the United States. *International Journal of Health Services,* 41(2), 231–238.

Manning WG. 1998. "The logged dependent variable, heteroscedasticity and the retransformation problem." *Journal of Health Economics* 17:283–295.

Manning WG, Mullahy J. 2001. "Estimating Log Models: To Transform or Not to Transform?" *Journal of Health Economics* 20(4): 461–494.

Mullahy J. 1998. "Much ado about two: Reconsidering retransformation and the two-part model in health econometrics." *Journal of Health Economics* 17:241–281.

National Heart, Lung, and Blood Institute. *Fact Book Fiscal Year 2010.* Bethesda, MD. : U.S. Dept. of Health and Human Services, National Heart, Lung, and Blood Institute, 2011.

National Partnership for Action. National Stakeholder Strategy for Achieving Health Equity; 2011.

Poisal JA, Truffer C, Smith S, Sisko A, Cowan C, Keehan S, Dickensheets B, and the National Health Expenditure Accounts Projections Team. 2007. "Health Spending Projections Through 2016: Modest Changes Obscure Part D's Impact." *Health Affairs* 26(2): w242–w253.

Smedley BD, Stith AY, Nelson AR, eds. 2002. "Unequal Treatment: Confronting Racial and Ethnic Disparities in Health Care." Washington, D.C.: National Academy Press.

Snyder L, Rudowitz R, Garfield R, Gordon T. "Why does Medicaid Spending vary across States: A Chartbook of Factors Driving State Spending." Kaiser Commission on Medicaid and the Uninsured November 2012.

U.S. Department of Health and Human Services (HHS). Office of Disease Prevention and Health Promotion, Healthy People 2020: Rockville, MD. Available at: *www.healthypeople.gov.*

U.S. Census Bureau, Population Division. U.S. population projections: Projected Population by Single Year of Age, Sex, Race, and Hispanic Origin for the United States: July 1, 2000 to July 1, 2050. *http://www.census.gov/population/projections/* Accessed November 2012.

Waidmann T. Estimating the Costs of Racial and Ethnic Health Disparities. Urban Institute September 2009. *http://www.urban.org/uploadedpdf/411962_health_disparities.pdf* Accessed November 2012.

DIGITIZING the DREAM: THE ROLE OF TECHNOLOGY IN EMPOWERING COMMUNITIES

CYNTHIA MARSHALL

This year is the 50th Anniversary of the *March on Washington for Jobs and Freedom* and while we all remember this seminal moment in our nation's history, I believe we must remain committed to tackling the challenges of today.

Progress in Black America relies on enabling everyone, especially those in predominately minority communities, to attain the education needed to secure well-paying jobs and contribute to the greater good.

Since the last *State of Black America* Report we have seen the re-election of President Obama and the beginnings of initiatives designed to narrow the education, employment and wealth gaps between the richest one percent and the rest of America. Because of the civic engagement efforts that resulted in a second term for President Obama, people of color will continue to progress toward educational, employment and wealth parity.

OUR COMMUNITY AS A WHOLE WILL THRIVE ONLY WHEN EVERYONE HAS ACCESS TO THE BEST EDUCATIONAL OPPORTUNITIES AND THE SKILLS NECESSARY TO EARN THE BEST EMPLOYMENT OPPORTUNITIES.

Our community as a whole will thrive only when everyone has access to the best educational opportunities and the skills necessary to earn the best employment opportunities. As President Obama said, "If we want America to lead in the 21st century, nothing is more important than giving everyone the best education possible—from the day they start preschool to the day they start their career." I would also emphasize the importance of continuing education during one's career, because in this fast changing world one must continuously acquire new skills. Educational initiatives must focus on the jobs of the future and equipping students to handle rapid developments in technology. In parallel, we must build an enduring infrastructure to support American competitiveness and robust job creation.

From my perspective, as a representative of AT&T, Black America's future success will be influenced in large part by our transition to a knowledge-based, technology-driven economy. Broadband and wireless technologies have become vitally important to educating our children, young adults and continuing education students. Without the requisite emphasis on infrastructure development, however, America will lag behind in providing both education and employment opportunities. Expanding access to high-speed broadband Internet and next-generation wireless and Internet Protocol (IP)-based networks will bolster achievement and lead to brighter futures for people of color.

Consider these facts: during the 2009–10 school year, more than 1.5 million K-12 students engaged in some form of online or blended learning, with more than a third of tweens and young teenagers in the United States using smartphones to do homework. Smartphones were employed for homework by 39 percent of 11 to 14 year olds; 31 percent said they completed assignments on a tablet, while nearly 65 percent used laptops. In addition, 50 percent of employers use e-learning for training new and existing workers.

To achieve better outcomes more of the time, we must facilitate investment in job-creating infrastructure programs. Not only will these investments facilitate increased educational opportunities, but they will also create a large number of jobs for communities of color and enhance the state of Black America. A study by economists Robert Shapiro and Kevin Hassett found that the infrastructure investment and transition from 2G to 3G wireless alone created approximately 1.6 million U.S. jobs.

The only way to achieve educational and employment success in Black America is by providing the investors and companies looking to embark on new infrastructure projects the incentive and certainty necessary to make major commitments.

At AT&T we recently announced Project Velocity IP (VIP), a plan to invest $14 billion over the next three years to significantly expand and enhance our wired and wireless IP broadband networks. IP stands for "Internet Protocol." It is the common "language" that advanced forms of technology can understand and use to communicate with each other. IP technology enables seamless communication of voice, data, and Internet applications among various devices, including televisions, phones, laptops, and tablets.

As a result of this planned investment, we expect Black America will be able to take advantage of a greater variety of advanced digital services at faster speeds than those delivered on old legacy copper-based telephone networks, helping to increase the effectiveness of education delivered over both wired and wireless connections. Imagine streaming videos for online classes or virtual job interviews. An all-IP network will help usher in a new era in education.

But these educational and employment benefits can only be realized if government and industry work together to improve and expand our digital infrastructure. A robust American IP infrastructure can generate hundreds of thousands of jobs at every stage of the process, from the physical installation of new network infrastructure, to network management, to the thousands of new businesses and jobs that will result from a burgeoning high-speed IP broadband economy.

As the senior executive vice president of human resources at AT&T, a company at the forefront of technology, I believe the transition to IP-enabled networks will assist people of color looking for employment by making it quicker to apply for work online at home or through job kiosks using broadband. By delivering wired and wireless broadband through the buildout of advanced digital infrastructure, more Black Americans will achieve success.

The types of educational and employment opportunities we are contemplating today are not merely to acquire fundamental knowledge or entry-level jobs. African Americans and other communities of color must aim high. The build-out of America's infrastructure, including its digital infrastructure, requires workers with sophisticated knowledge supported by a broad and deep education stressing quantitative and technological know-how. That is what we hope to deliver. Students all over the country, in rural and urban communities, will gain access to the best education, from virtual charter schools to top-tier universities to specialized continuing education institutions.

In order to make progress and succeed, job seekers and workers, including Black America, will need to call for more infrastructure build-out so all of us can gain access to the best education and employment opportunities this great country has to offer. Let's digitize the dreams embodied by the *March on Washington* and take advantage of the technological opportunities that can propel us toward economic prosperity.

FINANCIAL DIGNITY *in an* ECONOMIC AGE

JOHN HOPE BRYANT

"In the civil rights movement we succeeded in integrating the lunch counters, the stores, the universities and public facilities, but we failed to integrate the money. The new movement has to include making free enterprise relevant to the poor, and work for the poor."

–Ambassador Andrew Young

Empowering individuals and families with a new agenda of 'Silver Rights', to accompany their historic legacy of civil rights, has to be a key component of the new national Black agenda for 2013. More people have no bank account today (approximately 27M unbanked and underbanked)[1] than didn't have the right to vote in the civil rights movement in 1962 (approximately 26 million). For this reason, Operation HOPE and others also see financial literacy empowerment as important.

REAL MONEY, FALLING BETWEEN OUR OWN FINGERS

In 2004 alone, $10 billion of Earned Income Tax Credit (EITC) benefits went unclaimed by families who qualify in my home state of California.[2] What's more, national estimates indicate that 1 out of 4 people who qualify for EITC, never even ask for it[3]—and this is not government charity or hand outs. This is money earned as a cash credit for eligible working families.[4]

Who amongst us does not have a family member or friend who seems to always be asking for a loan for this or that? If that family member or friend works, and they make $50,000 or less and has dependent children there is a good chance that they qualify for EITC.[5] This means they can get the money they need, wired into a bank account of their choice within 3–4 weeks once they file their federal taxes.[6] For a family making $30,000 a year, receiving a check for as much as $12,000 in EITC benefits represents more money, as a lump sum, than they would ever see in a lifetime of work.[7] That's enough to cure a mortgage in foreclosure for the average family, or maybe pay off a car loan, or put a serious dent in college tuition.

In all the talk about the fiscal cliff in late 2012, the literal fiscal cliff that most struggling working class and middle class American families encounter every month as they make ends meet is seldom mentioned. This is the relevancy of financial literacy empowerment in our lives.

A NEW MOVEMENT FOR A NEW TIME

In the 20th century, the issue was empowerment through democracy and the right to vote. In the 21st century, the issue is economic empowerment. The newest version of freedom might well be self-determination. What our communities need most are good jobs and the income and benefits that flow from them. Following our emancipation from slavery, we were promised 40 acres and a mule, but arguably what we need now is 40 books and a bank account.

700 CREDIT SCORE COMMUNITIES

If you want to break up the conspiracy of check cashers, payday lenders, and rent-to-own stores and liquor stores preying on our communities, you must deprive them of their customer. These businesses represent a form of bad capitalism, targeting 550 credit score neighborhoods. It's not racism, its target marketing. A 550 credit score customer and neighborhood has a certain profile; low financial IQ, low levels of financial literacy and understanding, low self esteem, lack of access, low levels of hope, and tied to hope, low levels of aspiration. At Operation HOPE on average we are moving credit scores from 550 to 670, more than 120 points, over an 18 to 24 months period. This literally changes someone's life, and we believe it will transform communities too.

IF WE DON'T BRIDGE THE GAP BETWEEN THE 77% OF YOUTH WHO WANT TO BE THEIR OWN BOSS AND THE 5% WHO ACTUALLY RECEIVE A BUSINESS INTERNSHIP OR BUSINESS ROLE MODEL, WE ARE DONE.

If we did this all across America, in black and brown neighborhoods, five years after this experiment in Silver Rights started you would witness check cashers and payday lenders becoming credit unions and banks, through market forces (meaning you and me, demanding more, better). And, our so-called poor neighborhoods would become emerging market opportunities and examples of financial dignity and pride.

HOPE BUSINESS IN A BOX

We believe that kids are dropping out of high school at alarming rates for a reason. They don't believe that education is relevant to their futures. With the best of good intentions, we have disconnected education from aspiration. Most kids don't want a lecture about grades or graduation. They want to be successful, rich and famous. But, if the only examples of success in their communities are drug dealers, rap stars and athletes, then that is what they will model. The book, *The Tipping Point*, showed that with merely 5% role models, every community stabilizes.[8]

The 2011 Gallup-HOPE Index national poll (3% margin of error) showed that 91% of all kids are not afraid to take risk, 77% of all kids wanted to be their own boss, 45% of all kids wanted to own their own business, and 44% of all kids believed they would create something that changed the world. But only 5% of all youth had a business role model or business internship.[9] If we don't bridge the gap between the 77% of youth who want to be their own boss and the 5% who actually receive a business internship or business role model, we are done.

Our vision at Operation HOPE is to now connect financial literacy education with a course in dignity (values), and then a primer course in entrepreneurship. We follow that with 25 businesses we have designed that a kid can start for $500 or less. We schedule a pitch event in the school auditorium (think "Shark Tank" for kids), and every kid with a plan gets two minutes to pitch their idea before an audience of judges, their community, and peers. Our experience to date shows that this changes everything in the kids' brains, hearts and spirits. It rewires everything, and now the kid is wired for educational-sound and hooked on real success. Better still, they see school as a gateway to get theirs, and want to be at school because it is now cool to stay in school.

WHERE DO WE GO FROM HERE?

The work of eradicating poverty and empowering people is needed more today than in 1968, when Dr. King called forth this question in his last published book, *Where Do We Go From Here: Chaos or Community*. Operation HOPE, the National Urban League and others seek to answer this question now, and to do something about the problem in real time. To quote Rev. Cecil Murray, former pastor of the First AME Church in Los Angeles, "the best way to start living your dream, is to start by waking up."

Okay, let's go.

NOTES

[1] Federal Deposit Insurance Corporation, 2011 *FDIC National Survey of Unbanked and Underbanked Households*, September 2012 (see at *http://www.fdic.gov/householdsurvey/2012_unbankedreport.pdf*) (Last Accessed February 2013).

[2] California Legislative Information, AB-325 *Federal Earned Income Tax Credit*, February 18, 2009, (see at *http://leginfo.legislature.ca.gov/faces/billNavClient.xhtml?bill_id=200920100AB325*) (Last Accessed February 2013).

[3] *The National EITC Outreach Partnership*, The Earned Income Tax Credit: A Fact Sheet, Center for Budget and Policy Priorities (see at http://www.cbpp.org/eitc-partnership/eitcfactsheet.pdf)(Last Accessed February 2013).

[4] Ibid.

[5] Ibid.

[6] Ibid.

[7] The $12,000 EITC benefit is based on a maximum of $4000 per years times three years (1 current year and 2 retroactive years per IRS 2013 EITC Guidelines) (see at *http://www.irs.gov/Individuals/Preview-of-2012-EITC-Income-Limits,-Maximum-Credit--Amounts-and-Tax-Law-Updates*).

[8] Malcolm Gladwell, *The Tipping Point*, Little, Brown and Company, 2002, pgs 12-13.

[9] Gallup and Operation HOPE, 2012 Gallup-HOPE Index (see at *http://www.gallup.com/file/strategicconsulting/159902/2013%20Gallup%20HOPE%20Report.pdf*)(Last Accessed February 2013).

PROJECT ADVOCATE: A ROADMAP to CIVIC ENGAGEMENT

VINCENT WATTS AND EDITH WHITE

The 2012 Presidential campaign was threatened by numerous injustices and seemingly endless assaults on the democratic process. Changes to voter ID laws threatened to sideline many voters by creating confusion and apathy. In the 2012 election, many advocacy groups and political pundits forecasted a deep decline in voter participation and an increase in voter apathy.

As a response to this projection, the National Urban League launched the *Occupy the Vote* campaign with the goal of eradicating apathy by engaging targeted populations in pre-election activities.

THE URBAN LEAGUE OF HAMPTON ROADS

The Urban League of Hampton Roads, Inc. (ULHR) accepted the call to action and established strategic goals to dispel voting rights myths and provide voter education. Our response was multi-faceted, recognizing that it was critical that we engage with the possible electorate in as many different forms as many times as possible.

In order to roll out *Project Advocate*, we established a collaborative partnership between the ULHR and the State Board of Elections to help distribute the appropriate materials emphasizing that Virginia was a non-photo ID state. We also sought out partnerships with other organizations which had similar voter education aims and utilized the media for message delivery.

Two of our key media partners were Clear Channel Communications comprising multiple stations and Hampton University's WHOV 88.1 FM with a listening audience of over 125,000 local listeners and worldwide audience. Clear Channel Media+Entertainment-Norfolk provided interview opportunities for the ULHR and public service announcements. WHOV, which is the host station for the weekly broadcast of "Building A Better Life with Edith White" created a *Project Advocate* segment that aired in September, October and November.

ULHR also immediately provided over 4000 contacts for phone banking, connected with Voter Activation Network (VAN), planned street outreach, participated in Get Out the Vote (GOTV) activities in five cities, made appearances at 10 churches and collected over 600 Occupy the Vote surveys.

In order to strengthen our grassroots outreach, we utilized our Urban League Young Professionals and Guild network to provide the essential outreach to the community. The Young Professionals targeted precincts with a history of low voter turnout for canvassing and literature drops. They sponsored debate watch parties and campus visits resulting in the registration of hundreds of college students. Their success with college student registration was further buoyed by a Get Out the Vote (GOTV) rally done with Norfolk State University. They also coordinated with local churches and participated in the national partnership on voting with Alpha Kappa Alpha Sorority through mid-Atlantic regional activities.

IN ORDER TO STRENGTHEN OUR GRASSROOTS OUTREACH, WE UTILIZED OUR URBAN LEAGUE YOUNG PROFESSIONALS AND GUILD NETWORK TO PROVIDE THE ESSENTIAL OUTREACH TO THE COMMUNITY.

We believe that the Urban League effectively and efficiently utilized the necessary advocacy strategies to insure opportunities for participation in our democracy by all. Through *Project Advocate* we were able to create a strong grassroots organization to educate and inform our local electorate of their right to vote in Virginia. Ours was a swift and decisive response with a targeted focus to ensure that we accomplished the mission of the Urban League to eradicate inequality and injustice. Accomplishing these goals contributed to an increase in African American voting in Virginia from 18% in 2008 to 21% in 2012.[1]

GREATER STARK COUNTY URBAN LEAGUE, INC.

The goals for *Project Advocate* seemed simple and straightforward—contact eligible residents and encourage them to register to vote and then follow-up to ensure that they cast a ballot. Initially, we weren't really sure where to begin because so many groups were already involved on the ground here in Ohio. Indeed, everyone from labor unions to campaign staff were on the ground encouraging people to register. However, we realized that we still needed to engage with our clients because in the neighborhoods most represented by our affiliate, low voter participation was the norm. Therefore our challenge in 2012 was to convince unregistered voters in our community the importance of voting. They needed to hear from us not who to vote for, but that without being registered and without voting they played no active part in the process, no part in decisions that affect their lives.

So against the backdrop of the national discussion of voter suppression and lawsuits contesting every step of the election process, the Greater Stark County Urban League looked to engage inner-city residents through the relationships that we had built over years and generations. First, we obtained a copy of the voter purge list which had 5,800 names on it. To us, these were our family and friends, people we knew and talked to everyday. This wasn't a question of Democrat or Republican, conservative or liberal. It was a question of who gets to participate.

Our particular challenge was that our county was inundated with campaign literature and endless commercials, so many residents had largely tuned out the campaign as it seemed to be a discussion about them, not with them. Fortunately, our Urban League team, through *Project Advocate*, was able to convince voters that getting registered was in their best interest. We utilized our relationships with them to emphasize that this was their opportunity to speak back to the establishment in their own small voice, through their individual vote.

In the end while there weren't many undecided voters and President Obama won Stark County by less than 900 votes, it is our belief that our involvement with *Project Advocate* allowed us to use the one tool that makes our Urban League affiliate, and other affiliates, relevant—the ability to reach people on a personal level—to ensure that we were effective advocates in fighting voter registration challenges and apathy that would have decimated the voting rights of many.

NOTES

[1] Josh Mitchell, Black Turnout Key in Virginia, The Wall Street Journal, November 7, 2012 (see at *http://online.wsj.com/article/SB10001424052970204755404578103210057244462.html*) (Accessed January 2013).

CIVIL RIGHTS ENFORCEMENT *in the* 21ST CENTURY

ATTORNEY GENERAL ERIC H. HOLDER, JR.

On June 11, 1963, just hours after the first two African American students enrolled at the University of Alabama, President John F. Kennedy delivered a televised address from the Oval Office to ask the American people to join in support for the "moral issue" of civil rights.

"This nation was founded," President Kennedy said, "on the principle that all men are created equal, and that the rights of every man are diminished when the rights of one man are threatened." But for African Americans, he explained, reality fell far short of these principles, and justice was long overdue. He asked Congress to pass legislation that would make clear "that race has no place in American life or law" and ensure greater access to opportunity for all people.

This year, we will celebrate the 50th anniversaries of these and other notable events—some tragic and some inspiring, but all seminal in the march toward true equality. We will mourn the loss of life caused by the bombing of the 16th Street Baptist Church in Birmingham 50 years ago. We will honor the 50th anniversary of the Supreme Court's ruling in *Gideon v. Wainwright*, which has resulted in the provision of legal counsel to tens of thousands of indigent defendants who would otherwise go unrepresented. We will mark the 50 years that have passed since Dr. King marched on Washington and told the American people of his dream that "this nation will rise up and live out the true meaning of its creed: *We hold these truths to be self-evident, that all men are created equal.*"

We have made great progress in the five decades since that time. But every day that I serve as Attorney General reminds me of how much remains to be done before we can truly say that we have finished the job—that we have reached the high ground to which Dr. King's stirring words summoned us.

For these reasons, we must treat each of this year's milestones as a clarion call to further action—to secure access and opportunity to all citizens, to safeguard the most vulnerable among us, and to ensure protection of the infrastructure of our democracy, including the fundamental right to vote.

As Attorney General, I have the honor and great responsibility of enforcing many of the laws America's civil rights pioneers fought to secure. These laws protect people from discrimination based not only on the color of their skin, but based on their national origin, their sex, the language they speak, their disabilities or the religion they practice. Through the aggressive and evenhanded enforcement of these laws, the Civil Rights Division of the Department of Justice is

THROUGH THE AGGRESSIVE AND EVENHANDED ENFORCEMENT OF THESE LAWS, THE CIVIL RIGHTS DIVISION OF THE DEPARTMENT OF JUSTICE IS DOING MORE THAN EVER TO EXPAND ACCESS TO THE PROTECTIONS THESE LAWS GUARANTEE.

doing more than ever to expand access to the protections these laws guarantee.

In the wake of the national foreclosure crisis, for example, the Department found that mortgage lenders—including some of the nation's largest—had engaged in widespread discrimination against African American and Hispanic borrowers. We discovered lenders that charged African American and Hispanic borrowers as much as tens of thousands of dollars more for their mortgages than they charged similarly-qualified white borrowers. Others steered these borrowers into expensive and risky subprime loans. The Department has vigorously rooted out these fair lending violations, securing record relief—more than $660 million over the past four years—for victims and their communities, and sending a clear message to all lenders that all borrowers must be treated fairly.

Similarly, we have demonstrated that all qualified workers must be able to compete on equal terms. The Department has advanced challenges to discriminatory hiring and promotion procedures, triggering changes to the employment practices of public employers nationwide. At the same time, we have pursued cases across the country to combat continuing racial segregation in schools. Education is the great equalizer, but nearly 60 years after *Brown v. Board of Education*, far too many students are still denied the key that opens the door to a better future because of the color of their skin. That is why the Department is using every tool at our disposal to ensure that Brown's promise is realized in all aspects of a school district's operations—from its facilities and faculty, to its extracurricular activities, course offerings, and discipline practices.

For example, we are partnering with the Department of Education to dismantle the school-to-prison pipeline, in which children arrested in schools, often for minor infractions, become entangled in unnecessary cycles of incarceration. Through the Supportive School Discipline Initiative that I co-lead with the Secretary of Education, we are working with government, law enforcement, academic and community leaders to support good discipline practices and to foster safe and productive learning environments in every classroom.

WE CONVICTED 74 PERCENT MORE HATE CRIMES DEFENDANTS OVER THE LAST FOUR YEARS THAN DURING THE PRECEDING FOUR-YEAR PERIOD.

The Department is also taking decisive action in the criminal context. We convicted 74 percent more hate crimes defendants over the last four years than during the preceding four-year period, including the successful prosecution of a group of men who targeted and brutally murdered a Brandon, Mississippi man because of his race. And we are working with more police departments than ever before to address systemic law enforcement misconduct—such as racial profiling or the excessive use of force—and ensure effective, accountable policing. In 2012 alone, the Department entered into far-reaching, court-enforceable agreements with six jurisdictions that will serve as models for reform nationwide.

Equally important, we have moved both fairly and aggressively to safeguard the most basic right of our democracy: the right to vote. Through our vigorous enforcement of the Voting Rights Act of 1965—a signature achievement of the Civil Rights Movement that remains a powerful tool for preventing discrimination and disenfranchisement in our elections today—the Department has carefully reviewed a number of state and local voting changes, including redistricting plans, early voting procedures, and photo identification requirements, to evaluate whether they have discriminatory purpose or effect.

Through this work, we have taken important steps to protect Americans' voting rights when necessary. For example, the Department objected to a voter identification law enacted by the State of Texas—characterized by a court as "perhaps the most stringent in the country"—that would have required voters to identify themselves with one of only five forms of identification, some of which could be obtained only if voters could afford to pay for underlying documents. A three-judge panel blocked the implementation of that law, finding that it "will almost certainly have retrogressive effect," since "it imposes strict, unforgiving burdens on the poor—and racial minorities in Texas are disproportionately likely to live in poverty."

As we look back on these accomplishments—and celebrate the hard-won success of those who came before us—we must also look forward. Those who fought the civil rights battles we mark this year did so with the hope that the promise of "more perfect union" would be made real. We honor their legacy through our own actions to secure the rights we all cherish. And because we have more to do, and further to go, in the struggle for civil rights, each milestone we pass must inspire us to continue our journey with a stronger, more powerful commitment to the principles of equal justice and opportunity that motivate us all.

JONATHAN CAPEHART

"Race doesn't matter! Race doesn't matter," the young people chanted behind then Sen. Barack Obama after his hard-fought victory in the South Carolina primary in 2008. The remarkable display would touch off frenzied commentary that we were entering a post-racial society. But that mantra—"Race doesn't matter!"—was as hopeful as it was naive. Four years after the historic election and reelection of the first African American president, race still does matter—a lot.

Almost from the start of his administration, President Obama faced a level of disrespect not seen by his predecessors. During a Sept. 2009 address before a joint session of Congress on his health care reform plan, Rep. Joe Wilson (R-S.C.) yelled, "You lie!" when Obama said his plan would not insure illegal immigrants. And we saw the rise of the Tea Party and the far-right fringe whose adherents wanted to "take our country back" from a man they believed was usurping the Constitution.

Obama's most virulent critics questioned his presidency's legitimacy by questioning his citizenship. "Birthers" clung to the belief he was born in Kenya not Hawaii. It was a racist lie that was given staying power by the silence of the Republican establishment. The release of the President's long-form birth certificate in April 2011 snuffed the Birther movement but it did nothing to hush age-old racial dog whistles.

During the 2012 presidential election, Newt Gingrich called Obama a "Food Stamp President." John Sununu called him "lazy" and once said the President needed to "learn how to be an American." Sarah Palin accused Obama of a "shuck and jive shtick" to "cover up" the Sept. 11, 2011 attack on the American consulate in Benghazi.

Yet, the racial name-calling of President Obama also came from African Americans. Cornel West branded the President "a black mascot of Wall Street oligarchs and a black puppet of corporate plutocrats." Former front runner for the Republican presidential nomination Herman Cain told the *New York Times* that Obama wasn't the "strong black man that I'm identifying with."

This not-black-enough critique strayed into policy as many African Americans questioned the President's commitment to improving the lives of black people. In a June 2012 opinion piece for the *Washington Post* headlined "Still waiting for our first black president," Columbia University professor Fredrick Harris wrote, "Obama has pursued a racially defused electoral and governing strategy, keeping issues of specific interest to African Americans—such as disparities in the criminal justice system; the disproportionate impact of the foreclosure crisis on communities of color; black unemployment; and the persistence of HIV/AIDS—off the national agenda."

THE CLEAREST PROOF THAT RACE STILL MATTERED WAS THE CONCERTED EFFORT TO SUPPRESS VOTER TURNOUT IN THE 2012 ELECTION.

All of the issue areas Harris cites are being addressed by President Obama. And it is being done, as I wrote in response to Harris, "Not in the theatrical way Harris would like. But in the actions-speak-louder-than-words way of Obama." That the President won't present an identifiable "Black Agenda" or even speak about race directly rankles even his most ardent supporters.

President Obama has not waded as deeply in the pool of race since his beautifully nuanced speech during the 2008 Democratic primary campaign in response to the controversial remarks made by his former pastor, the Rev. Jeremiah Wright. Two events during his first term illustrate the perils of him doing so.

When he was asked at a press conference in 2009 for his reaction to the arrest of Dr. Henry Louis Gates Jr. in his own home, Obama said he thought the police "acted stupidly" in doing so. The uproar over his remarks and the ensuing controversy over the arrest led to the Beer Summit in the Rose Garden between Gates and the arresting officer with Vice President Biden and President Obama in attendance.

"You know, if I had a son, he'd look like Trayvon," the President said in March 2012, nearly one month after armed neighborhood watch volunteer George Zimmerman killed an unarmed 17-year-old Trayvon Martin in Sanford, FL. Gingrich and Rick Santorum, another 2012 Republican presidential aspirant, accused the president of "politicizing" the tragedy and using race to score political points.

The clearest proof that race still mattered was the concerted effort to suppress voter turnout in the 2012 election. State officials in Ohio tried to curb early voting. In ticking off a list of accomplishments, the Pennsylvania House majority leader told the Republican state committee, "Voter ID, which is going to allow Governor Romney to win the state of Pennsylvania. Done." And in Florida, the number of early voting days was cut from 14 days to eight. The hours were cut, as well.

But the attempt to disenfranchise black voters backfired. According to a post-2012 presidential election analysis by the Pew Research Center, "Blacks voted at a higher rate this year than other minority groups and for the first time in history may also have voted at a higher rate than whites." For instance, historic African American turnout in Ohio (15% in 2012 versus 11% in 2008) helped keep the state Romney needed to win the White House in President Obama's column.

It will take more than the election of a black President to transform America into a "post-racial" society. It will take demographic shifts, which are happening at lightning speed. And it will take adjustments in attitude, which are slower to change. Ultimately, what we must seek is not a "post-racial" America, but a "post-racist" one.

THE NEW ARITHMETIC of BLACK POLITICAL POWER

MICHAEL K. FAUNTROY, PH.D.

President Barack Obama's reelection confirmed many of the long-seen demographic changes occurring in the United States. The 2012 electorate was younger, more educated, and more racially diverse than any in our nation's history.[1] The lesson in all this for African Americans is just as profound: be prepared to use the new arithmetic of Black political power or watch it diminish in an increasingly diverse and more resource competitive nation.

SO WHILE AFRICAN AMERICAN TURNOUT HAS BEEN AT OR NEAR RECORD LEVELS IN THE LAST TWO ELECTIONS,[10] THE POST-OBAMA ERA WILL REQUIRE EVEN GREATER PARTICIPATION FROM AFRICAN AMERICANS, IN ALL ELECTIONS, AT ALL LEVELS, TO TRULY RESULT IN CHANGE.

FIRST, THE DEMOGRAPHICS

African Americans comprised 13 percent of the 2012 electorate, the same percentage as 2008; however, the 2012 national electorate and African American electorate were down relative to 2008.[2] There is still room for significant growth. According to U.S. Census Bureau data, there are roughly 26.6 million voting-age eligible African Americans as of 2008;[3] of that number 16.68 million (or 62.7 percent) cast ballots in 2012.[4]

Latinos comprised 10 percent of the 2012 electorate, building on the 2008 total of eight percent.[5] As the largest racial minority in the nation, and with projections indicating that 50,000 Latinos will turn 18 years of age each month for the next 20 years, their political impact relative to their proportion of the nation's population has not been fully realized.[6]

Whites comprised 72 percent of the 2012 general electorate, down from 87 percent in 1992.[7] The white share of the national electorate has consistently fallen for nearly a generation, from 87 percent in 1992, to 83 percent in 1996, to 81 percent in 2000, to 77 percent in 2004, to 74 percent in 2008, to 72 percent in 2012.[8]

Asian Americans comprise three percent of the 2012 electorate. However, they are America's fastest-growing ethnic group and are an important and underrated portion of the swing vote in states like Virginia and North Carolina.

Bottom line: With the white share of the electorate in continued decline, the Latino vote not yet solidified, and the Asian American vote still in growth-mode, African Americans are presented with an opportunity to apply political power, not just influence, in the years ahead by picking who wins elections.

NOW, THE POLITICS

Conventional wisdom has held that because African Americans comprise a relatively small segment of America's population, it cannot amass enough political power to make real, lasting, and effective change in some of the areas that still besiege our communities. I disagree. I think the power does exist, but has been unrealized because of low electoral turnout. Early analysis of the 2012 election returns suggests that the 2012 election is the first in recorded history in which the African American turnout rate exceeded the white turnout rate. If confirmed, that milestone may well prove to be the launching point for a new arithmetic of Black political power. African American turnout has increased in each of the last four presidential elections.[9] That has great potential for down ballot races and, if continued and coupled with further erosion of the White vote, greater political power for African Americans.

This, then, opens the door to real change on issues ranging from the prison-industrial complex, which warehouses Black men in community-damaging proportions, to access to college which, in an era of diminishing resources, has the power to be the salvation for Black people in America. Utilizing public policy to reroute the pipeline from community-to-prison to community-to-college can only occur with overwhelming electoral turnout that results in the elections of people who will put into practice those policies that reflect our collective ideals. So while African American turnout has been at or near record levels in the last two elections,[10] the post-Obama era will require even greater participation from African Americans, in all elections, at all levels, to truly result in change.

This will not be easy. Exercising power, and not just settling for symbols, is difficult. It requires that we sometimes be tough with our friends and punish our opponents. Ultimately, however, African Americans will have to be comfortable with the use of political power for achieving policy ends. Politics without policy change is nothing. Failing that, we will continue to get what we've always received.

NOTES

[1] David Bositis, "Blacks and the 2012 Elections: A Preliminary Analysis," (Washington, D.C.: Joint Center for Political and Economic Studies, 2012).

[2] Ibid, p. 3.

[3] Ibid, p. 5. Bositis also points out the gender imbalance in the 2012 Black electorate: Black women comprised 61.5 percent, while Black men represented 38.5 percent.

[4] Ibid.

[5] Ibid.

[6] Erin Zlomek, "Voting Focus Turns to Latino," *Arizona Republic*, September 8, 2012 (*http://www.azcentral.com/arizonarepublic/local/articles/2008/09/09/20080909immigrantvote0909.html?nclick_check=1, accessed online, February 22, 2013*).

[7] Bositis, p. 5.

[8] Ibid. See also, Ronald Brownstein, "The Hidden History of the American Electorate," *National Journal*, August 23, 2012 (*http://www.nationaljournal.com/2012-conventions/the-hidden-history-of-the-american-electorate-20120823*, accessed February 22, 2013).

[9] Bositis.

[10] Ibid.

STRATEGIC ALLIANCES for ADDRESSING THE SKILLS GAP

THE BUFFALO URBAN LEAGUE GREEN JOBS CONSTRUCTION TRAINING PROGRAM

BRENDA MCDUFFIE

"Now is the time to build a firmer, stronger foundation for growth that will not only withstand future economic storms, but one that helps us thrive and compete in a global economy. It's time to reform our community colleges so that they provide Americans of all ages a chance to learn the skills and knowledge necessary to compete for the jobs of the future."

—President Barack Obama

The economic recession that we are currently experiencing across the nation has hit the Buffalo Niagara Region especially hard. This challenge has required the Buffalo Urban League to develop new strategies and expand partnerships with our community colleges to prepare individuals to return to the workforce.

One of the emerging opportunities in the Buffalo Niagara Region is in the area of green jobs. Through partnerships with two local community colleges, Erie Community College and Niagara County Community College, our affiliate has successfully addressed the education and skill needs of businesses by preparing individuals to transition into green job employment opportunities and/or start businesses. The Buffalo Urban League Green Jobs Construction Training Program consists of 18 weeks of training, combining individuals in a variety of green construction areas that lead to certifications. These high-demand certifications provide each participant with skills that give them a competitive advantage to help secure employment in this emerging and growing industry. Some of the certifications are: HazWoper, National Electric Code, OSHA 10 for Construction, OSHA 30 for Construction, OSHA 10 General Industry, Ladder Safety and Weatherization.

Local businesses define the education and skills that are required to meet their workforce needs. Each certification granted through the program is a recognized credential; therefore our local businesses actively seek out individuals completing the program to satisfy their employment opportunities. In addition to hiring individuals who successfully complete the program, local businesses also provide

THESE HIGH-DEMAND CERTIFICATIONS PROVIDE EACH PARTICIPANT WITH SKILLS THAT GIVE THEM A COMPETITIVE ADVANTAGE TO HELP SECURE EMPLOYMENT IN THIS EMERGING AND GROWING INDUSTRY.

occupational skills (with a focus on the green construction skills) with education, life skills, hands-on work experience, job development, placement, follow-up case management and support services. This training program is a strategic allegiance between three entities—our local community colleges, local businesses and our Buffalo Urban League. Each entity has a distinct and important role in ensuring the success of the program.

Utilizing their ability to grant certifications, the community colleges offer courses to tools and supplies, as well as hands-on demonstrations and training.

Our partnership responsibility lies in recruiting and screening program participants, providing the basic education skills specific to the industry requirements, as well as delivering skills and services aimed at the holistic betterment of the participants—life skills, case management, job readiness training, job placement and supportive and follow-up services.

Of the 10 individuals who completed the first session of the program, one is now self employed, another is a licensed contractor and seven are employed within the green construction field.

Today we are fielding a new class of program participants. All 10 of our newest participants have already been placed in positions. One example of the program's immediate success is Khalif Swanson. Mr. Swanson was laid off and had limited prospects for employment. He previously worked in a variety of jobs and had some experience in a do-it yourself home improvement business. After successfully completing our first session, Mr. Swanson is now a licensed home improvement contractor and is giving back to the program by serving as a hands-on instructor in our second session.

We must continue to strengthen not only the network of America's community colleges, but also the ability of community partners like the Buffalo Urban League, to give a foundation for Mr. Swanson and many others to successfully compete in a global economy.

MENTORING MATTERS: WHY YOUNG PROFESSIONALS *and* OTHERS MUST MENTOR

DAVID MCGHEE

"The essence of true leadership is having the ability to establish and institute change—changes that go beyond the personal actions, development and well-being of the leader alone, but change that leads to sufficiency for the most marginalized groups of people. Leadership is the ability to be proactive, not just reactive."

Reflecting on the aforementioned quote by former National Urban League Executive Director, Whitney M. Young, Jr., I am inspired by his tenacious and relentless spirit in approaching the most pressing needs of African Americans. The breaking of segregation barriers and inequalities don't rest in taking a stand alone. Protesting, marching, picketing, and demonstrating are all great visuals, and indeed show that African Americans took a stand against the injustices that faced them. However, the next step after you take a stand is to take a walk to plot plans of strategy, opportunity, and policies that will change the scope of our nation.

WITHOUT THE HELP OF A CARING ADULT, THESE SAME YOUTH COULD MAKE CHOICES THAT WILL POSSIBLY DESTABILIZE THEIR FUTURE, AS WELL AS THE ECONOMIC AND SOCIAL WELL-BEING OF SOCIETY AS A WHOLE.

As a graduate of the National Urban League Emerging Leaders Program, a former Program Director at Big Brothers Big Sisters, and a current professor, the spirit of Whitney M. Young, Jr. has remained strategically present in my growth and development. Mr. Young demonstrated the type of courage and vision needed to look beyond day to day tasks, to implement models that would go on to become woven into the fabric of the movement. He also utilized this same courage and vision to serve as a role model and mentor.

Mentoring has the power to change the trajectory of human life—from the neighborhood corner in Flint, Michigan to the corner office. Mentors help guide you on life's journey, showing you the opportunity within the obstacles. Mentors speak up for you and speak out for you, at times when you aren't even around. While we know that our own education and insight takes us to great heights, having a mentor helps one see, and achieve, that much more. Mentoring, in essence, is one of the highest forms of leadership; the type of leadership that calls for us to think beyond ourselves.

Today America's youth are faced with problems and obstacles that we had never dreamed of when we were younger. As hectic and challenging as times may seem for our youth; there is something that can and must be done.

Too often children are living in situations where they lack access to being exposed to new things, access to new opportunities, and most importantly access to additional support from a caring adult figure in their lives. The access to a positive role model, on a consistent basis, can make a difference in developing self-esteem, resilience, and confidence—especially for black boys. Without the help of a caring adult, these same youth could make choices that will possibly destabilize their future, as well as the economic and social well-being of society as a whole.

Research shows that an estimated 8.5 million youth (about 20%) do not have caring adults in their lives.[1] Those from disadvantaged homes and communities are over-represented in this number. Young persons who lack a strong relationship with a caring adult while growing up are much more vulnerable to a host of difficulties, ranging from academic failure to involvement in serious risk behaviors. Research also finds that resilient youth—those who successfully transition from risk-filled backgrounds to the adult world of work and good citizenship—are consistently distinguished by the presence of a caring adult in their lives.[2]

As a lifelong resident of the City of Flint, I have benefited greatly from the best of what urban communities have to offer, and have witnessed what I refer to as the alley issues of urban communities. I feel fortunate to have been reared in a middle class household with two caring, hardworking parents, but I have friends and family members who were not afforded the same support system. In my opinion, if Flint and other urban communities are to become the nurturing, caring places that allow prosperity and opportunity for all people, mentoring is paramount. Individually, and collectively. Personally, and professionally. Academically, and socially. From peer-to-peer relationships, extending to senior and emerging leaders, its role cannot be overlooked.

As adults, many of us have been blessed. We've 'been there and done that'. Mentoring encourages us to help someone else get there and do it too.

NOTES

[1] Cavell, T., DuBois, D., Karcher, M., Keller, T., & Rhodes, J. (2009). *Strengthening Mentoring Opportunities for At-Risk Youth. Policy Brief.* (see at *http://www.mentoring.org/downloads/mentoring_1233.pdf*)(Accessed January 2013).

[2] Ibid.

COMMUNITY-BASED ORGANIZATIONS *and* CHILD WELFARE:

BUILDING COMMUNITIES *of* HOPE

WILLIAM C. BELL, PH.D.

Communities matter. Research in recent years has shown that where children live is one of the most significant influencers on their life potential and outcomes.[1] Studies have shown that where we live has a major impact on the quality of opportunities we are able to access; the quality of schools children will attend; the quality of public services we receive; the type, quality and cost of services immediately available; access to transportation; exposure to health risks; and access to and the quality of health care.

If where we live matters, then it stands to reason that strengthening the communities where our most vulnerable children live can help change the trajectory of their lives. If communities are isolated, under-resourced and suffering, the families living in those communities are most likely challenged and not doing well, or only marginally so, and the children in those families suffer the consequences.

On average, every 24 hours, in communities across America:

- ★ *Approximately 2,000 children are confirmed as victims of child abuse and neglect.*[2]
- ★ *Nearly 700 children are removed from their families and placed in foster care.*[3]
- ★ *About four children die as a result of child abuse and neglect; most of them before they reach their fifth birthday.*[4]
- ★ *Approximately 13 young people between the ages of 10 and 24 are murdered.*[5]
- ★ *Nearly 12 young people under the age of 25 take their own life.*[6]

Too often the systems we have in place to address children and youth in at-risk situations or who engage in risky behaviors take a rather narrow approach that focuses only on the child or his or her behavior. Historically, we've attempted to resolve child abuse and neglect and other issues that infringe upon a child's well-being without addressing the needs and challenges of their families and the needs and challenges present in the communities where those children and families live.

My years working in the child welfare arena have led me to conclude that in order to effectively address the issues of child abuse and neglect, we must secure the well-being and safety of children by adopting a holistic approach that includes the participation of communities and aims to secure their well-being by assisting their families in the communities where they live.

Just as Abraham Lincoln, 150 years ago, proclaimed an end to the institution of slavery in an effort to save a nation, so too must we commit ourselves to proclaiming an end to the social, economic and educational isolation of vulnerable children, families and communities. We must commit as a nation to build communities of hope if we are to fulfill the dreams of *all* our children.

This does not mean committing millions of new dollars in new government programs. Building communities of hope means:

1. Working together to strengthen struggling communities through a continuum of community-based resources in order to assist families in resolving the challenges they are facing—challenges such as unemployment, poverty, drug use, meeting basic needs, mental health and the lack of social supports.
2. Reforming our nation's child welfare finance system to allow child welfare and other professionals to respond to the needs of vulnerable children not just in the context of child rescue and foster care, but also in the broader context that includes prevention and meeting a child's family and community needs.

This is not a task for child welfare alone. Building communities of hope will require collaboration across various government systems and with non-profit, philanthropic, corporate and community-based institutions. Building communities of hope requires all of us to have shared ownership of the issues, shared responsibility for the solutions, and a shared vision for what is possible.

There is a critical role for all community-based and faith-based organizations in promoting the social and emotional well-being for vulnerable children and their families who need a whole host of effective alternatives that these entities can provide. They need community-supported and relevant programs, like the service programs of Urban League affiliates that comprise the National Urban League's Child Welfare Working Group (CWWG). Through a partnership with Casey Family Programs and funding by the Marguerite Casey Foundation, the CWWG is concentrating on making sure that families and children have a better chance; viable choices and opportunities; hope and possibility. Indeed, Casey Family Programs has been partnering with the National Urban League over the past five years to provide families with the strategies and resources they and their communities need to expand their opportunities.

Based on our experience, Casey Family Programs recommends three key actions that organizations can take to strengthen communities:

1. Build stronger collaborative partnerships with other community- and faith-based organizations within a one- to three-ZIP code radius of your organization.
2. Create and implement a collective impact strategy for improving life outcomes of vulnerable children and families within the one- to three-ZIP code radius of your organization.
3. Consistently collect, review, analyze and seek to improve data on the life outcomes for citizens living within the one- to three-ZIP code radius of your organization.

In his "I Have a Dream" speech, a speech rich in hopefulness, Dr. Martin Luther King, Jr. invoked his faith that a better, more just America will come and said, "with this faith we will be able to hew out of the mountain of despair a stone of hope." Fifty years later, Dr. King's dream still has meaning. Every child deserves a community of hope—their stone of hope carved out of what may seem to be their mountain of despair; and like Dr. King, every child deserves to dream and have faith and hope that their dreams will come true.

NOTES

[1] Jason Reece and Denis Rhoden, *Opportunity Matters: Place, Space and Life Outcomes*, The Kirwan Institute for the Study of Race and Ethnicity, The Ohio State University (see at *http://kirwaninstitute.osu.edu/*) (Assessed in 2010).

[2] U.S. Department of Health & Human Services, Administration for Children and Families, Administration on Children, Youth and Families, Children's Bureau, Child Maltreatment 2010, p.22 (see at *http://www.acf.hhs.gov/programs/cb/resource/child-maltreatment-2010*).

[3] U.S. Department of Health and Human Services, Administration for Children and Families, Administration on Children, Youth and Families, Children's Bureau, Child Welfare Outcomes 2007-2010 Report to Congress, p F-2 (see at *http://www.acf.hhs.gov/programs/cb/pubs/cwo07-10/cwo07-10.pdf).*

[4] U.S. Department of Health & Human Services, Administration for Children and Families, Administration on Children, Youth and Families, Children's Bureau, Child Maltreatment 2010, pp. 58-59 (see at *http://www.acf.hhs.gov/programs/cb/resource/child-maltreatment-2010*).

[5] Centers for Disease Control and Prevention, National Center for Injury Prevention and Control, Division of Violence Prevention, Youth Violence: Facts at a Glance 2012 (see at *http://www.cdc.gov/violenceprevention/*).

[6] Centers for Disease Control and Prevention, National Center for Injury Prevention and Control, Division of Violence Prevention, Suicide Prevention (see at *http://www.cdc.gov/ViolencePrevention/suicide/youth_suicide.html*).

★ ABOUT THE ★ AUTHORS

WILLIAM C. BELL, PH.D.

William C. Bell became President and CEO of Casey Family Programs in January 2006. He chairs the Executive Team, and is ultimately responsible for the vision, mission, strategies and objectives of the foundation. Dr. Bell has more than 30 years of experience in the human services field. Prior to becoming president and CEO of Casey Family Programs, he served as the foundation's executive vice president for child and family services, providing strategic direction to nine field offices and leading a staff working directly with young people from the public child welfare system. Prior to joining Casey, he served two-and-a-half years as commissioner of the New York City Administration for Children's Services (ACS). From 1996 to 2001, Dr. Bell was deputy commissioner of ACS's Division of Child Protection. From 1994 to 1996, he was deputy commissioner of field services and contract agency case management for the New York City Human Resources Administration. In the early 1990s, Dr. Bell was associate executive director for Miracle Makers, a private sector minority-owned, not-for-profit child and family services organization in New York City. Dr. Bell earned his Ph.D. in Social Welfare and his Master's of Social Work degree at Hunter College School of Social Work. He received a Bachelor's in Biology and Behavioral Science degree from Delta State University.

STEFANIE BROWN JAMES

Stefanie Brown James is the CEO of Vestige Strategies, LLC and served as the National African American Vote Director for the 2012 Obama for America campaign. Formerly the National Field Director and Director of the Youth & College Division for the NAACP, Ms. Brown James has dedicated her life to empowering people of color to organize and advocate for justice and equality in their communities. She has received numerous awards and recognitions including: The Grio 100, 2013 honoree; TheRoot 100, 2012 honoree; Young & Powerful Group's 2012 National Trailblazer Award; Essence.com's "Top 10 Emerging Political Leaders of 2010;" Howard University School of Business "Young Business Leaders Award 2010;" and *Ebony* Magazine's 2007 "Top 30 Young Leaders Under the Age of 30." A 2003 graduate of Howard University, Stefanie is the founder and Executive Director of Brown Girls Lead, a leadership development organization for collegiate women at Howard. She is also the founder of the Harvey & Delores Brown Scholarship Fund and a member of Delta Sigma Theta Sorority, Incorporated.
She resides in the Washington, D.C. area with her husband, Quentin James. Visit her online at *StefanieBrownJames.com* or on twitter @StefBrownJames.

JOHN HOPE BRYANT

John Hope Bryant is a thought leader, founder, chairman and CEO of Operation HOPE and Bryant Group Companies, Inc. Magazine/CEO READ bestselling business author of *LOVE LEADERSHIP: The New Way to Lead in a Fear-Based World* (Jossey-Bass), the only African American bestselling business author in America, and is chairman of the Subcommittee for the Under-Served and Community Empowerment for the U.S. President's Advisory Council on Financial Capability, for President Barack Obama. Mr. Bryant is the co-founder of the Gallup-HOPE Index, the only national research poll on youth financial dignity and youth economic energy in the U.S. He is also a co-founder of Global Dignity with HRH Crown Prince Haakon of Norway and Professor Pekka Himanen of Finland. Global Dignity is affiliated with the Forum of Young Global Leaders and the World Economic Forum. Mr. Bryant is represented by the Bright Sight Group for public speaking. Mr. Bryant serves on the board of directors of Ares Commercial Real Estate Corporation, an NYSE Euronext publicly traded company and a division of $54 billion Ares Capital.

ESTHER BUSH

Esther Bush is the President and CEO of the Urban League of Greater Pittsburgh. A graduate of Pittsburgh's Westinghouse High School, she began her career as a high school teacher. She also worked as a college administrator and corporate consultant. Ms. Bush has moved progressively up the ladder of the Urban League movement, starting in 1980 with the position of Assistant Director of the Labor Education Advancement Program for the National Urban League in New York City. During her tenure, the Urban League of Greater Pittsburgh has become one of the most accomplished affiliates in the country, leading by example with a perfect 5 out of 5 on a recent performance review conducted by the National Urban League. Ms. Bush was appointed by Governors to serve on the: Pennsylvania State Board of Education, PA Commission for Crime and Delinquency, Law Enforcement and Community Relations Task Force, the Governor's Commission on Academic Standards, and the Voting Modernization Task Force. She holds a Bachelor of Science in Education degree from Morgan State University and an M.A. in Guidance and Counseling from The Johns Hopkins University.

JONATHAN CAPEHART

Jonathan Capehart is a member of *The Washington Post* editorial board and writes about politics and social issues for the PostPartisan blog. He is also an MSNBC contributor, appearing regularly on "Morning Joe" and other dayside programs. Prior to joining *The Washington Post* in 2007, Capehart was the deputy editor of *New York Daily News's* editorial page from 2002 to 2005. He worked as a policy adviser to Michael Bloomberg in his successful campaign for mayor of New York City, he was a national affairs columnist for *Bloomberg News* from 2000 to 2001, and he was a member of the *Daily News* editorial board from 1993 to 2000. Capehart and the *Daily News* editorial board won the 1999 Pulitzer Prize for Editorial Writing for their series on the Apollo Theater in Harlem.

SHREE CHAUHAN

Shree Chauhan is the Legislative Manager for Education and Health Policy at the National Urban League Policy Institute (NULPI). Ms. Chauhan conducts legislative research and analysis to develop policy recommendations for federal and state policymakers, and actions for community-based partners. Her education portfolio spans grades PK-16, with a particular focus on Common Core State Standards, teacher effectiveness and accountability. Ms. Chauhan began her career as a Teach for America corps member after obtaining her Bachelor of Communications from the University of Miami. As an educator in Miami, she taught 6th grade reading and language arts, and her teaching experiences sparked her passion to improve education through policy. After leaving the classroom, she obtained her Master of Public Administration degree from American University. During her graduate studies, Ms. Chauhan worked at the Department of Education in the Office of Planning, Evaluation and Policy Development where she supported efforts to reauthorize the Elementary and Secondary Education Act and gained expertise on School Turnaround Grants. After graduating from American, she assisted several Senate offices' work in education policy and later supported the Data Quality Campaign's national and federal policy efforts.

GAIL CHRISTOPHER, PH.D.

Gail Christopher is Vice President for Programs at the W.K. Kellogg Foundation in Battle Creek, Michigan. In this role, she serves on the executive team that provides overall direction and leadership for the Foundation and provides leadership for Food, Health & Well-Being, and Racial Equity programming. Dr. Christopher is a nationally recognized leader in health policy, with particular expertise and experience in the issues related to social determinants of health, health disparities and public policy issues of concern to African Americans and other minority populations. A prolific writer and presenter, she is the author or co-author of three books, a monthly column in the *Federal Times*, and more than 250 articles, presentations, and publications. Her national print and broadcast media credits are numerous, and include *The Washington Post, Los Angeles Times, Dallas, Times, National Journal, Essence*, "Good Morning America," "The Oprah Winfrey Show," National Public Radio, and documentaries on PBS and CBS. Dr. Christopher holds a Doctor of Naprapathy degree from the Chicago National College of Naprapathy in Illinois and completed advanced study in the interdisciplinary Ph.D. program in holistic health and clinical nutrition at the Union for Experimenting Colleges and Universities at Union Graduate School of Cincinnati, Ohio.

MARIAN WRIGHT EDELMAN

Marian Wright Edelman, Founder and President of the Children's Defense Fund, has been an advocate for disadvantaged Americans for her entire professional life. A graduate of Spelman College and Yale Law School, Edelman was the first black woman admitted to the Mississippi Bar and directed the NAACP Legal Defense and Educational Fund office in Jackson, Mississippi. She has received over a hundred honorary degrees and many awards including the Albert Schweitzer Humanitarian Prize, the Heinz Award, a MacArthur Foundation Prize Fellowship, the Presidential Medal of Freedom, the nation's highest civilian award, and the Robert F. Kennedy Lifetime Achievement Award for her writings which include: *Families in Peril: An Agenda for Social Change*; *The Measure of Our Success: A Letter to My Children and Yours*; *Lanterns: A Memoir of Mentors*; *I'm Your Child, God: Prayers for Our Children*; *I Can Make a Difference: A Treasury to Inspire Our Children*; and *The Sea Is So Wide and My Boat Is So Small: Charting a Course for the Next Generation*.

MICHAEL K. FAUNTROY

Michael K. Fauntroy is an Associate Professor of Public Policy at George Mason University (GMU). Prior to joining the faculty at GMU, he was an analyst at the Congressional Research Service (CRS). From 1993 to 1996, he was a civil rights analyst at the U.S. Commission on Civil Rights, where he conducted research on issues such as voting rights and fair housing. Dr. Fauntroy is also the host of "The Forum with Michael Fauntroy," a 30-minute one-on-one interview show with local, national, and international policy makers, public intellectuals, and others who shape our world. His second book, *Republicans and the Black Vote*, analyzes the historical relationship between African Americans and the GOP. He is also the author of *Home Rule or House Rule? Congress and the Erosion of Local Governance in the District of Columbia*. A third book, *Living While Black: Reflections on a "Post-Racial" America* will be published in 2013. Dr. Fauntroy received a Bachelor of Arts in Political Science from Hampton University, a Master's degree in Public Affairs, specializing in public administration and public policy analysis and a Doctor of Philosophy degree in Political Science from Howard University. He currently lives in Washington, D.C. with his wife Lisa and their twins, Sunshine and Brett.

THE HONORABLE MARCIA L. FUDGE

Representative Marcia L. Fudge is a committed public servant who brings a hard-working, problem-solving spirit to Congress and to the task of creating jobs, attacking predatory lending, and improving health care, small business, and education. These characteristics were honed while serving as Warrensville Heights' first African American female Mayor. As the city's top executive, Representative Fudge led Warrensville Heights in building 200 new homes and shoring up a sagging retail base. Representative Fudge put her strong work ethic into practice in her appointments on House Committees and Caucus seats. On the Agriculture Committee, she continues her commitment to ending childhood obesity in a generation, stamping out hunger and monitoring the safety of our food supply. On the Education and the Workforce Committee, the Congresswoman is a strong advocate for policies to strengthen our education system and promote job creation. Additionally, she was an early, and continues to be a strong, voice for voter protection. Congresswoman Fudge is now serving in her third consecutive full term. She is highly respected by her congressional colleagues for her insight, wisdom, and honesty. She was elected unanimously in 2012 to serve as Chairwoman of the Congressional Black Caucus in the 113th Congress. Congresswoman Fudge is past National President of Delta Sigma Theta Sorority, Inc. She earned a Bachelor's degree in Business Administration from Ohio State University and a law degree from Cleveland-Marshall College of Law, Cleveland State University.

DARRELL J. GASKINS, PH.D.

Darrell J. Gaskin is Associate Professor of Health Economics and Deputy Director of the Center for Health Disparities Solutions at the Johns Hopkins Bloomberg School of Public Health. He is an international expert in healthcare disparities, access to care for vulnerable populations, and safety net hospitals. His goal is to identify and understand barriers to care for vulnerable populations; to develop and promote policies and practices that improve access to care for the poor, minorities and other vulnerable populations; and to eliminate race, ethnic, socioeconomic and geographic disparities in health and healthcare. His Ph.D. is in health economics from The Johns Hopkins University. He holds a M.S. degree in economics from the Massachusetts Institute of Technology, and a B.A. degree in economics from Brandeis University. Professor Gaskin is an ordained minister and Pastor of Beth Shalom AME Zion Church in Washington, D.C.

FREEMAN A. HRABOWSKI, III

Freeman A. Hrabowski, III, has served as President of the University of Maryland, Baltimore County (UMBC) since 1992. His research and publications focus on science and math education, with special emphasis on minority participation and performance. He recently was named by President Barack Obama to chair the newly created President's Advisory Commission on Educational Excellence for African Americans. In 2012, he was named by *TIME Magazine* as one of the "100 Most Influential People in the World," and also received the Heinz Award for his contributions to improving the "Human Condition" and was among the inaugural inductees into the *U.S. News & World Report* STEM Solutions Leadership Hall of Fame. He chaired the recent National Academies' committee that produced the report, *Expanding Underrepresented Minority Participation: America's Science and Technology Talent at the Crossroads.* A child-leader in the Civil Rights Movement, Hrabowski was prominently featured in Spike Lee's 1997 documentary, *Four Little Girls*, on the racially motivated bombing in 1963 of Birmingham's Sixteenth Street Baptist Church. He was born in 1950 in Birmingham, Alabama, and graduated at 19 from Hampton Institute with highest honors in mathematics. At the University of Illinois at Urbana-Champaign, he received his M.A. (mathematics) and his Ph.D. (higher education administration/statistics) at age 24.

CHANELLE P. HARDY, ESQ.

Chanelle P. Hardy is the National Urban League Senior Vice President for Policy and Executive Director of the National Urban League Policy Institute, with primary responsibility for developing the League's policy, research and advocacy agenda and expanding its impact and influence inside the beltway. She is Editor in Chief of the annual *State of Black America* report and is devoted to the League's mission to empower communities through education and economic development. She is the former Chief of Staff and Counsel to former U.S. Representative Artur Davis, who represented the Seventh Congressional District of Alabama and served on the powerful House Ways and Means Committee and the Committee on House Administration. Prior to coming to the Hill, Ms. Hardy was a Staff Attorney at the Federal Trade Commission, a Policy Fellow and Legislative Counsel at Consumers Union, and a Teach for America Corps member, teaching fifth graders in Washington, D.C. She received her Juris Doctorate from the Howard University School of Law, where she finished fifth in her class, and was a member of the Huver I. Brown Trial Advocacy Moot Court Team. Ms. Hardy is a member of the board of Excel Academy Public Charter School, the first all-girls public school in Washington, D.C.; the board of the Congressional Black Caucus Institute and a member of Alfred Street Baptist Church in Alexandria, VA.

THE HONORABLE DOT HARRIS

Dot Harris is the Director of the Office of Economic Impact and Diversity at the United States Department of Energy. Ms. Harris brings nearly 30 years of management and leadership experience to this position, having served at some of the world's largest firms and leading a successful energy, IT, and healthcare consulting firm. As an Assistant Secretary at the Office of Economic Impact and Diversity, Ms. Harris leads the Department of Energy's efforts to ensure minorities and historically underrepresented communities are afforded an opportunity to participate fully in energy programs. Ms. Harris oversees a corporate funding strategy for minority institutions, develops the current and future Departmental workforce, works closely to develop small business contracting opportunities at the Department, and protects the civil rights of Departmental employees and recipients of funding from the Department. Previously, Ms. Harris was the President and CEO of Jabo Industries, LLC, a minority-woman owned management consulting firm concentrated primarily in the energy, information technology and healthcare industries. Ms. Harris has also served as an executive at General Electric Company (GE). Before joining GE, Ms. Harris was an officer and Vice President of Operations & Production for ABB Service, Inc. She also spent twelve years as Field Services Engineer and Services Manager with Westinghouse Electric Company. Ms. Harris holds a B.S. in Electrical Engineering from the University of South Carolina in Columbia, SC and a M.S. in Technology Management from Southern Polytechnic State University in Marietta, GA.

THE HONORABLE ERIC H. HOLDER, JR.

Eric H. Holder, Jr. was sworn in as the 82nd Attorney General of the United States on February 3, 2009 by Vice President Joe Biden. President Barack Obama announced his intention to nominate Mr. Holder on December 1, 2008. In 1997, Mr. Holder was named by President Clinton to be the Deputy Attorney General, the first African American named to that post. Prior to that he served as U.S. Attorney for the District of Columbia. In 1988, Mr. Holder was nominated by President Reagan to become an Associate Judge of the Superior Court of the District of Columbia. Mr. Holder, a native of New York City, attended public schools there, graduating from Stuyvesant High School where he earned a Regents Scholarship. He attended Columbia College, majored in American History, and graduated in 1973. He graduated from Columbia Law School in 1976. While in law school, he clerked at the NAACP Legal Defense Fund and the Department of Justice's Criminal Division. Upon graduating, he moved to Washington and joined the Department of Justice as part of the Attorney General's Honors Program. He was assigned to the newly formed Public Integrity Section in 1976 and was tasked to investigate and prosecute official corruption on the local, state and federal levels. Prior to becoming Attorney General, Mr. Holder was a litigation partner at Covington & Burling LLP in Washington. Mr. Holder lives in Washington with his wife, Dr. Sharon Malone, a physician, and their three children.

FREDERICK S. HUMPHRIES JR.

Frederick S. Humphries Jr., is Vice President of U.S. Government Affairs, for Microsoft Corporation, in Washington, D.C. where he manages both the Federal and State Government Affairs teams. With almost twenty years of state, federal, campaign and association experience, Mr. Humphries' professional background includes serving as Senior Policy Advisor for Congressman Richard Gephardt's Leadership Staff in Washington, D.C. in the Office of the Minority Leader, as Southern Political Director for the Democratic National Committee, and as Chief of Staff for Congressman Sanford Bishop of Georgia. In addition, he worked on the staff of Governor Ned Ray McWherter of Tennessee and is the former Executive Director of Public Policy for U.S. West Communications. Mr. Humphries also has substantial experience in national politics, having served on the staffs of four presidential campaigns. He is a graduate of Morehouse College and Temple University School of Law.

AVIS A. JONES-DEWEEVER, PH.D.

Avis A. Jones-DeWeever is the Executive Director of the National Council of Negro Women. Both a membership and umbrella organization, the National Council galvanizes the collective power of more than 240 local sections along with 34 national Black women's organizations which together represent four million women of African descent in the U.S. and throughout the Diaspora. Prior to serving in the role of Executive Director, Dr. Jones-DeWeever served as the organization's Research and Policy Center Director and also held appointments with the Institute for Women's Policy Research, the Joint Center for Political and Economic Studies, and the Congressional Black Caucus Foundation. An accomplished scholar, writer, and public speaker, Dr. Jones-DeWeever is an authority on race and gender in the American economy, poverty in urban communities, inequality of educational and economic opportunity, and issues of privilege, power, and policy in the U.S. Dr. Jones-DeWeever is a Magna Cum Laude graduate of Virginia State University and holds a Ph.D. in Government and Politics from the University of Maryland, College Park.

AMBASSADOR RON KIRK

Ron Kirk is the U.S. Trade Representative (USTR). He is a member of President Obama's Cabinet and serves as the President's principal trade advisor, negotiator, and spokesperson on trade issues. Since Ambassador Kirk was confirmed by the U.S. Senate in March 2009, he has led the Obama Administration's market-opening negotiations and dialogue with trading partners around the world, including the conclusion and congressional passage of bilateral free trade agreements with Korea, Colombia, and Panama, advancing the ambitious regional Trans-Pacific Partnership talks, and sustaining serious U.S. engagement at the World Trade Organization. Ambassador Kirk has also simultaneously pursued robust enforcement of America's trade rights in support of U.S. businesses and workers, and he has focused efforts to better assist American small businesses seeking opportunities in international markets. Ambassador Kirk brings both public service and private sector experience to USTR. He served two terms as the first African American mayor of Dallas. Prior to becoming mayor, he served as Texas Secretary of State under Governor Ann Richards. In addition, Ambassador Kirk has practiced law as a partner in the international law firm Vinson & Elkins, LLP. He was named one of "The 50 Most Influential Minority Lawyers in America" by *The National Law Journal* in 2008. Originally from Austin, TX, Ambassador Kirk graduated from Austin College and earned his law degree at the University of Texas School of Law. Ambassador Kirk is married to Matrice Ellis-Kirk and they have two daughters.

THOMAS A. LAVEIST, PH.D.

Thomas A. LaVeist is Director of the Hopkins Center for Health Disparities Solutions and the William C. and Nancy F. Richardson Professor in Health Policy at the Johns Hopkins Bloomberg School of Public Health. He has been on the Johns Hopkins faculty since 1990. His research focuses on health inequalities and health policy. Dr. LaVeist is recipient of the "Knowledge Award" from the U.S. Department of Health and Human Services, Office of Minority Health. And, he was awarded the "Innovation Award" from the National Institute on Minority Health and Health Disparities of the National Institutes of Health. He received his Ph.D. in Medical Sociology from the University of Michigan in 1988.

THE HONORABLE JOHN LEWIS

John Lewis, often called "one of the most courageous persons the Civil Rights Movement ever produced," has dedicated his life to protecting human rights, securing civil liberties, and building what he calls "The Beloved Community" in America. Born the son of sharecroppers, Congressman Lewis transcended more than 40 arrests, numerous beatings and serious injuries to become a man whose ethical standards and moral principles have made him an indescribable public servant. From organizing sit-ins at segregated lunch counters, participating in the Freedom Rides and being an architect of and a keynote speaker at the historic *March on Washington*, John Lewis has truly lived through and made history. Congressman Lewis has had extensive experience within the public sector as he was elected to the Atlanta City Council in 1981 and went on to become U.S. Representative of Georgia's fifth congressional district in 1986, a position he has held since then. While holding a B.A. in Religion and Philosophy from Fisk University, Congressman Lewis also holds over 50 honorary degrees from prestigious colleges and universities throughout the United States. An author, and frequent contributor in documentaries, news broadcasts and journals, Congressman Lewis is also the recipient of several awards from prominent national and international institutions including the highest civilian honor granted by President Barack Obama, the Presidential Medal of Freedom.

JOHN W. MACK

John W. Mack was appointed to the Board of Police Commissioners by Mayor Antonio R. Villaraigosa in August of 2005. He held the position of President of the Police Commission for two consecutive years, and then the position of Vice President for two years, which he currently holds. Commissioner Mack served as President of the Los Angeles Urban League from August of 1969, until his retirement in 2005. During his tenure, the Los Angeles Urban League became one of the most successful non-profit community organizations in Los Angeles with an annual budget of $25 million. The Los Angeles Urban League served over 100,000 individuals each year and operated a number of innovative, result-oriented job training, job placement, education, academic tutorial, youth achievement and business development programs serving African Americans and other people of color. In 1997, United Way presented its Agency of the Year Award to the Los Angeles Urban League. Prior to heading the Los Angeles Urban League, he served on the Urban League's national staff for six months during the Whitney M. Young, Jr. era in Washington, D.C. Commissioner Mack was also a leader in the 1960 student civil rights movement in Atlanta—and Co-Founder and Vice Chairperson of the Committee on the Appeal for Human Rights. He received a Bachelor of Science degree in Applied Sociology from North Carolina A&T State University and a Master's Degree from Clark Atlanta University.

CYNTHIA G. MARSHALL

Cynthia Marshall, Senior Vice President of Human Resources, has responsibility for developing and directing human resource programs for AT&T's 240K employees. Through strategic partnerships, her organization implements and administers HR policies and practices to support AT&T's business strategy. Previously, Ms. Marshall served as President, AT&T North Carolina, where she was directly responsible for the company's regulatory, legislative and community affairs activities in the state. She has over 30 years of experience in the telecommunications industry, joining Pacific Bell in July 1981. Since then she has held a variety of management positions in operations, human resources, network engineering and planning, and regulatory/external affairs. Cynthia is a passionate advocate for education as the key to unlocking future economic and personal opportunities for all students. As President, AT&T North Carolina, she served as a co-chair of the General Assembly's Committee on Dropout Prevention and was named a "Friend of Education" by the State Board of Education in recognition of her untiring efforts on behalf of North Carolina's students and schools. Cynthia has received many awards and honors, including the Award of Excellence from the Thurgood Marshall Fund, and the Woman of Substance Award from Bennett College. She is a graduate of the University of California at Berkeley, where she earned degrees in Business Administration and Human Resources Management. Cynthia grew up in Richmond, California, and resides in the Dallas area. Cynthia is married to Kenneth Marshall. They have three children.

BRENDA W. MCDUFFIE

Brenda W. McDuffie has been serving as President and CEO of the Buffalo Urban League, Inc., since October 1998. Mrs. McDuffie started her career as a paralegal aide for Neighborhood Legal Services. She worked for the City of Buffalo Human Resources Department as Senior Manpower Coordinator and later served as Director of Planning at the Private Industry Council where she became Executive Director in 1994. From 1994 to 1998, Mrs. McDuffie was the Executive Director for the Buffalo and Erie County Private Industry Council, Inc. (PIC). While at the PIC, Mrs. McDuffie served as President of the New York State Association of Employment and Training Professionals (NYATEP). As President of NYATEP, she served as co-chair and member of the steering committee which produced the recommendations for New York State's future Workforce Development System. Mrs. McDuffie has received numerous awards and recognition including the Buffalo News Citizen of the Year, NAACP Community Service Award, Business First Forty Under 40, and United Way Volunteer of the Year. Mrs. McDuffie received her Bachelor of Science in Social Work from the State University College at Buffalo, and earned a graduate certificate in Human Resource Development from the State University of New York at Buffalo's School of Management. Mrs. McDuffie resides in Buffalo with her husband and three children.

DAVID MCGHEE

Faithful, focused, and fearless are just three words that describe David McGhee. As a former program director for Big Brothers Big Sisters, a current professor, and founder of 16th Letter Consulting, a non-profit and leadership development consulting firm, Mr. McGhee has built a national reputation as a servant leader who labors diligently to improve the quality of life for marginalized people. Proficient at building key relationships with non-profit agencies, he has extensive experience in program development, along with securing local, state, and federal grants. Mr. McGhee has more than 10 years of hands-on, practical experience working with youth and families. He is a well-respected, highly sought-after speaker who brings about change. A product of Flint, Michigan's unforgiving streets, Mr. McGhee relates to urban youth culture in ways many can't. He is indeed a much-needed change agent for children, youth and families—especially African American boys. His work with youth has been widely recognized throughout the country—recently being featured in the September 2012 issue of *Black Enterprise*. He received his Bachelor's degree in Public Administration & Public Policy from Oakland University and a Master's in Leadership degree from Central Michigan University.

MARC H. MORIAL

As President of the National Urban League since 2003, Marc H. Morial has been the primary catalyst for a transformation for the century-old civil rights organization. His energetic and skilled leadership is redefining civil rights in the 21st century with a renewed emphasis on closing the economic gaps between Whites and Blacks as well as rich and poor Americans. Under his stewardship the League has had record fundraising success towards a 250MM, five-year fundraising goal and he has secured the BBB non-profit certification, which has established NUL as a leading national non-profit. A graduate of the prestigious University of Pennsylvania with a degree in Economics and African American Studies, he also holds a law degree from the Georgetown University Law Center in Washington, D.C. Morial was elected Mayor of New Orleans in 1994, serving two terms as popular chief executive with a broad multi-racial coalition who led New Orleans' 1990's renaissance, and left office with a 70% approval rating. Elected by his peers as President of the bi-partisan U.S. Conference of Mayors (USCM), he served during the 9/11 Crisis and championed the creation of the Department of Homeland Security, and the federalization of airport security screeners. He serves as an Executive Committee member of the Leadership Conference on Civil Rights, the Black Leadership Forum, and Leadership 18, and is a Board Member of the Muhammad Ali Center, and the New Jersey Performing Arts Center. Morial, a history, arts, music and sports enthusiast, has an adult daughter, and is married to broadcast journalist Michelle Miller. Together they have two young children.

JANET MURGUÍA

Janet Murguía is President and CEO of the National Council of La Raza (NCLR), the largest national Hispanic civil rights and advocacy organization in the United States. Since 2005, she has sought to strengthen the Latino voice on issues affecting the Hispanic community such as education, health care, immigration, civil rights, the economy, and the rise of hate rhetoric and hate crimes targeting the Latino community. She has also focused on strengthening NCLR's relationships with its sister civil rights and advocacy organizations, spearheading efforts to build bridges between the African American and Latino communities. In her role as NCLR's spokesperson, Ms. Murguía has appeared on "ABC—World News Tonight," "CBS Evening News," "NBC Nightly News," NBC's "Today," CNN's "Larry King Live," PBS's "News Hour with Jim Lehrer," CNN's "Anderson Cooper 360°," and CNN's "Lou Dobbs Tonight." She began her career in Washington, D.C. as legislative counsel to former Kansas Congressman Jim Slattery. Ms. Murguía then worked at the White House from 1994 to 2000, ultimately serving as deputy assistant to President Clinton, providing strategic and legislative advice to the president on key issues. In 2001, Ms. Murguía joined the University of Kansas as executive vice chancellor for university relations, overseeing KU's internal and external relations with the public, including governmental and public affairs. She grew up in Kansas City, Kansas and has a Bachelor of Science in Journalism, a Bachelor of Arts in Spanish and a Juris Doctorate from Kansas University.

LAURA W. MURPHY

Laura W. Murphy is in her second tenure as Director of the ACLU's Washington Legislative Office, a position she first held from 1993–2005. Since returning Murphy has maintained strong relationships with leaders in the U.S. Congress and the Obama Administration to advance the ACLU's public policy priorities including national security, criminal justice, human rights, privacy, reproductive rights, civil rights and First Amendment issues. Prior to her return to the ACLU, she founded and directed her own firm, Laura Murphy & Associates, LLC, where she utilized her 30 years of policy-making and political expertise to guide and advise corporate and non-profit clients at the national, state and local levels. Murphy is well known for her notable legislative career advancing human rights and civil liberties. Both major newspapers on Capitol Hill, *Roll Call* and *The Hill*, selected Murphy as one of the 50 most influential lobbyists and one of 17 top non-profit lobbyists in 1997 and 2003, respectively. In 1997, and again in 2003, the Congressional Black Caucus honored her for her significant contributions to legislation that advances civil rights and civil liberties. In previous professional positions Murphy served as chief of staff to a California Assembly Speaker and a cabinet member for the Mayor of the District of Columbia. Murphy has testified more than a dozen times before Congress and is an experienced national spokesperson.

ANDREW NG

Andrew Ng is a Co-Founder of Coursera and an Associate Professor of Computer Science at Stanford University. He is also the Director of the Stanford Artificial Intelligence Lab, the main AI research organization at Stanford, with 15 professors and about 150 students/post docs. In 2008, together with SCPD he started SEE (Stanford Engineering Everywhere), Stanford's first major attempt at free, online distributed education, which made publicly available about a dozen Stanford engineering classes. At Stanford, he also led the development of the OpenClassroom and the ml-class/db-class online education platforms, which were the precursor to the Coursera platform. In addition to his work on online education, Ng also works on machine learning, specifically on building AI systems via large scale brain simulations. His previous work includes autonomous helicopters, the Stanford AI Robot (STAIR) project, and ROS (the most widely used open-source robotics software platform today). Ng is the author or co-author of over 150 published papers in machine learning, and his group has won best paper/best student paper awards at ICML, ACL, CEAS, 3DRR. He is a recipient of the Alfred P. Sloan Fellowship, and the 2009 IJCAI Computers and Thought award, one of the highest honors in AI.

JOHN A. POWELL

john a. powell is Executive Director of the Haas Institute for a Fair and Inclusive Society (HIFIS) and Robert D. Haas Chancellor's Chair in Equity and Inclusion at the University of California, Berkeley. Formerly, he directed the Kirwan Institute for the Study of Race and Ethnicity at Ohio State University and the Institute for Race and Poverty at the University of Minnesota. He led the development of an "opportunity-based" model that connects affordable housing to racialized spaces in education, health, health care, and employment. He is the author of *Racing to Justice: Transforming our Concepts of Self and Other to Build an Inclusive Society*.

PATRICK RICHARD, PH.D.

Patrick Richard is an Assistant Professor of Health Economics and Policy and Research Director at the Uniformed Services University of the Health Sciences (USUHS). He is also an adjunct faculty at the George Washington (GW) University Health Economics and Policy Program and an affiliate faculty at the Johns Hopkins Center for Health Disparities Solutions. Dr. Richard has taught and led several research projects in health economics, health services research, and health policy and has established a track record of translating empirical research into policy and peer-reviewed publications. Dr. Richard has more than fifteen years of experience in education, research, and program evaluation for public, private and non-profit organizations. Dr. Richard obtained his Doctoral degree in Health Economics from Johns Hopkins University (JHU) and completed post-doctoral research scholarship at the University of California, Berkeley.

REVEREND AL SHARPTON

Reverend Al Sharpton serves as the host of "PoliticsNation," on MSNBC. With over 40 years of experience as a community leader, politician, minister and advocate, the Rev. Al Sharpton is one of America's most-renowned civil rights leaders. His highly visible career began at the tender age of four when he preached his first sermon. A successful civil rights career soon followed helping him hold such notable positions as the Youth Director of New York's Operation Breadbasket, Director of Ministers for National Rainbow Push coalition, and founder of his own broad-based progressive civil rights organization, the National Action Network (NAN), one of the leading civil rights organizations in the world. Since its inception in 1991, NAN has expanded to encompass chapters throughout the United States and maintain important regional offices in Washington, D.C., Atlanta, GA, Detroit, MI, Chicago, IL, Dallas, TX, Las Vegas, NV, and Los Angeles, CA. Rev. Sharpton also hosts a nationally syndicated radio show that broadcasts in 40 markets, five days a week. He resides in New York and has two daughters, Dominique and Ashley.

PATRICIA STOKES

Patricia Stokes has served as CEO of the Urban League of Middle Tennessee since 2008. A graduate of Glynn Academy High School in Brunswick, GA, she earned a Bachelor's degree in Music Education from Howard University and her Master's degree in Clinical Social Work from Smith College. Ms. Stokes worked initially as a group home supervisor with Georgia CHARLEE, Inc. and as a family therapist with Charter Brook before joining Atlanta Area Health Education Center as director of special projects. In 1994, she joined Atlanta's American Red Cross, as director of metro-wide Youth Programs and leadership development. She started her own non-profit management consulting company in 2002 and was named program manager for Meharry Medical College's Center for Women's Health Research in 2006. Ms. Stokes is a member of the executive committee of the Interdenominational Ministerial Fellowship, serves on Nashville Chamber's Report Card committee, and is on the board of Centennial Medical Center. She also served as local chair and national corresponding secretary of The Society, Inc. and is an active member of the Nashville Chapter of Jack and Jill of America. Ms. Stokes was also an Athena nominee in 2011. She and her husband, Shereitte, are the parents of two daughters and two sons.

VINCENT E. WATTS

Vince Watts has served as the President and CEO of the Greater Stark County Urban League since 2008. Mr. Watts started his working career as a directory assistance operator with Ohio Bell in 1981. He left the company in 2003 as the Procurement Manager for Ohio and Michigan at the merger of SBC and AT&T. Mr. Watts organized the volunteer group Stark County Town Hall on Race Relations and incorporated it into Coming Together Stark County. Prior to coming to the Urban League Mr. Watts started Urban Hope Ohio an entrepreneurial program of Goodwill Industries of Greater Cleveland and East Central Ohio. In four years with the Urban League, Mr. Watts has a strong focus on bringing resources back to inner city neighborhoods through employment, education, financial literacy and health related programming. A 1980 graduate of Timken Senior High, Mr. Watts received his Bachelors degree in Business at Malone College and his Masters degree in Management from Walsh University. Mr. Watts is an ordained Elder in the Pentecostal church. He currently serves as the Assistant Pastor of the First Church of God in Christ in southeast Canton. He and his wife Debra have been married 29 years. They have four daughters and five grandchildren.

EDITH G. WHITE

Edith G. White is President and CEO of the Urban League of Hampton Roads, Inc. Since September 2000, she has lead the Urban League—one of the oldest and most successful organizations in creating opportunities for individuals to thrive and succeed. Under her leadership, new programs have been developed to enhance educational opportunities, provide technical assistance for business development, create wealth through homeownership and improve the quality of health. Additionally, many new partnerships have been developed within the non-profit sector and higher education, as well in the business community. She has spearheaded the development of new service sites throughout the region, new fundraising events and marketing/ communications campaigns. She is the recipient of numerous awards including the 2012 Citizen of the Year Award from Kappa Alpha Psi Fraternity, 2012 Outstanding Achievement in Community Service from Norfolk State University, 2011 Women of Power Award from the National Urban League, Champion of Diversity Award (United Way of Greater Richmond), Woman of Distinction Award (National Council of Negro Women), TRIO Achievers Award, the Zonta Award, 2010 Humanitarian Award (Virginia Center for Inclusive Communities) and the 2010 Women of Distinction Award (YWCASHR). Ms. White received a Bachelor of Science in Mass Communications and a Master of Science in Journalism Education from Virginia Commonwealth University. Additionally, she is a graduate of the Commonwealth Management Institute and the Management Excellence Program Center for Public Service at the University of Virginia. Ms. White is the proud mother of two children, Lauren and Anthony.

MADURA WIJEWARDENA

Madura Wijewardena is the Director of Research & Policy at the National Urban League Policy Institute (NULPI), where he uses quantitative analysis and research to promote NUL's legislative agenda in economic policy. He also assists in the production of the Equality Index and acts as the coordinator of the NUL's role as a Census Information Center. In addition to research, Mr. Wijewardena manages NUL's federal policy in telecoms/ technology, energy, and transportation. He also handles special partnerships with the Federal Communications Commission (FCC) and the U.S. Census Bureau to promote joint programs like the FCC's public-private broadband adoption programs. Prior to NULPI, he worked for a Chicago consulting firm where he used quantitative analysis of complex databases to assist state governments, foundations, and campaigns to micro-target services and messages. He has been interviewed on C-SPAN, ABC-TV, and Public Radio International, and his work has been quoted in *The New York Times* and in testimony before the U.S. Congress. For the first eight years of his career, Mr. Wijewardena was a corporate attorney in technology and telecommunications, where he structured and negotiated mergers, acquisitions, and joint ventures for global corporations. He has an M.A. in Public Policy from the University of Chicago (in statistics), and an LLB (equivalent of a Juris Doctorate) and a Bachelor of Economics degree from the University of Sydney, Australia.

VALERIE R. WILSON, PH.D.

Valerie Rawlston Wilson is an economist and Vice President of Research at the National Urban League Policy Institute in Washington, D.C. where she is responsible for planning and directing the Policy Institute's Research Agenda. She is also a member of the National Urban League President's Council of Economic Advisors, which assists the League in shaping national economic policy. Her fields of specialization include labor economics, racial and economic inequality, and economics of higher education. She has authored a number of publications on topics related to these areas and has appeared in print, television and radio media, including C-SPAN's "Washington Journal," National Public Radio, Fox News, *USA Today*, *Ebony* and *TIME Magazine*. Dr. Wilson earned a Ph.D. from the Department of Economics at the University of North Carolina at Chapel Hill.

★ OF ★

AUTHORS & ARTICLES

In 1987, the National Urban League began publishing ***The State of Black America*** in a smaller, typeset format. By doing so, it became easier to catalog and archive the various essays by author and article.

The 2013 edition of ***The State of Black America*** is the eighteenth to feature an Index of the Authors and Articles that have appeared since 1987. The articles have been divided by topic and are listed in alphabetical order by authors' names.

Reprints of the articles catalogued herein are available through the National Urban League Policy Institute, 300 New Jersey Avenue, N.W., Suite 650, Washington, D.C. 20001, (202) 629-5754.

Hanson, Renee, Mark McArdle, and Valerie Rawlston Wilson, "Invisible Men: The Urgent Problems of Low-Income African-American Males," 2007, pp. 209–216.

Holzer, Harry J., "Reconnecting Young Black Men: What Policies Would Help," 2007, pp. 75–87.

Johns, David J., "Re-Imagining Black Masculine Identity: An Investigation of the 'Problem' Surrounding the Construction of Black Masculinity in America," 2007, pp. 59–73.

Lanier, James R., "The Empowerment Movement and the Black Male," 2004, pp. 143–148.

———, "The National Urban League's Commission on the Black Male: Renewal, Revival and Resurrection Feasibility and Strategic Planning Study," 2005, pp. 107–109.

McGhee, David, "Mentoring Matters: Why Young Professionals and Others Must Mentor," 2013, pp. 162–165.

Morial, Marc H., "Empowering Black Males to Reach Their Full Potential," 2007, pp. 13–15.

Nutter, Michael A., "Black Men Are Killing Black Men. There, I Said It." 2012, pp. 106–109.

Reed, James, and Aaron Thomas, "The National Urban League: The National Urban League: Empowering Black Males to Reach Their Full Potential," 2007, pp. 217–218.

Rodgers III, William M., "Why Should African Americans Care About Macroeconomic Policy," 2007, pp. 89–103.

Wilson, Valerie Rawlston, "On Equal Ground: Causes and Solutions for Lower College Completion Rates Among Black Males," 2007, pp. 123–135.

BUSINESS

Blankfein, Lloyd, "Creating Jobs and Opportunities Through Minority Owned Businesses," 2012, pp. 70–73.

Bryant, John Hope, "Financial Dignity in an Economic Age," 2013, pp. 134–138.

Cofield, Natalie M. "What's in it for Us? How Federal Business Inclusion Programs and Legislation Affect Minority Entrepreneurs," 2011, pp. 100–109.

Emerson, Melinda F., "Five Things You Must Have to Run a Successful Business," 2004, pp. 153–156.

Glasgow, Douglas G., "The Black Underclass in Perspective," 1987, pp. 129–144.

Henderson, Lenneal J., "Empowerment through Enterprise: African-American Business Development," 1993, pp. 91–108.

Humphries, Frederick S., "The National Talent Strategy: Ideas to Secure U.S. Competitiveness and Economic Growth," 2013, pp. 86–90.

Marshall, Cynthia, "Digitizing the Dream: The Role of Technology in Empowering Communities," 2013, pp. 130–133.

Price, Hugh B., "Beacons in a New Millennium: Reflections on 21st-Century Leaders and Leadership," 2000, pp. 13–39.

Tidwell, Billy J., "Black Wealth: Facts and Fiction," 1988, pp. 193–210.

Turner, Mark D., "Escaping the 'Ghetto' of Subcontracting," 2006, pp. 117–131.

Walker, Juliet E.K., "The Future of Black Business in America: Can It Get Out of the Box?," 2000, pp. 199–226.

CASE STUDIES

Cleaver II, Emanuel, "Green Impact Zone of Kansas City, MO," 2011, pp. 88–93.

Patrick, Deval L., "Growing an Innovative Economy in Massachusetts," 2011, pp. 154–158.

CHILDREN AND YOUTH

Bell, William C., "How are the Children? Foster Care and African-American Boys," 2007, pp. 151–157.

———, "Community Based Organizations and Child Welfare: Building Communities of Hope," 2013, pp. 166–169.

Bryant, John Hope, "Financial Dignity in an Economic Age," 2013, pp. 134–138.

Chávez, Anna Maria, "Helping Girls Make Healthy Choices," 2012, pp. 124–126.

Comer, James P., "Leave No Child Behind: Preparing Today's Youth for Tomorrow's World," 2005, pp. 75–84.

Cox, Kenya L. Covington, "The Childcare Imbalance: Impact on Working Opportunities for Poor Mothers," 2003, pp. 197–224.

Dallas Highlight, "Urban Youth Empowerment Program," 2011, pp. 84–86.

Edelman, Marian Wright, "The State of Our Children," 2006, pp. 133–141.

———, "Losing Our Children in America's Cradle to Prison Pipeline," 2007, pp. 219–227.

———, "Time to Wake Up and Act: The State of Black America," 2013, pp. 68–69.

Fulbright-Anderson, Karen, "Developing Our Youth: What Works," 1996, pp. 127–143.

Hare, Bruce R., "Black Youth at Risk," 1988, pp. 81–93.

Harris, Dot, "Diversity in STEM: An Economic Imperative," 2013, pp. 92–95.

Howard, Jeff P., "The Third Movement: Developing Black Children for the 21st Century," 1993, pp. 11–34.

Hrabowski III, Dr. Freeman A., "The Power of Education to Empower Our Children," 2013, pp. 82–85.

Humphries, Frederick S., "The National Talent Strategy: Ideas to Secure U.S. Competitiveness and Economic Growth," 2013, pp. 86–90.

Kirk, Ron, "Education: The Critical Link between Trade and Jobs," 2013, pp. 76–80.

Knaus, Christopher B., "Still Segregated, Still Unequal: Analyzing the Impact of No Child Left Behind on African-American Students," 2007, pp. 105–121.

McGhee, David, "Mentoring Matters: Why Young Professionals and Others Must Mentor," 2013, pp. 162–165.

McMurray, Georgia L., "Those of Broader Vision: An African-American Perspective on Teenage Pregnancy and Parenting," 1990, pp. 195–211.

Moore, Evelyn K., "The Call: Universal Child Care," 1996, pp. 219–244.

Murphy, Laura, "Stop the Fast Track to Prison," 2013, pp. 96–100.

Obama, Michelle, "Let's Move Initiative on Healthier Schools," 2011, pp. 138–140.

Shaw, Jr., Lee, "Healthy Boys Stand SCOUTStrong™," 2012, pp. 126–128.

Scott, Kimberly A., "A Case Study: African-American Girls and Their Families," 2003, pp. 181–195.

Special Report. "Partnering to Empower Healthy Kids," 2012, pp. 120–123.

Williams, Terry M., and William Kornblum, "A Portrait of Youth: Coming of Age in Harlem Public Housing," 1991, pp. 187–207.

CIVIC ENGAGEMENT

Alton, Kimberley, "The State of Civil Rights 2008," 2008, pp. 157–161.

Brazile, Donna, "Fallout from the Mid-Term Elections: Making the Most of the Next Two Years," 2011, pp. 180–190.

Brown James, Stefanie, "Black Civic Engagement 2.0: In with the Old, in with the New," 2013, pp. 67–68.

Campbell, Melanie L., "Election Reform: Protecting Our Vote from the Enemy That Never Sleeps," 2008, pp. 149–156.

Capehart, Jonathan, "Race Still Does Matter—A Lot," 2013, pp. 150–153.

Chappell, Kevin, "'Realities' of Black America," 2011, pp. 192–195.

Fauntroy, Michael K., "The New Arithmetic of Black Political Power," 2013, pp. 154–157.

Fudge, Marcia L., "Unfinished Business," 2013, pp. 65.

Hardy, Chanelle P., "Introduction to Lift Ev'ry Voice: A Special Collection of Articles and Op-Eds.," 2013 pp. 60–61.

Holder, Jr., Eric H., "Civil Rights Enforcement in the 21st Century," 2013, pp. 144–148.

Lewis, John, "New Tactics, Same Old Taint," 2013, pp. 62–63.

Lindsay, Tiffany, "Weaving the Fabric: The Political Activism of Young African-American Women," 2008, pp. 47–50.

Scott, Robert C. "Bobby," "Minority Voter Participation: Reviewing Past and Present Barriers to the Polls," 2012, pp. 44–47.

Watts, Vincent and White, Edith, "Project Advocate: A Roadmap to Civic Engagement," 2013 pp. 140–143.

White, Edith and Watts, Vincent, "Project Advocate: A Roadmap to Civic Engagement," 2013 pp. 140–143.

Wijewardena, Madura and Kirk Clay, "Government with the Consent of All: Redistricting Strategies for Civil Rights Organizations," 2011, pp. 196–201.

Wijewardena, Madura, "Understanding the Equality Index," 2012, pp. 16–19.

———, "Understanding the Equality Index," 2013, pp. 22–25.

Wilson, Valerie Rawlston, "Introduction to the 2011 Equality Index," 2011, pp. 14–22.

———, "Introduction to the 2012 Equality Index," 2012, pp. 10–15.

———, "Introduction to the 2013 Equality Index," 2013, pp. 12–21.

Yearwood, Jr., Lennox,"The Rise and Fall and Rise Again of Jim Crow Laws," 2012, pp. 48–53.

CIVIL RIGHTS

Alton, Kimberley, "The State of Civil Rights 2008," 2008, pp. 157–161.

Archer, Dennis W., "Security Must Never Trump Liberty," 2004, pp. 139–142.

Brown James, Stefanie, "Black Civic Engagement 2.0: In with the Old, in with the New," 2013, pp. 67–68.

Burnham, David, "The Fog of War," 2005, pp. 123–127.

Campbell, Melanie L., "Election Reform: Protecting Our Vote from the Enemy That Never Sleeps," 2008, pp. 149–156.

Chappell, Kevin, " 'Realities' of Black America," 2011, pp. 192–195.

Edelman, Marian Wright, "Time to Wake Up and Act: The State of Black America," 2013, pp. 68–69.

Fudge, Marcia L., "Unfinished Business," 2013, pp. 65.

Grant, Gwen, "The Fullness of Time for a More Perfect Union: The Movement Continues," 2009, pp. 171–177.

Hardy, Chanelle P., "Introduction to Lift Ev'ry Voice: A Special Collection of Articles and Op-Eds.," 2013, pp. 60–61.

Holder, Jr., Eric H., "Civil Rights Enforcement in the 21st Century," 2013, pp. 144–148.

Jones, Nathaniel R., "The State of Civil Rights," 2006, pp. 165–170.

———, "Did I Ever" 2009, pp. 213–219.

Jones-DeWeever, Avis A., "The Enduring Icon: Dr. Dorothy Height," 2013, pp. 64.

Lewis, John, "New Tactics, Same Old Taint," 2013, pp. 62–63.

Mack, John W., "Reflections on National Urban League's Legacy and Service," 2013, pp. 66.

Ogletree, Jr., Charles J., "Brown at 50: Considering the Continuing Legal Struggle for Racial Justice," 2004, pp. 81–96.

Sharpton, Al, "Though We Have Achieved Much, the Battle Continues," 2013, pp. 63–64.

Shaw, Theodore M., "The State of Civil Rights," 2007, pp. 173–183.

Wijewardena, Madura and Kirk Clay, "Government with the Consent of All: Redistricting Strategies for Civil Rights Organizations," 2011, pp. 196–201.

CRIMINAL JUSTICE

Curry, George E., "Racial Disparities Drive Prison Boom," 2006, pp. 171–187.

Drucker, Ernest M., "The Impact of Mass Incarceration on Public Health in Black Communities," 2003, pp. 151–168.

Edelman, Marian Wright, "Losing Our Children in America's Cradle to Prison Pipeline," 2007, pp. 219–227.

———, "Time to Wake Up and Act: The State of Black America," 2013, pp. 68–69.

Lanier, James R., "The Harmful Impact of the Criminal Justice System and War on Drugs on the African-American Family," 2003, pp. 169–179.

Murphy, Laura, "Stop the Fast Track to Prison," 2013, pp. 96–100.

DIVERSITY

Bell, Derrick, "The Elusive Quest for Racial Justice: The Chronicle of the Constitutional Contradiction," 1991, pp. 9–23.

Capehart, Jonathan, "Race Still Does Matter—A Lot," 2013, pp. 150–153.

Cobbs, Price M., "Critical Perspectives on the Psychology of Race," 1988, pp. 61–70.

———, "Valuing Diversity: The Myth and the Challenge," 1989, pp. 151–159.

Darity, Jr., William, "History, Discrimination and Racial Inequality," 1999, pp. 153–166.

Harris, Dot, "Diversity in STEM: An Economic Imperative," 2013, pp. 92–95.

Humphries, Frederick S., "The National Talent Strategy: Ideas to Secure U.S. Competitiveness and Economic Growth," 2013, pp. 86–90.

Jones, Stephanie J., "Sunday Morning Apartheid: A Diversity Study of the Sunday Morning Talk Shows," 2006, pp. 189–228.

Stoute, Steve, "Tanning of America Makes Growth, Prosperity and Empowerment Easier," 2012, pp. 84–89.

Watson, Bernard C., "The Demographic Revolution: Diversity in 21st-Century America," 1992, pp. 31–59.

Wiley, Maya, "Hurricane Katrina Exposed the Face of Diversity," 2006, pp. 143–153.

DRUG TRADE

Lanier, James R., "The Harmful Impact of the Criminal Justice System and War on Drugs on the African-American Family," 2003, pp.169–179.

ECONOMICS

Alexis, Marcus and Geraldine R. Henderson, "The Economic Base of African-American Communities: A Study of Consumption Patterns," 1994, pp. 51–82.

Anderson, Bernard, "Lessons Learned from the Economic Crisis: Job Creation and Economy Recovery," 2010, pp. 60–65.

———, "William M. Rodgers III, Lucy J. Reuben, and Valerie Rawlston Wilson, "The New Normal? Opportunities for Prosperity in a 'Jobless Recovery,'" 2011, pp. 54–63.

Atlanta Highlight, "Economic Empowerment Tour," 2011, pp. 118–120.

Bradford, William, "Black Family Wealth in the United States," 2000, pp. 103–145.

———, "Money Matters: Lending Discrimination in African-American Communities," 1993, pp. 109–134.

Bryant, John Hope, "Financial Dignity in an Economic Age," 2013, pp. 134–138.

Buckner, Marland and Chanelle P. Hardy, "Leveraging the Greening of America to Strengthen the Workforce Development System," 2011, pp. 76–83.

Burbridge, Lynn C., "Toward Economic Self-Sufficiency: Independence Without Poverty," 1993, pp. 71–90.

Cleaver II, Emanuel, "Green Impact Zone of Kansas City, MO," 2011, pp. 88–93.

Corbett, Keith, "Economic Innovation: Finance and Lending Initiatives Point Paths to Prosperity for Underserved Communities," 2011, pp. 122–129.

Edwards, Harry, "Playoffs and Payoffs: The African-American Athlete as an Institutional Resource," 1994, pp. 85–111.

Graves, Jr., Earl, "Wealth for Life," 2009, pp. 165–170.

Hamilton, Darrick, "The Racial Composition of American Jobs," 2006, pp. 77–115.

Harris, Andrea, "The Subprime Wipeout: Unsustainable Loans Erase Gains Made by African-American Women," 2008, pp. 125–133.

Harris, Dot, "Diversity in STEM: An Economic Imperative," 2013, pp. 92–95.

Henderson, Lenneal J., "Blacks, Budgets, and Taxes: Assessing the Impact of Budget Deficit Reduction and Tax Reform on Blacks," 1987, pp. 75–95.

———, "Budget and Tax Strategy: Implications for Blacks," 1990, pp. 53–71.

———, "Public Investment for Public Good: Needs, Benefits, and Financing Options," 1992, pp. 213–229.

Herman, Alexis, "African-American Women and Work: Still a Tale of Two Cities," 2008, pp. 109–113.

Holzer, Harry J., "Reconnecting Young Black Men: What Policies Would Help," 2007, pp. 75–87.

Humphries, Frederick S., "The National Talent Strategy: Ideas to Secure U.S. Competitiveness and Economic Growth," 2013, pp. 86–90.

Jeffries, John M., and Richard L. Schaffer, "Changes in Economy and Labor Market Status of Black Americans," 1996, pp. 12–77.

Jones, Stephanie J., "The Subprime Meltdown: Disarming the 'Weapons of Mass Deception,'" 2009, pp. 157–164.

Kirk, Ron, "Education: The Critical Link Between Trade and Jobs," 2013, pp. 76–80.

Malveaux, Julianne, "Shouldering the Third Burden: The Status of African-American Women," 2008, pp. 75–81.

———, "The Parity Imperative: Civil Rights, Economic Justice, and the New American Dilemma," 1992, pp. 281–303.

Mensah, Lisa, "Putting Homeownership Back Within Our Reach," 2008, pp. 135–142.

Morial, Marc H. and Marvin Owens, "The National Urban League Economic Empowerment Initiative," 2005, pp. 111–113.

Myers, Jr., Samuel L., "African-American Economic Well-Being During the Boom and Bust," 2004, pp. 53–80.

National Urban League, "The National Urban League's Homebuyer's Bill of Rights," 2008, pp. 143–147.

National Urban League Research Staff, "African Americans in Profile: Selected Demographic, Social and Economic Data," 1992, pp. 309–325.

———, "The Economic Status of African Americans During the Reagan-Bush Era Withered Opportunities, Limited Outcomes, and Uncertain Outlook," 1993, pp. 135–200.

———, "The Economic Status of African Americans: Limited Ownership and Persistent Inequality," 1992, pp. 61–117.

———, "The Economic Status of African Americans: 'Permanent' Poverty and Inequality," 1991, pp. 25–75.

———, "Economic Status of Black Americans During the 1980s: A Decade of Limited Progress," 1990, pp. 25–52.

———, "Economic Status of Black Americans," 1989, pp. 9–39.

———, "Economic Status of Black 1987," 1988, pp. 129–152.

———, "Economic Status of Blacks 1986," 1987, pp. 49–73.

Patrick, Deval L., "Growing an Innovative Economy in Massachusetts," 2011, pp. 154–158.

Reuben, Lucy J., "Make Room for the New 'She'EOs: An Analysis of Businesses Owned by Black Females," 2008, pp. 115–124.

Richardson, Cy, "What Must Be Done: The Case for More Homeownership and Financial Education Counseling," 2009, pp. 145–155.

Rivlin, Alice M., "Pay Now or Pay Later: Jobs, Fiscal Responsibility and the Future of Black America," 2011, pp. 202–206.

Rodgers III, William, M., "Why Should African Americans Care About Macroeconomic Policy," 2007, pp. 89–103.

Shapiro, Thomas M., "The Racial Wealth Gap," 2005, pp. 41–48.

Sharpe, Rhonda, "Preparing a Diverse and Competitive STEM Workforce," 2011, pp. 142–152.

Spriggs, William, "Nothing Trickled Down: Why Reaganomics Failed America," 2009, pp. 123–133.

Stoute, Steve, "Tanning of America Makes Growth, Prosperity and Empowerment Easier," 2012, pp. 84–89.

Taylor, Robert D., "Wealth Creation: The Next Leadership Challenge," 2005, pp. 119–122.

Thompson, J. Phil, "The Coming Green Economy," 2009, pp. 135–142.

Tidwell, Billy J., "Economic Costs of American Racism," 1991, pp. 219–232.

Turner, Mark D., "Escaping the 'Ghetto' of Subcontracting," 2006, pp. 117–131.

Watkins, Celeste, "The Socio-Economic Divide Among Black Americans Under 35," 2001, pp. 67–85.

Webb, Michael B., "Programs for Progress and Empowerment: The Urban League's National Education Initiative," 1993, pp. 203–216.

EDUCATION

Allen, Walter R., "The Struggle Continues: Race, Equity and Affirmative Action in U.S. Higher Education," 2001, pp. 87–100.

Bailey, Deirdre, "School Choice: The Option of Success," 2001, pp. 101–114.

Bradford, William D., "Dollars for Deeds: Prospects and Prescriptions for African-American Financial Institutions," 1994, pp. 31–50.

Bush, Esther and Stokes, Patricia, "The Equity and Excellence Project: Community-Driven Education Reform," 2013, pp. 70–74.

Carr, Gregory E., "Sacrifice If You Must—The Reward Is Clear," 2012, pp. 137–139.

Chauhan, Shree, "Bringing Higher Education to the Masses: A Conversation with Coursera Co-Founder Andrew Ng," 2013, pp. 102–106.

Cole, Johnnetta Betsch, "The Triumphs and Challenges of Historically Black Colleges and Universities," 2008, pp. 99–107.

Comer, James P., Norris Haynes, and Muriel Hamilton-Leel, "School Power: A Model for Improving Black Student Achievement," 1990, pp. 225–238.

———, "Leave No Child Behind: Preparing Today's Youth for Tomorrow's World," 2005, pp. 75–84.

Dilworth, Mary E. "Historically Black Colleges and Universities: Taking Care of Home," 1994, pp. 127–151.

Duncan, Arne, "The Path to Success for African Americans," 2010, pp. 92–96.

Edelman, Marian Wright, "Black Children in America," 1989, pp. 63–76.

———, "Time to Wake Up and Act: The State of Black America," 2013, pp. 68–69.

Enyia, Amara, C. "College for All?" 2012, pp. 149–151.

Fattah, Chaka, "Needed: Equality in Education," 2009, pp. 57–60.

Freeman, Dr. Kimberly Edelin, "African-American Men and Women in Higher Education: 'Filling the Glass' in the New Millennium," 2000, pp. 61–90.

Gordon, Edmund W., "The State of Education in Black America," 2004, pp. 97–113.

Guinier, Prof. Lani, "Confirmative Action in a Multiracial Democracy," 2000, pp. 333–364.

Hanson, Renee R., "A Pathway to School Readiness: The Impact of Family on Early Childhood Education," 2008, pp. 89–98.

Hardy, Chanelle P., "Introduction: The Value of College," 2012, pp. 132–135.

Harris, Dot, "Diversity in STEM: An Economic Imperative," 2013, pp. 92–95.

Hrabowski III, Dr. Freeman A., "The Power of Education to Empower Our Children," 2013, pp. 82–85.

Humphries, Frederick S., "The National Talent Strategy: Ideas to Secure U.S. Competitiveness and Economic Growth," 2013, pp. 86–90.

Jackson, John, "From Miracle to Movement: Mandating a National Opportunity to Learn, 2009, pp. 61–70.

Jackson, Maria Rosario, "Arts, Culture, and Communities: Do Our Neighborhoods Inspire Our Children to Reach Higher?" 2012, pp. 153–154.

Journal of Blacks in Higher Education (reprint), "The 'Acting White' Myth," 2005, pp. 115–117.

Kirk, Ron, "Education: The Critical Link between Trade and Jobs," 2013, pp. 76–80.

Knaus, Christopher B., "Still Segregated, Still Unequal: Analyzing the Impact of No Child Left Behind on African American Students," 2007, pp. 105–121.

Legend, John, "The Show Me Campaign: A Conversation with John Legend," 2012, pp. 151–153.

Luckey, Desireé, "Communities, Schools and Families Make the Education-Career Connection," 2012, pp. 139–141.

McBay, Shirley M. "The Condition of African American Education: Changes and Challenges," 1992, pp. 141–156.

McKenzie, Floretta Dukes with Patricia Evans, "Education Strategies for the 90s," 1991, pp. 95–109.

Morial, Marc H. and Hal Smith, "Education is a Jobs Issue," 2011, pp. 130–137.

Murphy, Laura, "Stop the Fast Track to Prison," 2013, pp. 96–100.

Patrick, Deval L., "Growing an Innovative Economy in Massachusetts," 2011, pp. 154–158.

Perry, Dr. Steve, "Real Reform is Getting Kids One Step Closer to Quality Schools," 2012, pp. 147–149.

Powell, Kevin, "Why A College Education Matters," 2012, pp. 136–137.

Ransom, Tafaya and John Michael Lee, "College Readiness and Completion for Young Men of Color," 2012, pp. 141–147.

Ribeau, Sidney, "Foreword: A Competitive Foundation for the Future," 2011, pp. 8–9.

Robinson, Sharon P., "Taking Charge: An Approach to Making the Educational Problems of Blacks Comprehensible and Manageable," 1987, pp. 31–47.

Rose, Dr. Stephanie Bell, "African-American High Achievers: Developing Talented Leaders," 2000, pp. 41–60.

Ross, Ronald O., "Gaps, Traps and Lies: African-American Students and Test Scores," 2004, pp. 157–161.

Sharpe, Rhonda, "Preparing a Diverse and Competitive STEM Workforce," 2011, pp. 142–152.

Smith, Hal, "The Questions Before Us: Opportunity, Education and Equity," 2009, pp. 45–55.

Smith, Hal, Jacqueline Ayers, and Darlene Marlin, "Ready to Succeed: The National Urban League Project Ready: Post-Secondary Success Program," 2012, pp. 114–119.

Stokes, Patricia and Bush, Esther, "The Equity and Excellence Project: Community-Driven Education Reform," 2013, pp. 70–74.

Sudarkasa, Niara, "Black Enrollment in Higher Education: The Unfulfilled led Promise of Equality," 1988, pp. 7–22.

Thornton, Alvin, "The Nation's Higher Education Agenda: The Continuing Role of HBCUs," 2011, pp. 160–167.

Watson, Bernard C., with Fasaha M. Traylor, "Tomorrow's Teachers: Who Will They Be, What Will They Know?" 1988, pp. 23–37.

Willie, Charles V., "The Future of School Desegregation," 1987, pp. 37–47.

Wilson, Reginald, "Black Higher Education: Crisis and Promise," 1989, pp. 121–135.

Wilson, Valerie Rawlston, "On Equal Ground: Causes and Solutions for Lower College Completion Rates Among Black Males," 2007, pp. 123–135.

———, "Introduction to the 2011 Equality Index," 2011, pp. 14–22.

Wirschem, David, "Community Mobilization for Education in Rochester, New York: A Case Study," 1991, pp. 243–248.

EMERGING IDEAS

Huggins, Sheryl, "The Rules of the Game," 2001, pp. 65–66.

EMPLOYMENT

Anderson, Bernard E., "The Black Worker: Continuing Quest for Economic Parity, 2002, pp. 51–67.

———, "William M. Rodgers III, Lucy J. Reuben, and Valerie Rawlston Wilson, "The New Normal? Opportunities for Prosperity in a 'Jobless Recovery,'" 2011, pp. 54–63.

Atlanta Highlight, "Economic Empowerment Tour," 2011, pp. 118–120.

Cleaver II, Emanuel, "Green Impact Zone of Kansas City, MO," 2011, pp. 88–93.

Coulter, Patricia, "Small Business Growth = Job Growth," 2010, pp. 118–124.

Dallas Highlight, "Urban Youth Empowerment Program," 2011, pp. 84–86.

Darity, Jr., William M., and Samuel L. Myers, Jr., "Racial Earnings Inequality into the 21st Century," 1992, pp. 119–139.

Dodd, Christopher, "Infrastructure as a Job Creation Mechanism," 2009, pp. 101–108.

Gillibrand, Kirsten, "A Dream Not Deferred," 2012, pp. 60–63.

Hamilton, Darrick, "The Racial Composition of American Jobs," 2006, pp. 77–115.

Hammond, Theresa A., "African Americans in White-Collar Professions," 2002, pp. 109–121.

Herman, Alexis, "African-American Women and Work: Still a Tale of Two Cities," 2008, pp. 109–113.

Marshall, Cynthia, "Digitizing the Dream: The Role of Technology in Empowering Communities," 2013, pp. 130–133.

Morial, Marc H. and Hal Smith, "Education is a Jobs Issue," 2011, pp. 130–137.

National Urban League, "12 Point Urban Jobs Plan," 2011, pp. 46–52.

National Urban League Policy Institute, "Where Do We Go From Here? Projected Employment Growth Industries and Occupations," 2011, pp. 64–75.

———, The National Urban League 8-Point Education and Employment Plan: Employment and Education Empower the Nation, 2012, pp. 54–59.

Nightingale, Demetra S., "Intermediaries in the Workforce Development Systsem," 2010, pp. 84–91.

Patrick, Deval L., "Growing an Innovative Economy in Massachusetts," 2011, pp. 154–158.

Reuben, Lucy J., "Make Room for the New 'She'EOs: An Analysis of Businesses Owned by Black Females," 2008, pp. 115–124.

Rivlin, Alice M., "Pay Now or Pay Later: Jobs, Fiscal Responsibility and the Future of Black America," 2011, pp. 202–206.

Rodgers, William, "Why Reduce African-American Male Unemployment?," 2009, pp. 109–121.

Sharpe, Rhonda, "Preparing a Diverse and Competitive STEM Workforce," 2011, pp. 142–152.

Solis, Hilda, "Creating Good Jobs for Everyone," 2010, pp. 66–72.

Taylor, Barton, "Opening New Doors Through Volunteerism," 2010, pp. 126–131.

Thomas, Jr., R. Roosevelt, "Managing Employee Diversity: An Assessment," 1991, pp. 145–154.

Tidwell, Billy, J., "Parity Progress and Prospects: Racial Inequalities in Economic Well-Being," 2000, pp. 287–316.

———, "African Americans and the 21st-Century Labor Market: Improving the Fit," 1993, pp. 35–57.

———, "The Unemployment Experience of African Americans: Some Important Correlates and Consequences," 1990, pp. 213–223.

———, "A Profile of the Black Unemployed," 1987, pp. 223–237.

Wilkins, Ray, "Jobs, the Internet, and Our Exciting Future," 2011, pp. 94–99.

Wilson, Valerie Rawlston, "Introduction to the 2011 Equality Index," 2011, pp. 14–22.

ENVIRONMENT

Buckner, Marland and Chanelle P. Hardy, "Leveraging the Greening of America to Strengthen the Workforce Development System," 2011, pp. 76–83.

Cleaver II, Emanuel, "Green Impact Zone of Kansas City, MO," 2011, pp. 88–93.

McDuffie, Brenda, "The Strategic Alliances for Addressing the Skills Gap: The Buffalo Urban League Green Jobs Construction Training Program," 2013, pp. 158–161.

EQUALITY

Capehart, Jonathan, "Race Still Does Matter—A Lot," 2013, pp. 150–153.

Edelman, Marian Wright, "Time to Wake Up and Act: The State of Black America," 2013, pp. 68–69.

Fudge, Marcia L., "Unfinished Business," 2013, pp. 65.

Hardy, Chanelle P., "Introduction to Lift Ev'ry Voice: A Special Collection of Articles and Op-Eds.," 2013, pp. 60–61.

Holder, Jr., Eric H., "Civil Rights Enforcement in the 21st Century," 2013, pp. 144–148.

Jones-DeWeever, Avis A., "The Enduring Icon: Dr. Dorothy Height," 2013, pp. 64.

Lewis, John, "New Tactics, Same Old Taint," 2013, pp. 62–63.

Mack, John W., "Reflections on National Urban League's Legacy and Service," 2013, pp. 66.

Raines, Franklin D., "What Equality Would Look Like: Reflections on the Past, Present and Future, 2002, pp. 13–27.

Sharpton, Al, "Though We Have Achieved Much, the Battle Continues," 2013, pp. 63–64.

EQUALITY INDEX

Christopher, Gail, "Commentary on 2013 Black–White Equality Index: Mobilizing our Nation toward Racial Healing and Equity," 2013, pp. 28–29.

Global Insight, Inc., "The National Urban League Equality Index," 2004, pp. 15–34.

———, "The National Urban League Equality Index," 2005, pp. 15–40.

———, "The National Urban League Equality Index," 2010, pp. 18–39.

———, "The National Urban League 2012 Equality Index," 2012, pp. 20–43.

IHS Global Insight, "The National Urban League 2013 1963 to Now Equality Index," 2013, pp. 26–27.

———, "The National Urban League 2013 Black–White Equality Index," 2013, pp. 32–43.

———, "The National Urban League 2013 Hispanic–White Equality Index," 2013, pp. 46–57.

Murguía, Janet, "Commentary on 2013 Hispanic–White Equality Index: Partners in a Shared Plight," 2013, pp. 44–45.

powell, john a., "Commentary on 2013 Black–White Equality Index: A Theory of Change," 2013, pp. 30–31.

Thompson, Rondel and Sophia Parker of Global Insight, Inc., The National Urban League Equality Index, 2006, pp. 13–60.

Thompson, Rondel and Sophia Parker of Global Insight, Inc., The National Urban League Equality Index, 2007 pp. 17–58.

Wijewardena, Madura, "Understanding the Equality Index," 2013, pp. 22–25.

Wilson, Valerie Rawlston, "The National Urban League 2008 Equality Index: Analysis," 2008, pp. 15–24.

———, "The National Urban League 2008 Equality Index," 2009, pp. 15–24.

———, "Introduction to the 2013 Equality Index," 2013, pp. 12–21.

FAMILIES

Battle, Juan, Cathy J. Cohen, Angelique Harris, and Beth E. Richie, "We Are Family: Embracing Our Lesbian, Gay, Bisexual, and Transgender (LGBT) Family Members," 2003, pp. 93–106.

Bell, William C., "Community Based Organizations and Child Welfare: Building Communities of Hope," 2013, pp.166–169.

Billingsley, Andrew, "Black Families in a Changing Society," 1987, pp. 97–111.

———, "Understanding African-American Family Diversity," 1990, pp. 85–108.

Cox, Kenya L. Covington, "The Childcare Imbalance: Impact on Working Opportunities for Poor Mothers," 2003, pp. 197–224d.

Drucker, Ernest M., "The Impact of Mass Incarceration on Public Health in Black Communities," 2003, pp. 151–168.

Dyson, Eric Michael, "Sexual Fault Lines: Robbing the Love Between Us," 2007, pp. 229–237.

Hanson, Renee R., "A Pathway to School Readiness: The Impact of Family on Early Childhood Education," 2008, pp. 89–98.

Hill, Robert B., "Critical Issues for Black Families by the Year 2000," 1989, pp. 41–61.

———, "The Strengths of Black Families' Revisited," 2003, pp. 107–149.

Ivory, Steven, "Universal Fatherhood: Black Men Sharing the Load," 2007, pp. 243–247.

Lorain County Highlight, "Save Our Sons," 2011, pp. 176–178.

Rawlston, Valerie A., "The Impact of Social Security on Child Poverty," 2000, pp. 317–331.

Scott, Kimberly A., "A Case Study: African-American Girls and Their Families," 2003, pp. 181–195.

Shapiro, Thomas M., "The Racial Wealth Gap," 2005, pp. 41–48.

Stafford, Walter, Angela Dews, Melissa Mendez, and Diana Salas, "Race, Gender and Welfare Reform: The Need for Targeted Support," 2003, pp. 41–92.

Stockard, Jr., Russell L. and M. Belinda Tucker, "Young African-American Men and Women: Separate Paths?," 2001, pp. 143–159.

Teele, James E., "E. Franklin Frazier: The Man and His Intellectual Legacy," 2003, pp. 29–40.

Thompson, Dr. Linda S. and Georgene Butler, "The Role of the Black Family in Promoting Healthy Child Development," 2000, pp. 227–241.

West, Carolyn M., "Feminism is a Black Thing"?: Feminist Contribution to Black Family Life, 2003, pp. 13–27.

Willie, Charles V. "The Black Family: Striving Toward Freedom," 1988, pp. 71–80.

FOREWORD

Height, Dorothy I., "Awakenings," 2008, pp. 9–10.

Obama, Barack, Foreword, 2007, pp. 9–12.

King III, Martin Luther, Foreword, 2009, pp. 9–10.

Ribeau, Sidney, "A Competitive Foundation for the Future," 2011, pp. 8–9.

FROM THE PRESIDENT'S DESK

Morial, Marc H., "The State of Black America: The Complexity of Black Progress," 2004, pp. 11–14.

———, "The State of Black America 2012: Occupy the Vote to Educate, Employ & Empower," 2012, pp. 6–9.

———, "The State of Black America: Prescriptions for Change," 2005, pp. 11–14.

———, "The National Urban League Opportunity Compact," 2006, pp. 9–11.

———, "Empowering Black Males to Reach Their Full Potential," 2007, pp. 13–15.

———, From the President's Desk, 2008, pp. 11–14.

———, From the President's Desk, 2009, pp. 11–13.

———, From the President's Desk, 2010, pp. 6–7.

———, From the President's Desk, 2011, pp. 10–12.

———, From the President's Desk, 2012, pp. 6–9.

———, From the President's Desk, 2013, pp. 8–11.

HEALTH

Browne, Doris, "The Impact of Health Disparities in African-American Women," 2008, pp. 163–171.

Carnethon, Mercedes R., "Black Male Life Expectancy in the United States: A Multi-Level Exploration of Causes," 2007, pp. 137–150.

Chávez, Anna Maria "Helping Girls Make Healthy Choices," 2012, pp. 124–126.

Christmas, June Jackson, "The Health of African Americans: Progress Toward Healthy People 2000," 1996, pp. 95–126.

Cooper, Maudine R., "The Invisibility Blues' of Black Women in America," 2008, pp. 83–87.

Gaskin, Darrell, "Improving African Americans Access to Quality Healthcare," 2009, pp. 73–86.

Gaskins, Darrell J., LaVeist, Thomas A. and Richard, Patrick, "The State of Urban Health: Eliminating Health Disparities to Save Lives and Cut Costs," 2013, pp. 108–128.

Hamilton, Darrick, Goldsmith, Arthur H., and Darity, William, "An Alternative 'Public Option'," 2010, pp. 98–110.

Johnston, Haile, and Tatiana Garcia-Granados, "Common Market: The New Black Farmer," 2012, pp. 100–105.

Leffall, Jr., LaSalle D., "Health Status of Black Americans," 1990, pp. 121–142.

Lorain County Highlight, "Save Our Sons," 2011, pp. 176–178.

McAlpine, Robert, "Toward Development of a National Drug Control Strategy," 1991, pp. 233–241.

Morris, Eboni D., "By the Numbers: Uninsured African-American Women," 2008, pp. 173–177.

——— and Lisa Bland Malone, "Healthy Housing," 2009, pp. 87–98.

Nobles, Wade W., and Lawford L. Goddard, "Drugs in the African-American Community: A Clear and Present Danger," 1989, pp. 161–181.

Obama, Michelle, "Let's Move Initiative on Healthier Schools," 2011, pp. 138–140.

Patrick, Deval L., "Growing an Innovative Economy in Massachusetts," 2011, pp. 154–158.

Primm, Annelle and Marisela B. Gomez, "The Impact of Mental Health on Chronic Disease," 2005, pp. 63–73.

Primm, Beny J., "AIDS: A Special Report," 1987, pp. 159–166.

———, "Drug Use: Special Implications for Black America," 1987, pp. 145–158.

Ribeau, Sidney, "Foreword: A Competitive Foundation for the Future," 2011, pp. 8–9.

Richard, Patrick, Gaskins, Darrell J. and LaVeist, Thomas A., "The State of Urban Health: Eliminating Health Disparities to Save Lives and Cut Costs," 2013, pp. 108–128.

Shaw, Jr., Lee, "Healthy Boys Stand SCOUTStrong™," 2012, pp. 126–128.

Smedley, Brian D., "In the Wake of National Health Reform: Will the Affordable Care Act Eliminate Health Inequities?" 2011, pp. 168–175.

———, "Race, Poverty, and Healthcare Disparities," 2006, pp. 155–164.

Williams, David R., "Health and the Quality of Life Among African Americans," 2004, pp. 115–138.

Wilson, Valerie Rawlston, "Introduction to the 2011 Equality Index," 2011, pp. 14–22.

———, "Introduction to the 2012 Equality Index," 2012, pp. 10–15.

Wijewardena, Madura ,"Understanding the Equality Index," 2012, pp. 16–19.

HIGHLIGHTS

Atlanta, "Economic Empowerment Tour," 2011, pp. 118–120.

Braswell, Allie L., and James T. McLawhorn, Jr., "A Call to Advocate for America's Military Veterans," 2012, pp. 94–99.

Buffalo, McDuffie, Brenda, "The Strategic Alliances for Addressing the Skills Gap: The Buffalo Urban League Green Jobs Construction Training Program," 2013, pp. 158–161.

Dallas, "Urban Youth Empowerment Program," 2011, pp. 84–86.

Greater Stark County, Watts, Vincent and White, Edith, "Project Advocate: A Roadmap to Civic Engagement," 2013 pp. 140–143.

Hampton Roads, White, Edith and Watts, Vincent, "Project Advocate: A Roadmap to Civic Engagement," 2013 pp. 140–143.

Lorain County, "Save Our Sons," 2011, pp. 176–178.

Middle Tennessee, Stokes, Patricia and Bush, Esther, "The Equity and Excellence Project: Community-Driven Education Reform," 2013, pp. 70–74.

Obama, Michelle, "Let's Move Initiative on Healthier Schools," 2011, pp. 138–140.

Pittsburgh, Bush, Esther and Stokes, Patricia, "The Equity and Excellence Project: Community-Driven Education Reform," 2013, pp. 70–74.

Rollins, Nolan V., "The Economic Winds of Change: New Markets for an Old Problem," 2012, pp. 90–93.

Runner, Shari, "Inspiring Innovation: The Chicago Urban League Youth Investor/Entrepreneurs Project (YIEP)," 2012, pp. 110–113.

HOUSING

Calmore, John O., "To Make Wrong Right: The Necessary and Proper Aspirations of Fair Housing," 1989, pp. 77–109.

Clay, Phillip, "Housing Opportunity: A Dream Deferred," 1990, pp. 73–84.

Cooper, Maudine R., "The Invisibility Blues' of Black Women in America," 2008, pp. 83–87.

Corbett, Keith, "Economic Innovation: Finance and Lending Initiatives Point Paths to Prosperity for Underserved Communities," 2011, pp. 122–129.

Freeman, Lance, "Black Homeownership: A Dream No Longer Deferred?," 2006, pp. 63–75.

———, "Housing in the Post-Bubble Economy," 2010, pp. 74–83.

Harris, Andrea, "The Subprime Wipeout: Unsustainable Loans Erase Gains Made by African-American Women," 2008, pp. 125–133.

James, Angela, "Black Homeownership: Housing and Black Americans Under 35," 2001, pp. 115–129.

Jones, Stephanie J., "The Subprime Meltdown: Disarming the 'Weapons of Mass Deception,'" 2009, pp. 157–164.

Leigh, Wilhelmina A., "U.S. Housing Policy in 1996: The Outlook for Black Americans," 1996, pp. 188–218.

Morris, Eboni and Lisa Bland Malone, "Healthy Housing," 2009, pp. 87–98.

Richardson, Cy, "What Must Be Done: The Case for More Homeownership and Financial Education Counseling," 2009, pp. 145–155.

——— and Garrick Davis, "Rescue: The Case for Keeping Families in Their Homes by Confronting the Foreclosure Crisis," 2011, pp. 110–117.

Spriggs, William, "Nothing Trickled Down: Why Reaganomics Failed America," 2009. pp. 123–133.

Wilson, Valerie Rawlston, "Introduction to the 2011 Equality Index," 2011, pp. 14–22.

IN MEMORIAM

National Urban League, "William A. Bootle, Ray Charles, Margo T. Clarke, Ossie Davis, Herman C. Ewing, James Forman, Joanne Grant, Ann Kheel, Memphis Norman, Max Schmeling," 2005, pp. 139–152.

———, "Renaldo Benson, Shirley Chisholm, Johnnie Cochran, Jr., Shirley Horn, John H. Johnson, Vivian Malone Jones, Brock Peters, Richard Pryor, Bobby Short, C. Delores Tucker, August Wilson, Luther Vandross, and NUL members Clarence Lyle Barney, Jr., Manuel Augustus Romero;" 2006, pp. 279–287.

———, "Ossie Davis: Still Caught in the Dream," 2005, pp. 137–138.

———, "Ed Bradley, James Brown, Bebe Moore Campbell, Katherine Dunham, Mike Evans, Coretta Scott King, Gerald Levert, Gordon Parks, June Pointer, Lou Rawls, and Helen E. Harden," 2007, pp. 249–257.

———, "Effi Barry, Jane Bolin, Daniel A. Collins (NUL Member), Oliver Hill, Yolanda King, Calvin Lockhart, Mahlon Puryear (NUL Member), Max Roach, Eddie Robinson, William Simms (NUL Member), Darryl Stingley, and Ike Turner," 2008, pp. 205–217.

———, In Memoriam, 2009, pp. 225–241.

Jones, Stephanie J., "Rosa Parks: An Ordinary Woman, An Extraordinary Life," 2006, pp. 245–246.

MILITARY AFFAIRS

Braswell, Allie L., and James T. McLawhorn, Jr., "A Call to Advocate for America's Military Veterans," 2012, pp. 94–99.

Butler, John Sibley, "African Americans and the American Military," 2002, pp. 93–107.

MUSIC

Boles, Mark A., "Breaking the 'Hip Hop' Hold: Looking Beyond the Media Hype," 2007, pp. 239–241.

Brown, David W., "Their Characteristic Music: Thoughts on Rap Music and Hip-Hop Culture," 2001, pp. 189–201.

Bynoe, Yvonne, "The Roots of Rap Music and Hip-Hop Culture: One Perspective," 2001, pp. 175–187.

OP-ED/COMMENTARY

Archer, Dennis W., "Security Must Never Trump Liberty," 2004, pp. 139–142.

Bailey, Moya, "Going in Circles: The Struggle to Diversify Popular Images of Black Women," 2008, pp. 193–196.

Bernard, Michelle, "An Ode to Black America," 2009, pp. 203–207.

Boles, Mark A., "Breaking the 'Hip Hop' Hold: Looking Beyond the Media Hype," 2007, pp. 239–241.

Burnham, David, "The Fog of War," 2005, pp. 123–127.

Capehart, Jonathan, "Race Still Does Matter—A Lot," 2013, pp. 150–153.

Chappell, Kevin, " 'Realities' of Black America," 2011, pp. 192–195.

Cooke, Cassye, "The Game Changer: Are We Beyond What is Next to What is Now?," 2009, pp. 209–212.

Covington, Kenya L., "The Transformation of the Welfare Caseload," 2004, pp. 149–152.

Dyson, Eric Michael, "Sexual Fault Lines: Robbing the Love Between Us," 2007, pp. 229–237.

Edelman, Marian Wright, "Losing Our Children in America's Cradle to Prison Pipeline," 2007, pp. 219–227.

Emerson, Melinda F., "Five Things You Must Have to Run a Successful Business," 2004, pp. 153–156.

Fauntroy, Michael K., "The New Arithmetic of Black Political Power," 2013, pp. 154–157.

Hardy, Chanelle P., "Introduction to Lift Ev'ry Voice: A Special Collection of Articles and Op-Eds.," 2013, pp. 60–61.

Holder, Jr., Eric H., "Civil Rights Enforcement in the 21st Century," 2013, pp. 144–148.

Ivory, Steven, "Universal Fatherhood: Black Men Sharing the Load," 2007, pp. 243–247.

Jones, Nathaniel R., "Did I Ever? Yes I Did," 2009, pp. 213–219.

Journal of Blacks in Higher Education (reprint), "The 'Acting White' Myth," 2005, pp. 115–117.

Kirk, Ron, "Education: The Critical Link between Trade and Jobs," 2013, pp. 76–80.

Lanier, James R., "The Empowerment Movement and the Black Male," 2004, pp. 143–148.

Lee, Barbara, "President Obama and the CBC: Speaking with One Voice," 2009, pp. 193–197.

Lewis, John, "New Tactics, Same Old Taint," 2013, pp. 62–63.

Lindsay, Tiffany, "Weaving the Fabric: the Political Activism of Young African-American Women," 2008, pp. 187–192.

Malveaux, Julianne, "Black Women's Hands Can Rock the World: Global Involvement and Understanding," 2008, pp. 197–202.

Rivlin, Alice M., "Pay Now or Pay Later: Jobs, Fiscal Responsibility and the Future of Black America," 2011, pp. 202–206.

Ross, Ronald O., "Gaps, Traps and Lies: African-American Students and Test Scores," 2004, pp. 157–161.

Sharpton, Al, "Though We Have Achieved Much, the Battle Continues," 2013, pp. 63–64.

Taylor, Susan L., "Black Love Under Siege," 2008 pp. 179–186.

Taylor, Robert D., "Wealth Creation: The Next Leadership Challenge," 2005, pp. 119–122.

West, Cornel, "Democracy Matters," 2005, pp. 129–132.

Wijewardena, Madura and Kirk Clay, "Government with the Consent of All: Redistricting Strategies for Civil Rights Organizations," 2011, pp. 196–201.

Wilkins, Ray, "Jobs, the Internet, and Our Exciting Future," 2011, pp. 94–99.

OVERVIEW

Morial, Marc H., "Black America's Family Matters," 2003, pp. 9–12.

Price, Hugh B., "Still Worth Fighting For: America After 9/11," 2002, pp. 9–11.

POLITICS

Alton, Kimberley, "The State of Civil Rights 2008," 2008, pp. 157–161.

Brazile, Donna, "Fallout from the Mid-Term Elections: Making the Most of the Next Two Years," 2011, pp. 180–190.

Brown James, Stefanie, "Black Civic Engagement 2.0: In with the Old, in with the New," 2013, pp. 67–68.

Campbell, Melanie L., "Election Reform: Protecting Our Vote from the Enemy Who Never Sleeps," 2008, pp. 149–156.

Capehart, Jonathan, "Race Still Does Matter—A Lot," 2013, pp. 150–153.

Coleman, Henry A., "Interagency and Intergovernmental Coordination: New Demands for Domestic Policy Initiatives," 1992, pp. 249–263.

Fauntroy, Michael K., "The New Arithmetic of Black Political Power," 2013, pp. 154–157.

Fudge, Marcia L., "Unfinished Business," 2013, pp. 65.

Hamilton, Charles V., "On Parity and Political Empowerment," 1989, pp. 111–120.

———, "Promoting Priorities: African-American Political Influence in the 1990s," 1993, pp. 59–69.

Henderson, Lenneal J., "Budgets, Taxes, and Politics: Options for the African-American Community," 1991, pp. 77–93.

Holden, Jr., Matthew, "The Rewards of Daring and the Ambiguity of Power: Perspectives on the Wilder Election of 1989," 1990, pp. 109–120.

Holder, Jr., Eric H., "Civil Rights Enforcement in the 21st Century," 2013, pp. 144–148.

Kilson, Martin L., "African Americans and American Politics 2002: The Maturation Phase," 2002, pp. 147–180.

———, "Thinking About the Black Elite's Role: Yesterday and Today," 2005, pp. 85–106.

Lee, Silas, "Who's Going to Take the Weight? African Americans and Civic Engagement in the 21st Century," 2007, pp. 185–192.

Lewis, John, "New Tactics, Same Old Taint," 2013, pp. 62–63.

Lindsay, Tiffany, "Weaving the Fabric: The Political Activism of Young African-American Women," 2008, pp. 187–192.

Mack, John W., "Reflections on National Urban League's Legacy and Service," 2013, pp. 66.

McHenry, Donald F., "A Changing World Order: Implications for Black America," 1991, pp. 155–163.

Persons, Georgia A., "Blacks in State and Local Government: Progress and Constraints," 1987, pp. 167–192.

Pinderhughes, Dianne M., "Power and Progress: African-American Politics in the New Era of Diversity," 1992, pp. 265–280.

———, "The Renewal of the Voting Rights Act," 2005, pp. 49–61.

———, "Civil Rights and the Future of the American Presidency," 1988, pp. 39–60.

Price, Hugh B., "Black America's Challenge: The Re-Construction of Black Civil Society," 2001, pp. 13–18.

Rivlin, Alice M., "Pay Now or Pay Later: Jobs, Fiscal Responsibility and the Future of Black America," 2011, pp. 202–206.

Scott, Robert C. "Bobby," "Minority Voter Participation: Reviewing Past and Present Barriers to the Polls," 2012, pp. 44–47.

Tidwell, Billy J., "Serving the National Interest: A Marshall Plan for America," 1992, pp. 11–30.

Watts, Vincent and White, Edith, "Project Advocate: A Roadmap to Civic Engagement," 2013 pp. 140–143.

West, Cornel, "Democracy Matters," 2005, pp. 129–132.

White, Edith and Watts, Vincent, "Project Advocate: A Roadmap to Civic Engagement," 2013 pp. 140–143.

Wijewardena, Madura and Kirk Clay, "Government with the Consent of All: Redistricting Strategies for Civil Rights Organizations," 2011, pp. 196–201.

Williams, Eddie N., "The Evolution of Black Political Power," 2000, pp. 91–102.

Yearwood, Jr., Lennox, "The Rise and Fall and Rise Again of Jim Crow Laws," 2012, pp. 48–53.

POVERTY

Cooper, Maudine R., "The Invisibility Blues' of Black Women in America," 2008, pp. 83–87.

Edelman, Marian Wright, "The State of Our Children," 2006, pp. 133–141.

PRESCRIPTIONS FOR CHANGE

Bell, William C., "Community Based Organizations and Child Welfare: Building Communities of Hope," 2013, pp. 166–169.

Capehart, Jonathan, "Race Still Does Matter—A Lot," 2013, pp. 150–153.

Fauntroy, Michael K., "The New Arithmetic of Black Political Power," 2013, pp. 154–157.

Marshall, Cynthia, "Digitizing the Dream: The Role of Technology in Empowering Communities," 2013, pp. 130–133.

McGhee, David, "Mentoring Matters: Why Young Professionals and Others Must Mentor," 2013, pp. 162–165.

National Urban League, "Prescriptions for Change," 2005, pp. 133–135.

RELATIONSHIPS

Taylor, Susan L., "Black Love Under Siege," 2008, pp. 179–186.

RELIGION

Lincoln, C. Eric, "Knowing the Black Church: What It Is and Why," 1989, pp. 137–149.

Richardson, W. Franklyn, "Mission to Mandate: Self-Development through the Black Church," 1994, pp. 113–126.

Smith, Dr. Drew, "The Evolving Political Priorities of African-American Churches: An Empirical View," 2000, pp. 171–197.

Taylor, Mark V.C., "Young Adults and Religion," 2001, pp. 161–174.

REPORTS FROM THE NATIONAL URBAN LEAGUE

Gaskins, Darrell J., LaVeist, Thomas A. and Richard, Patrick, "The State of Urban Health: Eliminating Health Disparities to Save Lives and Cut Costs," 2013, pp. 108–128.

Hanson, Renee, Mark McArdle, and Valerie Rawlston Wilson, "Invisible Men: The Urgent Problems of Low-Income African-American Males," 2007, pp. 209–216.

Hardy, Chanelle P., Dr. Valerie Rawlston Wilson, Madura Wijewardena, and Garrick T. Davis, "At Risk: The State of the Black Middle Class," 2012, pp. 74–83.

Jones, Stephanie J., "Sunday Morning Apartheid: A Diversity Study of the Sunday Morning Talk Shows" 2006, pp. 189–228.

Lanier, James, "The National Urban League's Commission on the Black Male: Renewal, Revival and Resurrection Feasibility and Strategic Planning Study," 2005, pp. 107–109.

LaVeist, Thomas A., Richard, Patrick and Gaskins, Darrell J., "The State of Urban Health: Eliminating Health Disparities to Save Lives and Cut Costs," 2013, pp. 108–128.

National Urban League, "12 Point Urban Jobs Plan," 2011, pp. 46–52.

National Urban League Council of Economic Advisors, Bernard E. Anderson, William M. Rodgers III, Lucy J. Reuben, and Valerie Rawlston Wilson, "The New Normal? Opportunities for Prosperity in a 'Jobless Recovery,'" 2011, pp. 54–63.

National Urban League Policy Institute, The Opportunity Compact: A Blueprint for Economic Equality, 2008, pp. 43–74.

———, "Putting Americans Back to Work: The National Urban League's Plan for Creating Jobs" 2010, pp. 40–44.

———, "African Americans and the Green Revolution" 2010, pp. 46–59.

———, "Where Do We Go From Here? Projected Employment Growth Industries and Occupations," 2011, pp. 64–75.

———, "The 2012 National Urban League 8-Point Education and Employment Plan: Employment and Education Empower the Nation" 2012, pp. 54–59.

———, "The National Urban League Introduces New Reports on the State of Urban Business" 2012, pp. 64–69.

National Urban League Policy Institute, LaVeist, Thomas A., Richard, Patrick and Gaskins, Darrell J., "The State of Urban Health: Eliminating Health Disparities to Save Lives and Cut Costs," 2013, pp. 108–128.

Richard, Patrick, Gaskins, Darrell J. and LaVeist, Thomas A., "The State of Urban Health: Eliminating Health Disparities to Save Lives and Cut Costs," 2013, pp. 108–128.

REPORTS

Joint Center for Political and Economic Studies, A Way Out: Creating Partners for Our Nation's Prosperity by Expanding Life Paths for Young Men of Color—Final Report of the Dellums Commission, 2007, pp. 193–207.

Reed, James and Aaron Thomas, The National Urban League: Empowering Black Males to Meet Their Full Potential, 2007, pp. 217–218.

Wilson, Valerie Rawlston,"Introduction to the 2011 Equality Index," 2011, pp. 14–22.

SEXUAL IDENTITY

Bailey, Moya, "Going in Circles: The Struggle to Diversify Popular Images of Black Women," 2008 pp. 193–196.

Battle, Juan, Cathy J. Cohen, Angelique Harris, and Beth E. Richie, "We Are Family: Embracing Our Lesbian, Gay, Bisexual, and Transgender (LGBT) Family Members," 2003, pp. 93–106.

Taylor, Susan L., "Black Love Under Siege," 2008, pp. 179–186.

SOCIOLOGY

Cooper, Maudine R., "The Invisibility Blues' of Black Women in America," 2008, pp. 83–87.

Taylor, Susan L., "Black Love Under Siege," 2008, pp. 179–186.

Teele, James E., "E. Franklin Frazier: The Man and His Intellectual Legacy," 2003, pp. 29–40.

SPECIAL SECTION: BLACK WOMEN'S HEALTH

Browne, Doris, "The Impact of Health Disparities in African-American Women," 2008, pp. 163–171.

Morris, Eboni D., "By the Numbers: Uninsured African-American Women," 2008, pp. 173–177.

SPECIAL SECTION: KATRINA AND BEYOND

Brazile, Donna L., "New Orleans: Next Steps on the Road to Recovery," 2006, pp. 233–237.

Morial, Marc H., "New Orleans Revisited," 2006, pp. 229–232.

National Urban League, "The National Urban League Katrina Bill of Rights," 2006, pp. 239–243.

SPECIAL SECTION: LIFT EV'RY VOICE

Brown James, Stefanie, "Black Civic Engagement 2.0: In with the Old, in with the New," 2013, pp. 67–68.

Edelman, Marian Wright, "Time to Wake Up and Act: The State of Black America," 2013, pp. 68–69.

Fudge, Marcia L., "Unfinished Business," 2013, pp. 65.

Hardy, Chanelle P., "Introduction to Lift Ev'ry Voice: A Special Collection of Articles and Op-Eds.," 2013, pp. 60–61.

Jones-DeWeever, Avis A., "The Enduring Icon: Dr. Dorothy Height," 2013, pp. 64.

Lewis, John, "New Tactics, Same Old Taint," 2013, pp. 62–63.

Mack, John W., "Reflections on National Urban League's Legacy and Service," 2013, pp. 66.

Sharpton, Al, "Though We Have Achieved Much, the Battle Continues," 2013, pp. 63–64.

SURVEYS

The National Urban League Survey, 2004, pp. 35–51.

Stafford, Walter S., "The National Urban League Survey: Black America's Under-35 Generation," 2001, pp. 19–63.

———, "The New York Urban League Survey: Black New York—On Edge, But Optimistic," 2001, pp. 203–219.

TECHNOLOGY

Dreyfuss, Joel, "Black Americans and the Internet: The Technological Imperative," 2001, pp. 131–141.

Patrick, Deval L., "Growing an Innovative Economy in Massachusetts," 2011, pp. 154–158.

Ramsey, Rey, "Broadband Matters to All of Us," 2010, pp. 112–116.

Ribeau, Sidney, "A Competitive Foundation for the Future," 2011, pp. 8–9.

Wilkins, Ray, "Jobs, the Internet, and Our Exciting Future," 2011, pp. 94–99.

Wilson III, Ernest J., "Technological Convergence, Media Ownership and Content Diversity," 2000, pp. 147–170.

URBAN AFFAIRS

Allen, Antoine, and Leland Ware, "The Geography of Discrimination: Hypersegregation, Isolation and Fragmentation Within the African-American Community," 2002, pp. 69–92.

Bates, Timothy, "The Paradox of Urban Poverty," 1996, pp. 144–163.

Bell, Carl C., with Esther J. Jenkins, "Preventing Black Homicide," 1990,pp. 143–155.

Bell, William C., "Community Based Organizations and Child Welfare: Building Communities of Hope," 2013, pp. 166–169.

Bryant Solomon, Barbara, "Social Welfare Reform," 1987, pp. 113–127.

Brown, Lee P., "Crime in the Black Community," 1988, pp. 95–113.

Bryant, John Hope, "Financial Dignity in an Economic Age," 2013, pp. 134–138.

Bullard, Robert D. "Urban Infrastructure: Social, Environmental, and Health Risks to African Americans," 1992, pp. 183–196.

Chambers, Julius L., "The Law and Black Americans: Retreat from Civil Rights," 1987, pp. 15–30.

———, "Black Americans and the Courts: Has the Clock Been Turned Back Permanently?" 1990, pp. 9–24.

Edelin, Ramona H., "Toward an African-American Agenda: An Inward Look," 1990, pp. 173–183.

Fair, T. Willard, "Coordinated Community Empowerment: Experiences of the Urban League of Greater Miami," 1993, pp. 217–233.

Gaskins, Darrell J., LaVeist, Thomas A. and Richard, Patrick, "The State of Urban Health: Eliminating Health Disparities to Save Lives and Cut Costs," 2013, pp. 108–128.

Gray, Sandra T., "Public-Private Partnerships: Prospects for America...Promise for African Americans," 1992, pp. 231–247.

Harris, David, "'Driving While Black' and Other African-American Crimes: The Continuing Relevance of Race to American Criminal Justice," 2000, pp. 259–285.

Harris, Dot, "Diversity in STEM: An Economic Imperative," 2013, pp. 92–95.

Henderson, Lenneal J., "African Americans in the Urban Milieu: Conditions, Trends, and Development Needs," 1994, pp. 11–29.

Hill, Robert B., "Urban Redevelopment: Developing Effective Targeting Strategies," 1992, pp. 197–211.

Johnston, Haile, and Tatiana Garcia-Granados, "Common Market: The New Black Farmer," 2012, pp. 100–105.

Jones, Dionne J., with Greg Harrison of the National Urban League Research Department, "Fast Facts: Comparative Views of African-American Status and Progress," 1994, pp. 213–236.

Jones, Shirley J., "Silent Suffering: The Plight of Rural Black America,"1994, pp. 171–188.

LaVeist, Thomas A., Richard, Patrick and Gaskins, Darrell J., "The State of Urban Health: Eliminating Health Disparities to Save Lives and Cut Costs," 2013, pp. 108–128.

Mack, John W., "Reflections on National Urban League's Legacy and Service," 2013, pp. 66.

Massey, Walter E. "Science, Technology, and Human Resources: Preparing for the 21st Century," 1992, pp. 157–169.

Mendez, Jr., Garry A., "Crime Is Not a Part of Our Black Heritage: A Theoretical Essay," 1988, pp. 211–216.

Miller, Jr., Warren F., "Developing Untapped Talent: A National Call for African-American Technologists," 1991, pp. 111–127.

Murray, Sylvester, "Clear and Present Danger: The Decay of America's Physical Infrastructure," 1992, pp. 171–182.

Pemberton, Gayle, "It's the Thing That Counts, Or Reflections on the Legacy of W.E.B. Du Bois," 1991, pp. 129–143.

Pinderhughes, Dianne M., "The Case of African-Americans in the Persian Gulf: The Intersection of American Foreign and Military Policy with Domestic Employment Policy in the United States," 1991, pp. 165–186.

Richard, Patrick, Gaskins, Darrell J. and LaVeist, Thomas A., "The State of Urban Health: Eliminating Health Disparities to Save Lives and Cut Costs," 2013, pp. 108–128.

Robinson, Gene S. "Television Advertising and Its Impact on Black America," 1990, pp. 157–171.

Sawyers, Dr. Andrew and Dr. Lenneal Henderson, "Race, Space and Justice: Cities and Growth in the 21st Century," 2000, pp. 243–258.

Schneider, Alvin J., "Blacks in the Military: The Victory and the Challenge," 1988, pp. 115–128.

Smedley, Brian, "Race, Poverty, and Healthcare Disparities," 2006, pp. 155–164.

Stafford, Walter, Angela Dews, Melissa Mendez, and Diana Salas, "Race, Gender and Welfare Reform: The Need for Targeted Support," 2003, pp. 41–92.

Stewart, James B., "Developing Black and Latino Survival Strategies: The Future of Urban Areas," 1996, pp. 164–187.

Stone, Christopher E., "Crime and Justice in Black America," 1996, pp. 78–94.

Tidwell, Billy J., with Monica B. Kuumba, Dionne J. Jones, and Betty C. Watson, "Fast Facts: African Americans in the 1990s," 1993, pp. 243–265.

Wallace-Benjamin, Joan, "Organizing African-American Self-Development: The Role of Community-Based Organizations," 1994, pp. 189–205.

Walters, Ronald, "Serving the People: African-American Leadership and the Challenge of Empowerment," 1994, pp. 153–170.

Allen, Antoine, and Leland Ware, "The Geography of Discrimination: Hypersegregation, Isolation and Fragmentation within the African-American Community," 2002, pp. 69–92.

Wiley, Maya, "Hurricane Katrina Exposed the Face of Poverty," 2006, pp. 143–153.

WELFARE

Bell, William C., "Community Based Organizations and Child Welfare: Building Communities of Hope," 2013, pp. 166–169.

Bergeron, Suzanne, and William E. Spriggs, "Welfare Reform and Black America," 2002, pp. 29–50.

Cooper, Maudine R., "The Invisibility Blues' of Black Women in America," 2008, pp. 83–87.

Covington, Kenya L., "The Transformation of the Welfare Caseload," 2004, pp. 149–152.

Spriggs, William E., and Suzanne Bergeron, "Welfare Reform and Black America," 2002, pp. 29–50.

Stafford, Walter, Angela Dews, Melissa Mendez, and Diana Salas, "Race, Gender and Welfare Reform: The Need for Targeted Support," 2003, pp. 41–92.

WOMEN'S ISSUES

Bailey, Moya, "Going in Circles: The Struggle to Diversify Popular Images of Black Women," 2008, pp. 193–196.

Browne, Doris, "The Impact of Health Disparities in African-American Women," 2008, pp. 163–171.

Cooper, Maudine R., "The Invisibility Blues' of Black Women in America," 2008, pp. 83–87.

Harris, Andrea, "The Subprime Wipeout: Unsustainable Loans Erase Gains Made by African-American Women," 2008, pp. 125–133.

Herman, Alexis, "African-American Women and Work: Still a Tale of Two Cities," 2008, pp. 109–113.

Lindsay, Tiffany, "Weaving the Fabric: The Political Activism of Young African-American Women," 2008, pp. 187–192.

Malveaux, Julianne, "Black Women's Hands Can Rock the World: Global Involvement and Understanding," 2008, pp. 197–202.

———, "Shouldering the Third Burden: The Status of African-American Women," 2008, pp. 75–81.

Mensah, Lisa, "Putting Homeownership Back Within Our Reach," 2008, pp. 135–142.

Morris, Eboni D., "By the Numbers: Uninsured African-American Women," 2008, pp. 173–177.

Reuben, Lucy J., "Make Room for the New 'She'EOs: An Analysis of Businesses Owned by Black Females," 2008, pp. 115–124.

Stafford, Walter, Angela Dews, Melissa Mendez, and Diana Salas, "Race, Gender and Welfare Reform: The Need for Targeted Support," 2003, pp. 41–92.

Taylor, Susan L., "Black Love Under Siege," 2008, pp. 179–186.

West, Carolyn M., "Feminism is a Black Thing?": Feminist Contribution to Black Family Life, 2003, pp. 13–27.

WORLD AFFAIRS

Malveaux, Julianne, "Black Women's Hands Can Rock the World: Global Involvement and Understanding," 2008, pp. 197–202.

★ NATIONAL URBAN LEAGUE ★

BOARD of TRUSTEES

★ NATIONAL URBAN LEAGUE ★

EXECUTIVE STAFF

EXECUTIVE TEAM

President & CEO
Marc H. Morial

Senior Vice President & Executive Director
Policy Institute
Chanelle P. Hardy, Esq.

Senior Vice President
Marketing & Communications
Rhonda Spears Bell

Senior Vice President
Programs
Donald E. Bowen

Senior Vice President & Chief Talent Officer
Human Resources
Wanda H. Jackson

Senior Vice President
Affiliate Services
Herman L. Lessard, Jr.

Senior Vice President
Strategy, Innovation & Technology
Michael E. Miller

Senior Vice President
Development
Dennis Serrette

Senior Vice President
Finance & Operations
Paul Wycisk

POLICY INSTITUTE STAFF

Senior Vice President & Executive Director
Chanelle P. Hardy, Esq.

Senior Director, Operations & Chief of Staff
Cara M. McKinley

Vice President, Communication & External Relations
Pamela Rucker Springs

Vice President, Research & Economist
Valerie Rawlston Wilson, Ph.D.

Director, Research & Policy
Madura Wijewardena

Senior Legislative Director, Workforce, Civil Rights & Social Services
Suzanne M. Bergeron, MSW

Legislative Director, Education & Health Policy
Jacqueline Ayers

Legislative Director, Financial & Economic Policy
Garrick T. Davis

Legislative Director, Research & Analysis
Hazeen Y. Ashby, Esq.

Special Assistant to the Executive Director
Courtney O'Neal

Legislative Manager, Education & Health Policy
Shree Chauhan

Broadband & Technology Fellow
Patric Taylor

Research Assistant
Tiffany Harrison

★ **ROSTER OF** ★

NATIONAL URBAN LEAGUE *affiliates*

AKRON, OHIO
Akron Community Service Center and Urban League

ALEXANDRIA, VIRGINIA
Northern Virginia Urban League

ALTON, ILLINOIS
Madison County Urban League

ANDERSON, INDIANA
Urban League of Madison County, Inc.

ATLANTA, GEORGIA
Urban League of Greater Atlanta

AURORA, ILLINOIS
Quad County Urban League

AUSTIN, TEXAS
Austin Area Urban League

BALTIMORE, MARYLAND
Greater Baltimore Urban League

BATTLE CREEK, MICHIGAN
Southwestern Michigan Urban League

BINGHAMTON, NEW YORK
Broome County Urban League

BIRMINGHAM, ALABAMA
Birmingham Urban League

BOSTON, MASSACHUSETTS
Urban League of Eastern Massachusetts

BUFFALO, NEW YORK
Buffalo Urban League

CANTON, OHIO
Greater Stark County Urban League, Inc.

CHARLESTON, SOUTH CAROLINA
Charleston Trident Urban League

CHARLOTTE, NORTH CAROLINA
Urban League of Central Carolinas, Inc.

CHATTANOOGA, TENNESSEE
Urban League Greater Chattanooga, Inc.

CHICAGO, ILLINOIS
Chicago Urban League

CINCINNATI, OHIO
Urban League of Greater Southwestern Ohio

CLEVELAND, OHIO
Urban League of Greater Cleveland

COLORADO SPRINGS, COLORADO
Urban League of Pikes Peak Region

COLUMBIA, SOUTH CAROLINA
Columbia Urban League

COLUMBUS, GEORGIA
Urban League of Greater Columbus, Inc.

COLUMBUS, OHIO
Columbus Urban League

DALLAS, TEXAS
Urban League of Greater Dallas and North Central Texas

DENVER, COLORADO
Urban League of Metropolitan Denver

DETROIT, MICHIGAN
Urban League of Detroit and Southeastern Michigan

ELIZABETH, NEW JERSEY
Urban League of Union County

ELYRIA, OHIO
Lorain County Urban League

ENGLEWOOD, NEW JERSEY
Urban League for Bergen County

FARRELL, PENNSYLVANIA
Urban League of Shenango Valley

FLINT, MICHIGAN
Urban League of Flint

FORT LAUDERDALE, FLORIDA
Urban League of Broward County

FORT WAYNE, INDIANA
Fort Wayne Urban League

GARY, INDIANA
Urban League of Northwest Indiana, Inc.

GRAND RAPIDS, MICHIGAN
Grand Rapids Urban League

GREENVILLE, SOUTH CAROLINA
Urban League of the Upstate, Inc.

HARTFORD, CONNECTICUT
Urban League of Greater Hartford

HOUSTON, TEXAS
Houston Area Urban League

INDIANAPOLIS, INDIANA
Indianapolis Urban League

JACKSON, MISSISSIPPI
Urban League of Greater Jackson

JACKSONVILLE, FLORIDA
Jacksonville Urban League

JERSEY CITY, NEW JERSEY
Urban League of Hudson County

KANSAS CITY, MISSOURI
Urban League of Kansas City

KNOXVILLE, TENNESSEE
Knoxville Area Urban League

LANCASTER, PENNSYLVANIA
Urban League of Lancaster County

LAS VEGAS, NEVADA
Las Vegas-Clark County
Urban League

LEXINGTON, KENTUCKY
Urban League of Lexington-
Fayette County

LONG ISLAND, NEW YORK
Urban League of Long Island

LOS ANGELES, CALIFORNIA
Los Angeles Urban League

LOUISVILLE, KENTUCKY
Louisville Urban League

MADISON, WISCONSIN
Urban League of Greater Madison

MEMPHIS, TENNESSEE
Memphis Urban League

MIAMI, FLORIDA
Urban League of Greater Miami

MILWAUKEE, WISCONSIN
Milwaukee Urban League

MINNEAPOLIS, MINNESOTA
Minneapolis Urban League

MORRISTOWN, NEW JERSEY
Morris County Urban League

NASHVILLE, TENNESSEE
Urban League of Middle Tennessee

NEW ORLEANS, LOUISIANA
Urban League of Greater
New Orleans

NEW YORK, NEW YORK
New York Urban League

NEWARK, NEW JERSEY
Urban League of Essex County

NORFOLK, VIRGINIA
Urban League of Hampton Roads

OKLAHOMA CITY, OKLAHOMA
Urban League of Greater
Oklahoma City

OMAHA, NEBRASKA
Urban League of Nebraska, Inc.

ORLANDO, FLORIDA
Central Florida Urban League

PEORIA, ILLINOIS
Tri-County Urban League

PHILADELPHIA, PENNSYLVANIA
Urban League of Philadelphia

PHOENIX, ARIZONA
Greater Phoenix Urban League

PITTSBURGH, PENNSYLVANIA
Urban League of Greater Pittsburgh

PORTLAND, OREGON
Urban League of Portland

PROVIDENCE, RHODE ISLAND
Urban League of Rhode Island

RACINE, WISCONSIN
Urban League of Racine &
Kenosha,Inc.

RICHMOND, VIRGINIA
Urban League of Greater
Richmond, Inc.

ROCHESTER, NEW YORK
Urban League of Rochester

SACRAMENTO, CALIFORNIA
Greater Sacramento Urban League

SAINT LOUIS, MISSOURI
Urban League Metropolitan
St. Louis

SAINT PAUL, MINNESOTA
St. Paul Urban League

SAINT PETERSBURG, FLORIDA
Pinellas County Urban League

SAN DIEGO, CALIFORNIA
Urban League of San Diego County

SEATTLE, WASHINGTON
Urban League of
Metropolitan Seattle

SPRINGFIELD, ILLINOIS
Springfield Urban League, Inc.

SPRINGFIELD, MASSACHUSETTS
Urban League of Springfield

STAMFORD, CONNECTICUT
Urban League of Southern
Connecticut

TACOMA, WASHINGTON
Tacoma Urban League

TALLAHASSEE, FLORDIA
Tallahassee Urban League

TOLEDO, OHIO
Greater Toledo Urban League

TUCSON, ARIZONA
Tucson Urban League

TULSA, OKLAHOMA
Metropolitan Tulsa Urban League

WARREN, OHIO
Greater Warren-Youngstown
Urban League

WASHINGTON, D.C.
Greater Washington Urban League

WEST PALM BEACH, FLORIDA
Urban League of Palm Beach
County, Inc.

WHITE PLAINS, NEW YORK
Urban League of
Westchester County

WICHITA, KANSAS
Urban League of Kansas, Inc.

WILMINGTON, DELAWARE
Metropolitan Wilmington
Urban League

WINSTON-SALEM,
NORTH CAROLINA
Winston-Salem Urban League

THE 2013 STATE OF BLACK AMERICA® REPORT WAS BROUGHT TO LIFE WITH LIVE AND DIGITAL EVENTS.

PLEASE SCAN TO VIEW

2013 STATE OF BLACK AMERICA WEBSERIES

DIGITAL EVENT TEAM

Rhonda Spears Bell
Amber C. Jaynes
Pamela Rucker Springs
Kristian Buchanan
Simone Jordan
Beatriz Mota
Will Ashley
Candece Monteil